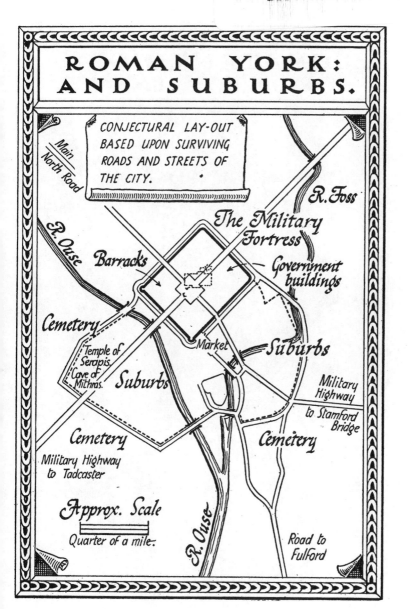

ROMAN YORK: AND SUBURBS.

CONJECTURAL LAY-OUT BASED UPON SURVIVING ROADS AND STREETS OF THE CITY.

Main North Road

R. Foss

The Military Fortress

R. Ouse

Barracks

Government buildings

Cemetery

Temple of Serapis, Cave of Mithras.

Market

Suburbs

Suburbs

Military Highway to Stamford Bridge

Cemetery

Cemetery

Military Highway to Tadcaster

Approx. Scale

Quarter of a mile.

R. Ouse

Road to Fulford

CONSTANTINOPLE OR NEW ROME.

EUROPE.

N

W E

S

To the Euxine or Black Sea

BOSPORUS

GOLDEN HORN

Galata

WALL OF CONSTANTINE

St Sophia

"Golden Gate"

Chrysopolis

ASIA

Constantinople

Chalcedon

PROPONTIS

To the Aegean Sea

CONSTANTINE
THE GREAT

and the Christian Revolution

BY

G. P. BAKER

ILLUSTRATED

Cooper Square Press

Published by Cooper Square Press
An Imprint of the Rowman & Littlefield Publishing Group
150 Fifth Avenue, Suite 817
New York, New York 10011

Distributed by National Book Network

Library of Congress Cataloging-in-Publication Data available

ISBN 0-8154-1158-8 (pbk. : alk. paper)

♾™ The paper used in this publication meets the minimum requirements of
American National Standard for Information Sciences—Permanence of
Paper for Printed Library Materials, ANSI/NISO Z39.48-1992.
Manufactured in the United States of America.

OTHER
COOPER SQUARE PRESS
TITLES OF INTEREST

SULLA THE FORTUNATE
Roman General and Dictator
G. P. Baker
328 pp., 4 b/w photos, 8 maps &
    diagrams
0-8154-1147-2
$18.95

TIBERIUS CAESAR
Emperor of Rome
G. P. Baker
344 pp., 1 b/w photo, 5 maps &
    charts
0-8154-1113-8
$18.95

HANNIBAL
G. P. Baker
366 pp., 3 illustrations; 5 maps
0-8154-1005-0
$16.95

AUGUSTUS
The Golden Age of Rome
G. P. Baker
378 pp., 17 b/w illustrations
0-8154-1089-1
$18.95

MUSSOLINI
Jasper Ridley
464 pp., 24 b/w photos
0-8154-1081-6
$19.95

THE LIFE AND TIMES OF
AKHNATON
Pharaoh of Egypt
Arthur Wiegall
322 pp., 26 b/w photos; 7 line
    drawings
0-8154-1092-1
$17.95

GANDHI
A Biography
Geoffrey Ashe
432 pp., 18 b/w photos
0-8154-1107-3
$18.95

THE DREAM AND THE TOMB
A History of the Crusades
Robert Payne
456 pages, 34 b/w illustrations
0-8154-1086-7
$19.95

HISTORY OF THE CONQUEST
OF MEXICO & PERU
William H. Prescott
1330 pp., 2 maps
0-8154-1004-2
$32.00

T. E. LAWRENCE
A Biography
Michael Yardley
308 pp., 71 b/w photos, 5 maps
0-8154-1054-9
$17.95

GENGHIS KAHN
R. P. Lister
256 pp., 1 b/w illustration
0-8154-1052-2
$16.95

Cooper Square Press

150 Fifth Avenue
Suite 817
New York, NY 10011

Available at bookstores;
or call 1-800-462-6420

Constantius 1,   Galerius,
as Caesar.   as Caesar.

Constantine the Great.

HOC OPVS
GVLIELMO
GARTHWAITIO
DVNELMIAE
BARONETTO
EQVITI COR·
ONAE BELGICAE
INSCRIPTVM EST
QVI VT GRATIAS PATRIAE
SVAE AGAT SALVTEMQVE
COMMVNEM CIVITATIS
ADIUVET STVDIA HISTORIAE
GVBERNATIONIS ORIGINIS·
QVE ET AVCTVS DIGNITATIS
REGIAE FOVET.

PREFACE

WHAT interest has Constantine the Great for a modern reader? This:—that all the social institutions under which we live have in some way been modified by him. He stands at the point of focus upon which all the influences of the ancient world concentrate and from which they radiate again to us. The American Constitution, the plan of Parliament Square, and the history of the Place de la Concorde would all be different but for him.

The halo, with which rightly grateful enthusiasts have surrounded the head of Constantine, is of less importance to posterity than the intelligence which was once inside it. He was no pale curate. He was a clever, strong and determined man who may or may not have performed miracles, but who seldom made mistakes. The only serious error he ever made is narrated in this book. It was typical of the man in that we can form no adequate conception either of the magnitude or of the results of such a mistake as the death of Crispus; but in any case, he himself was the principal sufferer.

We are accustomed to recognize a certain number of episodes which we call Revolutions. We can most of us count them off—the Russian Revolution, the French Revolution, the English Revolution of 1688; and all these important historical crises have certain features in common—the violent overthrow of an old-established system of government, and the institution of a new. The Protestant reformation was a revolution; the

Norman Conquest likewise; but both had features which distinguish them from the former three, and to find accurate parallels to these three we have to go back a long way. The Roman world knew three great revolutions of the first importance. One was the Expulsion of the Kings; another was the Cæsarian, which established the empire; the third was that by which Constantine made Christianity the typical religion of Europe. These had all the characteristics which are notes of the true revolutions in the sense we commonly mean. All were civil contests evolved from within the state. All were party triumphs. All of them permanently altered the principles of government.

This book is a description of the Christian revolution, of its causes and some, at any rate, of its results.

Not all revolutions are equally successful. The French, great as it was in its indirect and its moral effects, directly and materially affected only the government of a small part of Europe. The Russian revolution will, in all probability, prove in the end to be still more local and limited in its direct effects. But the Cæsarian and the Constantinian had results which affected the whole of western civilization from that day to this. Christianity did not make the world safe for itself merely by singing hymns and distributing tracts to the heathen. It employed several other additional precautions. It might today be as obscure a sect as Nestorianism is in the East, had it not been for Constantine. By making himself the champion of the Church he won an empire for himself and his sons, and immortal fame for his name, and he settled for many a century to come the lines along which civilization should evolve.

The majority of people do not regard revolution as a desirable activity deserving of cultivation for its own sake. Some kind of explanation is needed from those who attempt it, and no less from those who have successfully achieved it. The assertion of the Christians is that a genuine attempt was made to root out their religion. It is nowadays the fashion to argue that the persecutions were much lighter and less important than the old authorities declare them to have been: and a good case can be made out for the contention that some of them were comparatively trifling. It may be that the earlier persecutions were not exhaustive, nor pushed home with consistent energy. Howsoever this may be, the contention does not apply to the persecution of A.D. 303-313. This last was a quite serious attempt to extirpate Christianity—and in self-defence the Christians resorted to the only possible means of avoiding their fate. That is to say, they brought about a revolution and themselves seized power. This is their own statement.

If anyone should doubt the possibility of extirpating a religion, their attention may be drawn to cases in which it has successfully been done. It was done in Japan, which in the sixteenth century almost absolutely suppressed Christianity. It was done in many Mohammedan countries. Buddhism was suppressed in India. There is no reason to suppose that in the ordinary course of events the attempt of Galerius would have been less successful.

Some of the practical point of Constantine's story is given it by its relation to the situation in Russia. The present Russian government has set itself a task even greater than that which was undertaken by Galerius. It has proposed to itself the abolition, not only of Christianity, but of all religion. This is a highly interesting programme. Whether it will be pushed home to its logical conclusion remains to be seen. But this book depicts the conduct of just such an effort which was pushed home to its logical conclusion. It shows some of the problems involved; some of the unavoidable expedients, the uncontemplated stumbling blocks, the blind ditches, the subtle embarrassments. Above all, it illustrates precisely what those factors were, which brought Christianity to victory then. No religion can expect to survive unless it is able to go to the secular statesman with full demonstration that it can enrich and glorify the material every-day life of men. None, probably, can live save upon the foundation of those incredible and amazing men whose stories fill the old martyrologies sometimes with startling pathos, and sometimes with earthquake and eclipse. Christianity has never survived anywhere save by producing results: especially results upon character.

Constantine's second claim to immortality is his foundation of Constantinople. Yet although a far larger and more variegated jury will acknowledge the justice of this claim, we must remember that Constantinople is inseparable from the Christian religion. She was the Christian citadel, the fighting-home of the faith, the castle of the church militant. Constantinople, if any earthly city, was that New Jerusalem which descended from Heaven adorned as a bride for her husband. She overthrew the Fire-Worshipping Persian, and broke the power of the Arab and the Bulgarian and the

Avar: she was the immovable rock that turned back
all assault upon the new Europe which was slowly,
ignorantly, ungratefully forming under her protection.
She civilized the new east as well as the new west. If
Arab scholarship was for a time the highest in the world,
the Arab got his skill from Constantinople.

More than this: Constantine has yet another claim
to immortality in that he was the principal agent in
shaping and disseminating the later European system of
monarchy. He assembled the elements and combined
them into one coherent idea. To him is due the peculiar
political organism which, until the English Parliamentary War thirteen centuries later, was the prevailing
form of government in Europe.

It is less certain that Constantine, as a secular statesman, created general conditions favourable to the free
development of institutions and men. But if he failed
to give the state the *élan vital* which would carry it to
fresh forms and higher manifestations of civilization, he
was marvellously successful in conserving and stabilizing. Hardly any other man, coming to the control of
affairs when all seemed slipping into ruin, pulled them
together again with such effect, and saved them for so
long a period of time. We are not called upon to adopt
any air of superiority over this. The Byzantine empire,
which was indirectly his work, was the foster-mother of
modern civilization. But for that armed and christened
Athene, beautiful and barren, protectress and creator of
civilization, none of us might be here; we might have
much less to boast of, and much less to enjoy. Constantine taught at all events the political science of con-
servation. If we wish to know how to hold a civiliza-

tion intact against all assaults for eleven hundred years, to hold it steady, unalterable, unflinching and almost incorruptible, so that it never dies, but is slain sword-in-hand—then the life of Constantine has something to tell us.

Thanks ought here to be given to Dr. Meredith Hanmer, who in the year 1584 did translate out of the Greek the works of the ecclesiastical historians, beginning with Eusebius; which, bound up in the year 1650 with Mr. Wye Saltonstall's version of Eusebius' *Life of Constantine,* and published by Edw. Dod and Nath. Ekins at the Signe of the Gunne in Ivie Lane, hath greatly lightened and enchanted the work of preparing the present volume. Both Dr. Hanmer and Mr. Saltonstall, like others their contemporaries, had the prettiest turn of style, and even dull passages of the Greek issue from their pens with a brightness and sparkle pleasing to the English taste.

Elmer, Sussex,   G. P. B.
    1930.

CONTENTS

ILLUSTRATIONS, MAPS AND DIAGRAMS

CHAPTER I

THE FIRST DEATH

I

AFTER New York has sunk and vanished on the skyline, a modern liner ploughs her way for nine days through the waste of waters. On the ninth day she raises Cape Clear and the Old Head of Kinsale. Passing up St. George's Channel, the traveller sees Snowdon to the eastward, and comes slowly into the Mersey, between the long dark wilderness of buildings on the Cheshire shore and the endless sea wall of Liverpool Docks, surmounted with its crowded achievement of shipping. From Liverpool it is a short day, or thereabouts, by rail, over the Lancashire flats and through the hills of the south riding of Yorkshire—a land still one of the centres of human energy and industry. Towards the end of the day, in a wide flat country bordered by low and far-off hills, we may find a strange, most ancient city, bearing in it the visible marks of another world and another age—with its battlemented and banquetted ring-wall, its huge castle, and its vast cathedral, standing like some miraculous jewel in the sunset. Over its gates still hang the shields blazoned with the heraldry of its prime—the red cross on the silver ground, the sign of St. George.

It is old York.

From the new to the old

II

It was no mean city which gave its name to that wondrous daughter across the Atlantic. The men who

I

carried her renown abroad did so in no idle mood. Old York had a long history of commerce and battle and statesmanship. But her name and fame, which made that history, were built upon those of a still older and more venerable city which stood there before her. Long before her walls were built, or her cathedral began to grow to the sky, ancient walls, now long dust, stood there, and a city which also gave rise to a mighty city.

That mother was Roman York—Eburacum: and the daughter-city was Constantinople.

Eburacum was first built on the river flats during the reign of those rulers who ever since have been a pattern for magistrates and kings—the Roman emperors Antoninus Pius and Marcus Aurelius. It was a small, an almost unknown fortress when it began. When Marcus Aurelius, having fought the foes of his country, governed his realm and written his books, died, it was not much larger.

Let us watch the events which made her the starting point from which the builder of Constantinople set out—events which first gave to Eburacum the name and fame that men afterwards carried to build a modern Constantinople in the west.

III

Mankind progresses in a series of reactions. The reaction from Marcus Aurelius was violent to a degree as **Commodus** tremendous as his virtues. His son was by far the most sensational of his works. Commodus was a tall, handsome, athletic man, with a loathing for all the things his father had loved, and a passion for all those that his father had despised. He loved the fierceness of wild beasts, the strength of men, the nakedness of women, the scent of blood—he loved almost anything that was not like Marcus Aurelius. He was even persuaded to take a benevolent interest in Christianity—a vulgar religion of which his father disapproved. Can we blame him? He had received one of those careful educations which are more dangerous than none.

The career of Commodus is one of the most scarlet scandals of antiquity. Our shocked amazement at the sensational particulars may, however, be somewhat tempered when we ask ourselves whether their lurid colour has received any assistance from human art. Few of us will be conscious of very great surprise when we learn that more than one party had an interest in damaging the reputation of Commodus. The son of Marcus Aurelius was nothing like the monster depicted by his foes. He would probably have attracted attention in any age as a distinguished Buck or Corinthian; but he had the misfortune to be entangled in a political contest from which both his person and his repute emerged a wreck.

IV

The Roman emperors, from Nerva to Marcus Aurelius, represented a compromise between the army and the senate. The battle which had raged during the reign of Tiberius was suspended, but not terminated. Throughout the reign of Marcus this compromise had been dying. With the accession of Commodus the compromise was dead. A new generation had arisen which had forgotten the civil wars of Galba, Otho,

The compro-mise

Vitellius and Vespasian, and all that those wars had meant. Men were once more ready to try for their extreme claims.

Commodus himself was not a co-opted emperor. He ruled by hereditary right as the son of Marcus, accepted by the senate and the army. His very person was a revolution. When it became evident that he was little likely to have a son, and still less likely to co-opt a successor acceptable to the senate, the imperial succession, for the first time since the end of Nero's reign, was thrown open to doubt and intrigue. Long before the death of Commodus the protagonists were preparing to struggle for the throne as soon as his light should be blown out.

Dissolution of the compromise

Commodus was not an easy emperor to dethrone. He was a popular fellow who never did any of those things which alienate the common people. He was capable of fighting his weight in men—and was only too happy to do so. It was difficult to find a woman who would betray him. In the earlier days of his reign he was no nervous tyrant fidgeting about personal danger. The lost secretary of the rebel Avidius Cassius was run to earth, after having lain in concealment for years, and was captured with his papers upon him. The young emperor showed generosity and good feeling by refusing to follow up the case. He burned the correspondence unread, considerably to the relief of many persons in Rome. . . . The answer to this gesture was the knife of a man who sprang at him out of a dark corner, crying: "The senate sends you this!" . . . The attempt failed; but it set going the wheels of war and destiny.

V

Although investigation failed to reveal any direct complicity on the part of the senate, and indeed proved that his sister Lucilla had armed the assassin, Commodus evidently did not think that these facts exhausted the case. It is difficult to see what Lucilla had to gain, and what her motives were; and Commodus looked further for the full truth.

Conflict between emperor and senate

The delators—who had not been employed on political cases since the days of Domitian—were accordingly set to work: and the historians began to enter in their diaries the usual improbabilities concerning the gentle senators of beautiful character and perfect innocence, who were unexpectedly arrested by the brutal myrmidons of the young emperor. . . . The Prætorian prefect, Perennis, began a policy of excluding the senatorial class from military commands. The senate was powerful enough to force the downfall and death not only of Perennis, but of his successor Cleander. A second attempt, of a very curious nature, was made to assassinate Commodus. The assassins, men of the Rhine army, were to assemble secretly at Rome during the festival of Cybele. . . . This attempt, too, miscarried. Some one "blew the gaff" at the last moment. The third attempt succeeded.

Commodus had a shrewd idea that his immediate entourage was being tampered with, but the persons really implicated he was not able to discover. They proved to be his mistress Marcia, Eclectus his chamberlain, and Lætus, the new Prætorian prefect. They did not dare to give the athletic young emperor a chance for his life.

Marcia drugged him; and he was then strangled by a professional wrestler brought in for the task. The body was removed without anyone else in the palace being the wiser. The Prætorian prefect, who seems to have been the leading spirit, proceeded to report to Publius Helvius Pertinax, a senator. Pertinax convoked the senate, and informed it that he had been accepted by the army. The senate joyfully confirmed him in his new rank.

VI

The murder of Commodus is one of the determining events in history. It was the beginning of a process of action and reaction which, as we shall see, almost involved the running-down and stopping of that immense machine which we call the Roman empire. And that it was the work of the senate is fairly sure. According to the emperor Julian, Pertinax was accessory to the murder; [1] and although Julian is by no means an impeccable historian, he may be allowed, on such a point, to speak with a certain amount of authority. The murder of Commodus was a senatorial *coup d'état*. . . . The army certainly thought so. . . . All the efforts of Pertinax to make his government popular and acceptable were fruitless. Eighty-six days later he was assassinated by the men of the Prætorian guard.

The events which followed are famous. So little had the Prætorians any concerted plan of their own, or any considered programme, that as a last resort they put the throne up for sale and sold it to an able man named Didius Julianus. The Rhine, the Syrian and the Illyrian

[1] Julian, *Cæsars*, 312 D; Hist. Aug. *Pertinax*, IV, 4; VI, 7.

armies at once moved to suppress this proceeding. After a little disorder, Septimius Severus, the Illyrian commander, was placed upon the throne of Augustus. There is not much doubt about the political significance of Septimius Severus. He was the nominee of the army, a military emperor, who came with a mandate to avenge Commodus and to recover control of the empire. In his person, and under his government, the compromise with the senate was utterly destroyed.[1] Thinking to grasp at power, the senate had lost even that which it had.

Septimius Severus was an extraordinarily able man, but the government instituted by him and his sons possessed one or two defects fatal to its permanency. He had not sufficiently thought out the problem of the succession, or at all events he could not grapple with it, and his sons were not able to make good the lack. Hence, the new military rule began to disintegrate as soon as it was formed. So great was the moral impress left by Septimius himself—the last Roman of the earlier age—that his mere prestige was enough to uphold, for a few years, two strange Syrian youths who claimed the throne in virtue of an alleged connection with his family. At last the world could wait no longer. A vigorous soldier, Maximin, overthrew the confectionery Stoic emperor, Alexander Severus. With Maximin, the struggle between senate and principate reached its culmination; and before we proceed further we shall do well to examine what this contest was, why it occurred,

Failure of Severus

---

[1] Hist. Aug. *Severus*, XIII, 1-8, tells us that forty-one senators were proscribed —a number equal to the Sullan list. Prof. Bury (f.n. to Gibbon, I, p. 120) thinks it safer to follow Dion in the number twenty-nine. In any case something had happened to involve a good many senators.

and who were its leaders—for all these are matters important to have clearly in mind.

VII

The power of the army and the power of the senate did not rest upon fancy or opinion, but upon the services which they were able respectively to render to the state. The relative value of these services varied a good deal from time to time. There had been periods—such as that following the battle of Magnesia in 192 B.C., or that following the death of Domitian—when the army had very little to give, and had occupied a back seat in the estimation of men. At other times the army had been the heart and soul of Rome, the protection of all her gifts to mankind, and the repository of her traditions. Such clear cut distinctions led to equivalent clear cut political conditions. The case was harder to deal with when both the competing powers could put forward claims to importance. . . . If they had been able so to arrange their affairs that they both wielded power alternately, as modern party governments do, in and out in turn, both of them might have done their work without injury to the other or to the state. But this was beyond their horizon. The Roman world had to accept one and to reject the other, in each case with a good deal more finality and absoluteness than was good for anyone concerned—or, perhaps, than anyone wished.

It ought to be needless to say that the army was certainly not able to impose its arbitrary will by the mere process of stamping with its boots and issuing its orders.

Questions
at issue

Senators controlled the formidable bloodless weapons which are employed in the market-place and the exchange. Both parties needed to appeal to the public opinion of the world at large. The supremacy of army or of senate was thus to be achieved only by demonstration of benefits to be conferred. . . . What were these? They fell into two categories. First, the economic maintenance and strengthening of the empire; secondly, the protection of the empire from external force. If the latter is at times a much more spectacular service, and liable to more dramatic publicity, the former has the advantage of coming much closer home. To the average Roman, the Rhine and the Danube were as remote as the Yang-tse-Kiang or the Orinoco are to us. Who cares about such places? But all men care to find their income increasing; all are interested in moving into a larger house, and patronizing a more expensive seat at the theatre. Economic benefits touch men on a very sensitive nerve. Hence the senate was far from being a delicate unprotected thing, obliged to suffer meekly the arrows of outrageous fortune. The soldier on the Rhine probably felt it to be a power of tremendous magnitude, straddling the world.

The appeal to public opinion

VIII

The senate represented that ancient tradition which had come down from the days of the city states: the tradition of the self-governing city with its trading, manufacturing, agricultural population, fighting tooth and nail for its own hand, the founder of the world's arts, literature, laws and philosophy: in short, the senate stood for civilization. Unfortunately, civilization had proved a most unreliable thing: it could not be trusted alone. Its history had been the tale of one step after another in the process of disarming, cautioning, policing and controlling the lethal activities of the more civilized classes in the interests of the less. It was always undercutting the ground it stood upon, and kicking away the ladder on which it had climbed. This self-destructive tendency was a marked characteristic in its nature.

So far, it had noticeably failed to reach any permanent equilibrium. For short periods, such as the age of Pericles or that immediately preceding the Punic Wars, the statesman and the commercial man seemed to have found a *modus vivendi*. But it had turned restlessly away. Its activity had a streak of femininity in its savage egoism and its inconsequence, its proud defiance of common-sense, its charm and its exactingness. Sulla had tempered some of its enterprise by a little blood-letting. Augustus had calmed it with a considerably freer use of the scalpel. The civil wars of the Cæsarean revolution had implied the downfall of the immense fortunes which had dominated the Roman world, and the subordination of the economic power to the political power. The imperial period ushered in a golden age for the small capitalist and farmer. The impulse then given to finance and commerce had covered the Roman world with flourishing towns and crowded ports. Civilization, education, intelligence and morals had all taken a good step forward.

But there are certain limits to the work that can be done by small capitalists and small farmers. Some

The economic power

forms of enterprise demand the huge capital and the large estate. Moreover, the small men, having duly earned their returns, quite naturally proceeded to eat, drink and be merry—or at least, to attend philosophic lectures. They had no scope for anything more. The emperors ensured that it should be an age of moderate fortunes and a certain genial enjoyment of life. No great schemes were formed; no big enterprises were floated. The days of the giants were over.

IX

No point of human experience is clearer than the necessity of building up reserves against emergency. Such reserves can be built up in various ways. They can be packed away into human flesh and blood and training; they can be stored away in material form; they can be treasured as bullion, or kept in the more ethereal form of credit. But Roman civilization had not built up any adequate reserve at all. The human quality, originally matchless, had by degrees become inferior to that of the tribal north, whence its Dempseys and its Deerfoots were derived. Neither in bullion nor in credit had it much to show. The strain came before the death of Marcus Aurelius. During the wars upon the Danube and in the east, a certain inadequacy became visible in the economic resources of the world-state. Everything was bespoken. There was nothing that could be called upon without injuring the processes of daily life and common prosperity. . . . The emperors tried the old and effective expedient of broadening the agricultural basis. They settled men upon waste

Strain on the economic system

land. . . . Apparently something went wrong, for a few years later the land was still waste. . . . The economic scheme would not expand.

We all know what the average boy does when his engine will not go. He *makes* it go. It is not surprising that the emperors did likewise. They proceeded to *make* the economic scheme expand. At any rate, they taxed it just as if it had duly expanded when told to.

Economic systems respond very sensitively to taxation. The Roman capitalist and landlord objected, upon general principles, to the ruinous expenses he had to meet. To pass them on to the consumer only partially met the problem. He had already, in all likelihood, passed on to the consumer all that the unfortunate brute would bear. Further burdens merely broke his back and left the producer without a customer. As most men are both producers and consumers, the solution amounted to men mutually passing the burden along to one another. The only resource was to resist the new taxation.

It was for these reasons that slowly, from the reign of Marcus Aurelius onwards, the old struggle between the economic and the political power was renewed. The inability of the economic world to expand, and the growing burden of taxation it had to meet, were in the reign of Marcus intensified by a new trouble. Plague ravaged the empire: and we know by later experience how serious such an event can be. All these difficulties piled themselves upon the man of commerce and finance.

Marginal note: Revolt of the economic power

X

There were two aspects to the claims of the army: one was strictly military; the other was political. The army—that is, the empire—embodied the democratic tradition of Rome; the tradition of the small farmer and small trader, who demanded of government that kind of justice and administration which safeguards the small man against the big one. The empire, throughout its days, made a systematic point of checking the big man. There are limits to the process—not only limits of will and prudence, but limits of power and possibility. Nevertheless, whithersoever we turn we find the emperors and their administrators supporting the small farmer and business man, and receiving from them that support which made imperial rule indestructible.

The political power

This claim upon the support of the people at large was strengthened, from time to time, by the strictly military one. Augustus and Tiberius had made the Rhine frontier. Trajan and Hadrian had completed the Danube frontier and had made the world safe for Rome against the dangers of invasion by the tribally organized peoples of northern Europe. But just about the time when Commodus was murdered, and Septimius Severus reigned, and Maximin rose to power, something began to happen which made the wars of Tiberius and Trajan seem small and unimportant. . . . The tide of ethnic migration from Asia, which has ebbed and flowed for thousands of years in a curiously regular pulsation, began to flow.

The educated Roman (like, until recently, everyone else too) was not prepared for any such event. He

knew of no regular recurrence of these migrations; he
had no reason to expect them; least of all was he fore-
warned of their possible immensity. His tradition only
just spanned the period from the Scythian and Cim-
merian wars to the Marcomannic war of Marcus
Aurelius. He would have smiled at the notion of connecting fabulous legends of centaurs and Cimmeri with
the military situation on the Danube. He would have
found it hard to believe any theory about the regular
recurrence of ethnic migration out of the pastoral regions. Yet such a theory was true. The Roman was
feeling the first breath of what, when it came, was to
be a tornado.

Against this new aggressive force the task of the
Roman was to call up his reserves and to take the lead.
He needed to do at once all those things which cen-
turies afterwards were done by the Frankish emperor
Charles the Great and the German king Henry the
Fowler. He could not do them. He had not the money
or the organization, and he hardly knew whither to turn
to get either.

Although they had no knowledge of the full import
of what was coming, the heads of the Roman army instinctively responded to the call of necessity. They demanded reorganization, reform and the bringing up to
date of the old military machinery which had been
created for purposes of a quite different nature. They
might have had some difficulty in making this demand
effective against the scepticism of men still less aware
of the need for it: but at this point the political aspect
of the army came to its help. The military chiefs could
carry public opinion with them by raising some suitable,

even if irrelevant, slogan. Translated into practice, this meant the murder of Alexander Severus, for until Alexander was gone, the necessary steps could not be taken.

XI

Young Alexander was an admirable example of the ornamental or gingerbread Roman emperor. He might have been created by a committee of typical middle-class Romans who aimed at producing the Perfect Man. Educated by his strong-minded mother and his august aunt, he had no vices, and only the more decorous virtues. His private chapel contained a statuette of Abraham, as well as one of Apollo. He possessed, in fact, that beautiful spirit which is developed by a generous belief in everything. He illustrates the profound though natural error of the notion that amiability is the first, instead of the last, of the virtues. He was sincerely deplored by many who did not miss him in the least.

The new emperor Maximin had some of the less lovable characteristics of a Prussian drill sergeant. When he directed the senate to efface itself from the scene, the senators fell over one another in their haste to comply, and the less eager members of the illustrious body came to a regrettable and frequently abrupt end. It is no matter of surprise that the character of Maximin has been painted by the survivors in the darkest colours. He was, however, on the other hand, a man of unblemished character, and he certainly had a softer side to him. We might sum him up as a soldier quite in the tradition of Gaius Marius, with the same stern democratic temper, and the same large military ideas. He projected nothing less than the conquest of Germany right up to the shores of the Baltic. Under his administration the necessary military reforms were begun.

An attempt to assassinate Maximin was repressed with energy. The next answer of the senate came from a very fitting quarter—Africa, the province **The Gordians** furthest removed from the danger of invasion. The two Gordians, who raised the revolt, were eminent examples of the Petticoat Man which grew up in the protected and slightly hot-house atmosphere of the Roman provinces: a sentimental, domestic, sensual atmosphere, heavy with a stuffy material prosperity.[1] They formed an admirable dramatic foil to Maximin. . . . She-men of this type are much less efficient than the hundred per cent feminine woman who can get her way from Samson. The local garrison of Africa suppressed the Gordians: and the senatorial party dropped a sympathetic tear over the sad fate of the twenty-two widows and sixty-six children of the younger Gordian, who had lost their breadwinner.[2]

XII

Promptly upon the death of the Gordians two men—emperors in name; republican consuls in spirit—were elected by the senate to take their place. The choice of Balbinus and Pupienus was by no means a bad one,

---

[1] The elder Gordian celebrated the age of the Antonines in a poem of thirty books. It is, fortunately, lost. (Hist. Aug. *Gordiani Tres*, III, 3-4.)

[2] Hist. Aug. *Gordiani Tres*, XVIII-XIX. Rostovtzeff, *Social and Economic History of the Roman Empire*, p. 402, well brings out the fact that the revolt of the Gordians was engineered by a few rich men.

but it provoked, in the populace of Rome, certain
memories every whit as keen as those which persisted
among the senators. If the republican era were to be
restored, it should be completely restored. The mob
proceeded to claim a share in the election by enforcing
the choice of a nephew of the younger Gordian as
Cæsar.

Neither of the two emperors adopted young Gordian, **Revolt**
and it remained a problem what status and power (if **of the**
any) were in these circumstances possessed by a Cæsar. **senate**
Solution of these puzzles was postponed by the advance
of Maximin from Sirmium to repress the whole amazing
affair. He laid siege to Aquileia too early in the season.
The morale of the troops suffered from the hardship.
Exactly what happened is uncertain. Some say that
Maximin was murdered by his men. Some say that he
killed himself. In any case, killed he was.

Maximin's army, without its leader, and without a
candidate to take his place, surrendered to the victors.
The senate's triumph was unprecedented. The work
of Cæsar and his successors seemed to be reversed. The
republic was restored; and had the senatorial party been
equal to the emergency, it is quite conceivable that the
restoration might have been permanent. Where it
fumbled and lost control of the situation was in its
undue haste. It proceeded to reduce taxation regard-
less of the purpose for which it had been imposed; and
it went on to limit and tie up the power of the army
by legislation. This was imprudent, and was far ahead
of its mandate. Worse than this, individual senators,
rendered over-confident by their victory, came to blows
with the Prætorians. The gladiators and bruisers of the

senatorial party besieged the Prætorian camp, broke the
water-pipes, and attacked the garrison. Behind their
defences, the professional soldiers held their own, and
repulsed every effort to oust them. . . . Peace, after
desperate efforts, was patched up by Balbinus. It was
not a cordial peace.

When the army of Maximin arrived in Rome, the
views of the military party rapidly took definite form.
As soon as the Prætorians were assured of support, they
acted. Balbinus and Pupienus were separately murdered, and the senatorial counter-revolution was at an
end.

XIII

The termination of the senatorial triumph did not
provide the army with a new policy or a new leader.
The Prætorians filled up the vacant throne by proclaim-
ing young Gordian, who lasted a few years, as a stop-
gap and fell to Philip, a soldier of the Persian wars. But
a man of the Persian border was not what the empire
needed. Philip fell in turn to Decius, a man—himself
Illyrian by birth—put forward by the Illyrian army.
By this time, however, the dissensions between the senate and the army had gone so far, and had wrought
such mischief, that the whole position of the empire
was in peril. Gothic invasions were growing more and
more formidable. They threatened to destroy one of
the rich and prosperous divisions of the empire, and to
cut the Roman dominion into two dissevered halves.
Decius, in these circumstances, represented a "move to
the right."

His programme was one of general reform. He revived the office of censor, allowed (or rather ordered) the senate to elect a censor whom it would accept, and projected a general overhaul of the whole machinery of taxation and administration. It was high time. What he would have accomplished remains unknown to us, for after achieving the celebrity of being the first Roman emperor who ever had to bolt before the barbarian, he won the yet greater fame of being the first who ever lost his life in battle against them. He was slain in battle against the Goths, and his body was never found. His successor, Gallus, was a nominee of the senate; and it is hardly surprising, though it may be grieving, to find that Gallus negotiated a peace which left the Goths all their loot and prisoners, fed them while the negotiations were proceeding, and paid them an annual tribute afterwards. As the terms were not observed on the Gothic side, even such a peace as this was useless. . . . The disgusted governor of Pannonia thereupon assumed responsibility and the purple. He threw the Goths out of the Danubian provinces, and shared the tribute money among his own stout fellows. After slaying Gallus in a battle at Spoleto, he was overthrown by Valerian, the censor whom the senate had consented to trust. Valerian established a record exceeding even that of Decius. This elect of the senate was the first Roman emperor, and the only Roman emperor, who ever fell alive into the hands of foreign foes. He was (as we shall presently see) captured by the gratified Persians in the year A.D. 260.

The Anarchy increases

The reign of Valerian was the lowest gulf into which Roman repute ever descended.

XIV

In spite of his misfortunes, Valerian was far from being a fool or an idler. Had he died before he became emperor, his fame would be secure as a man of brilliant parts and worldly success. His son Gallienus, whom he associated with himself as co-emperor, was an even more brilliant man, with something of the peculiar quality of François I: a soldier, a rake, a cynic, a poet, an orator, a gardener, a cook, an antiquarian, and a man capable of receiving pleasure from conversations with the philosopher Plotinus—which is a good deal more than most of us can boast of. The father and the son were of parts as good as any two such men who ever sat upon the imperial throne.

Gallienus

But the disaster that was overtaking Rome was no respecter of brilliant parts. Valerian's reign was not three years old before the Goths overran Dacia north of the Danube, and that famous conquest of Trajan vanished from its place on the map of the Roman empire. A year later, the Franks launched their attack upon the Rhine frontier.[1] Gallienus took the Rhine command, having under him an assistant of remarkable ability, one Postumus. The same year the Alamanni, the successors of Marbod's Suevi, carried the attack eastward along the upper Danube, and the Persians came up to Antioch. . . . The Persians retired, to come again; but the Frankish raiders had a wilder and stranger

---

[1] The Franks enter the historical scene with this war, A.D. 256. They were the old German tribes of Sigambri and Chamavi, joined by the Chatti, the Chattuarii, Ampsivarii, and part of the Bructeri. Their career lasted some six hundred years. As suddenly and as definitely they vanished from history with the battle of Fontenay in A.D. 841.

history. Unable to get home through the lines that Postumus had drawn along the Rhine, they pressed on south, living by the strong hand on one of the richest and loveliest countries in the world. Coming to Spain, they fought and caroused their way from the Pyrenees to Ceuta, and then got ships, and continued the good work in Africa. . . . Incidentally, they destroyed the Spanish tin trade, with the result that the Cornish tin mines were reopened, to the great increase of British prosperity. . . .[1] They had twelve years of it; but the glorious epic has not come down to us, for none of them survived to bring it home. Among the world's best buccaneering stories this tale of the first Franks takes a high place.

XV

Amid the wild anarchy that was now the Roman empire, Valerian and Gallienus set out with amazing courage to restore order and civilization. Two men can seldom have confronted a more hopeless task. Valerian started for the east to deal with the Persian menace, while Gallienus made his headquarters on the upper Danube, whence he could superintend the whole range of the northern frontier. This scheme of defence was wrecked when Postumus decided to take the charge of the western provinces into his own hands. Postumus set up as emperor at Trèves, and for years to come ruled Britain, Gaul and Spain. . . . At the same time one Ingenuus set up independently upon the lower Danube —and the realm of Gallienus was unexpectedly shortened to Italy, Africa, and Greece. One result was that

The tactics of Gallienus

[1] Rostovtzeff, *op. cit.*, p. 583, note 86.

Britain, Gaul and Spain were secured. Postumus was a capital ruler, and looked well after them.

The cheerful cynicism of Gallienus was no doubt a help to him when the world was crumbling about his ears. Although the positions of Postumus and Ingenuus were highly irregular, they did hold their ground; but the first effect was to divert the whole stream of invasion upon Gallienus. The Alamanni threw their force upon him. With his Italian army he made his "retreat from Mons" over the Alps and down into Italy, fighting as he went. He retreated almost to the gates of Rome before his chance came, and he turned, advanced, fought his battle of the Marne near Milan, and drove the invaders back across the Danube. He maintained an optimistic outlook even when the news came that his father was a prisoner in the hands of the Persians. His optimism was adversely commented upon in some quarters.

The northern frontier held

Who can blame these critics? The disasters which had already happened were child's play to all that was to come. The angel of judgment poured out the vial of his wrath with exhaustive completeness. The loss of the west, the revolt of Illyria, and the devastation of northern Italy were followed by general disorder in Sicily and something resembling civil war in Alexandria, besides rebellion in Asia Minor. Posterity would have forgiven Gallienus if he had jumped into the Tiber. It has found it harder to forgive him because when things were at their worst he merely sent for another drink and went on fighting. The Persians, having captured Valerian, advanced as far as Cæsarea, and only retired because they found the country uninteresting. But the greatest event of all was the great raid of the Goths.

XVI

The defence of the Rhine frontier by Postumus had not been more efficient than the defence of the Danube by Ingenuus; but while the action of Postumus had no effects beyond his own province, that of Ingenuus set going a surprising chain of events. Fended off from the Danube, the Goths turned their attention further east, and occupied the Tauric Chersonese—the land which nowadays is the Crimea. Ships and pilots were available, and so, probably, was reliable information upon the subject of geography. After sacking the rich Asiatic city of Trapezus, the Goths made a test of the straits that led into the Mediterranean.

The Danube frontier turned

A highly successful expedition induced them to return in the following year with strong forces. Though defeated by the local troops in a sea-fight, the Goths made their way through the straits and nearly took Thessalonica. Gallienus gave hasty orders for the instant repair throughout Greece of the ancient fortifications which for several centuries had been mouldering happily away into obsolescence. Before very much could be done, the Goths spread themselves throughout the peninsula. They were surprised at Athens by some enterprising Greeks. Claudius, afterwards the emperor, headed off and captured several parties who were attempting to return home across the Danube. Gallienus himself arrived with troops. Having collected as much as they could carry of everything that struck their fancy, the Goths sailed back again through the straits, and arrived at their starting point.

There was now hardly any corner of the Roman Collapse

dominions, no matter how remote or how protected from the blasts of ordinary adversity, which had not felt the fire and sword of savage foes. The raid of the Goths into Greece put the final touch to the horrible picture. . . . Countries as peaceful and as unaccustomed to violence as our own modern homes had been swept by the Franks, the Alamanni, the Goths and the Persians, or by civil dissension hardly less ferocious. The end of the world seemed to be at hand. Terrifying prodigies warned men of the evil yet to come. Famine stalked abroad, and with famine, starvation, and with starvation pestilence. . . . The material injury done was catastrophic; but perhaps still worse was the damage done to the spiritual fabric of credit and confidence upon which industry is ultimately built. Money collapsed as we have seen the German mark and the Russian rouble collapse.[1] Almost at a stroke, with terrifying suddenness and unexpectedness, the civilized world was plunged to the lips in the barbarism it had well-nigh forgotten.

XVII

Such was the reign of Gallienus. If that cheerful cynic had no other virtue, he had at least the gift of boundless hope. When matters were at their worst, he acted as though all were well. He abated no jot or tittle of right from the imperial sovereignty. When, after fighting and intriguing for fifteen years, the great-

---

[1] The denarius fell to less than one thirty-second part of its normal value. The fall was sometimes worse than this. Even in Diocletian's time, Egyptian wheat was 15,000 per cent over its normal price, or money one fifteen thousandth of its normal value. See Rostovtzeff, *loc. cit.*, pp. 417-420. This was no doubt temporary and exceptional.

est optimist in history fell to the missile of an unknown hand outside Milan, he named, before he died, a successor—M. Aurelius Claudius.

Whatsoever secret history may conceivably have lain behind the nomination of Claudius, it was a turning point in the tide of events. He was not a brilliant man; it is doubtful if he was even clever. He had few personal gifts, but he had that peculiar thing, the kingly mind. He had just that elusive and indefinable combination of qualities which will make men act in unison. *The first Illyrian emperor*

Gallienus, the son of a nominee of the senate, had been gradually forced by the pressure of events into an anti-senatorial policy. He had made the defence of the empire and the preservation of its unity the aim of his life. In doing so, he adopted the policy of the army. Under his government the old opposition between army and senate had taken the form of a complete exclusion of the old senatorial class from military employment. He had changed the army into a guild far more exclusive than it ever had been before. These were some of the reasons for that quite peculiar hatred of Gallienus which the senatorial party always showed. . . . The disasters of his reign were scarcely his fault. Something much more than the enterprise and ability of a single man was needed to defend the empire from external invasion and inward disruption. New organization and new plans were necessary, suited to the new era; and it would take more than one man's life to elaborate these. Money was wanted; and this was where the shoe pinched the worst. The accession of Claudius allowed the senate to surrender with a good grace. It expressed its delight in his manly virtues and solid worth. *Significance of Gallienus*

XVIII

The brief reign of Claudius was singularly crowded with events for a man so stolid and prudent. He was just in time to meet and defeat the great coalition of northern nations which broke upon the Roman frontier in the year of his accession. He beat the Alamanni and their allies near Lake Garda. Proceeding into Illyria, he swept the Goths out of the peninsula. He died of the plague which was ravaging the starving and ruined empire. But before he died he nominated a successor, L. Domitius Aurelianus, whom the army obediently proceeded to elect and to force (if necessary) upon the empire. The senate had backed a rival, a brother of Claudius, but hastened to submit.

Aurelian restores the empire to normal

Aurelian was a peasant by birth, and a particularly tough specimen of the Illyrian breed. Claudius had reigned only two years; Aurelian reigned only four and three-quarters—but every week was full of important events. In that brief time Aurelian suppressed the Alamanni, imposed order on the northern frontiers, recovered the east, put down the troubles in Egypt, received the surrender of Gaul, and restored the empire outwardly to its normal state. He was a hard man with no feelings save those dictated by expedience: a disciplinarian whose word was law. He might have lived many years if he had not frightened a dishonest secretary. He was assassinated near Byzantium, in the year A.D. 275.

It was almost at once recognized that the murder of Aurelian was a mistake—even an irregularity. The murderers apologized, and explained that they had been misled. The result was that the army had no candidate ready. An interregnum of some six months followed, while army and senate watched one another.

Aurelian had been highly obnoxious to the senate, who had been at daggers drawn with him for a good part of his reign. He was too obviously the candidate of the army. Yet things were not now as they had been. Faced now by the polite request of the army to select **Position of the** an acceptable successor, the senate could not make up **senate** its mind. It contained, apparently, no one passionately desirous of power. Not a single senator, burning with prophetic zeal, pressed forward to serve his country. . . . This was strange. The military habit of murdering one's predecessor was at any rate testimony to a keen interest in politics. . . . At length the senate elected M. Claudius Tacitus, a venerable old gentleman of seventy-five. . . . Six months of campaigning in Asia Minor were enough for Tacitus. He died of worry and hard work at Tyana. His brother Florianus somewhat irregularly appointed himself his successor. The senate seemed to have nothing very decided to say upon the subject, but the unfortunate army sent a wild appeal to Probus, a popular officer, who at once answered the call. He arrived to find that the grateful army had done away with Florianus, and now proceeded to clap the crown upon his own head.

XIX

Probus, like Aurelian, was an Illyrian and a realist. He had no particular desire to be emperor. Life had already given him all the substantial rewards she can shower upon a brilliant career; and the imperial sovranty only meant more work and responsibility, without more pleasure. But he accepted the dignity thus thrust upon him. His policy was to respect the authority and tradition of the senate; and the senate was delighted with a man who was ready to do all the work and leave it all the credit.

The reign and the death of Probus were very similar to those of Aurelian. Like Aurelian, he spent his days in incessant activity in every part of the empire. Like Aurelian, he was successful in all that he began. His most important contribution to the future lay outside war and administration. Long after his death he continued to rule the Roman world in the persons of men whose feet he had first set upon the road to success. He was that greatest of men—a judge of other men. We shall soon meet with their names—Carus, Diocletian, Maximian, Constantius and Galerius. . . . These were the amazing General Staff which Probus picked.

And he died like Aurelian. He was too strict a disciplinarian, and he was slain in a sudden mutiny. The mutineers regretted their act as soon as it was done.

Peculiar importance of Probus *(margin note)*

XX

And now a new and remarkable figure enters the arena; a dry, grim, shabby, bald-headed old wolf of a man, who notified the senate, with indifference, that he had been elected emperor, and it could do what it liked about it. With a few murmurs, it proceeded to do nothing. Carus reveals in his actions that new ideas were growing in the minds of the more intelligent offi-

Transformation *(margin note)*

cers. The days were over when, for lack of a policy, the army was ready to give the senate its chance. Carus created his two sons "Cæsars," and gave the eldest, Carinus, the government of the western provinces of the empire. The younger, Numerian, accompanied his father to the east. Carus apparently intended—for the plan was never carried out—to create a Cæsar for the west and a Cæsar for the east, over whom the Augustus should exercise a final authority. Had he lived, he might have tackled the whole thorny question of the succession—and much else. The need was crying.

The reign of Carus, though successful, was short. He died during his eastern campaign, and was at once succeeded by the two Cæsars, Carinus and Numerian. Exactly what arrangement they would or could have made between them with regard to the empire cannot now be guessed, for stronger hands pushed them aside.

On the march home from Persia, rumours began to circulate through the Roman army. At last the truth came to light. Numerian was dead, and Arrius Aper, the Prætorian prefect, had for some time been issuing fictitious orders in his name. Aper was swiftly brought to justice. He was charged before an assembly of the army with the murder of Numerian, and was cut down before he had made his defence.

His accuser and slayer was Diocletian.

Election of Diocletian, Sept. 17th, A.D. 284

CHAPTER II

DIOCLETIAN

I

BUT who was Diocletian? That he was an accident, or that he was totally unconnected with all that went before, it is hard to believe. His entry upon the stage has all the air of being the entry of the star player. After this and that forerunner has busied himself in keeping warm the Roman imperial throne, and has spoken a short part that seems to have been learned by rote—suddenly enters this man, with stern authentic words; and with a shock we realize that here at length is the master.

Master of what? . . . It is not easy to say. He had some power which was not his obvious and official power. He was commander of the imperial Household Guards—the Domestici. This post did not give him officially the contact with and control over the imperial service which the Prætorian prefect possessed. Arrius Aper had counted upon his rank to give him the reversion of the imperial throne. All went for nothing.[1] Though he was of a lower grade and a lower office, Diocletian

Diocletian

Identity of Diocletian

---

[1] If a commission of investigation had ever sat upon the deaths of Carus and Numerian, the evidence would have been sensational. Carus died under extremely mysterious circumstances. During a thunderstorm his tent was seen to be on fire, and one set of witnesses say that he was killed by lightning. His private secretary, on the other hand, asserts that he died naturally, but forgets to say of what, and makes the interesting statement that the fire was caused by the emperor's servants in their grief. All this is a highly suspicious tale, on which a cross-examining counsel would work great havoc. A little later, Numerian also died in some way

had an influence over men which made his path easy. He may have been the head of some Mithraistic order. He was tired of seeing his delegates strut their little hour. He took openly the control which he had for long past exercised in secret. The world was not long in realizing the difference.

II

Before Diocletian could regard himself as settled in power he had to remove the surviving son of Carus. . . . Young Carinus had no intention of submitting meekly. All the material advantages of numbers and resources were in his hands. After a winter of negotiations, plans and intrigues, the two rivals met in Illyria, where the river Morawa falls into the Danube. Carinus all but won the battle. The army of Diocletian was already beaten when Carinus was stabbed by one of his own

not perfectly clear to us. As Diocletian was commander of the guard, he cannot but have known the circumstances, and his sworn evidence before the commission would have been interesting. He would also have been asked to tell the court—(i) Why he killed Arrius Aper before the latter could make any statement; (ii) How he had the power to carry this off without provoking enquiry; (iii) Why he said, "Great Æneas slays you!" (iv) Why he said, "I have slain the boar [Aper] at last!" (Vopiscus, *Numerian* XV.) (v) Whether the grandfather of Vopiscus the historian was correct in his testimony.

The grandfather of Vopiscus could have told the Court: When they were all private soldiers together in the ranks, their landlady at Tongres was a Druidess. She kept a shop. Diocletian lodged there. Once, when paying his bill, he seemed slow to part with his money, and she said: "Don't get stuck to it," or words to that effect. Diocletian said: "I shall part with it quicker when I am emperor," or words to that effect. She said: "You will be emperor when you have killed the boar." He smiled and said nothing, because, said Vopiscus' grandfather, he was a deep one (erat altus). And on another occasion Diocletian said: "I always kill the boar, but some one else gets the skin." . . . Finally, Vopiscus' grandfather (possibly feeling that he had spoken too freely) said that Diocletian told him that he only killed Aper because of the Druidess's prophecy. . . . The Commission could then have considered its verdict. Most of us could make an intelligent anticipation of its substance.

The boar was a sacred animal in the old Celtic religion, and "killing the boar" may easily have had a technical sense in some quarters.

officers: by which deed the course of history was changed.

The battle of Margus extinguished the last trace of opposition to Diocletian. His first actions were significant. He proscribed no one. The officers of Carinus were welcomed. It may have been the gentle benevolence of the new emperor which inspired this mood; but it may no less have been the approval of a master satisfied with the service he has received.

With the accession of Diocletian the Roman world emerged from the night of disaster and disorder. He represented a definite policy of reform and reconstruction, which he put into force by the imperial authority. The economic power had done nothing. The political power accordingly took the reins. A subtle transformation was already passing over it. In the person of Diocletian it was renewing a dazzling youth.

III

There was appropriateness in this; for Diocletian had a personality which in some of its qualities recalled with strange distinctness the first, the great Augustus—far though in others it might diverge from that classic pattern. His parents had been slaves in the household of a prosperous Roman senator named Anulinus; and his father rose to be a freedman and the family secretary. The future emperor himself had no haughtier name than that which he derived from the town in Illyricum where his mother was born—Doclia. Young Docles, as he grew in ambition, became Diocles, and at last Diocletianus.

As might be inferred from the occupation of his father, Diocletian was, if not precisely of scholarly temperament, at any rate distinguished by some of those more subtle intellectual qualities which are unpopular with rough and robust men.[1] Discussion and persuasion were his methods. He disliked violence and usually avoided responsibility for its use. He possessed naturally that polish of manner and decorum of conduct which some men need to assume as a mask that is always slipping off. . . . He had many of the instincts of the shop-walker. It was his mission in life to conduct his customers with ceremony and in the most suitable ways to the departments they needed.

IV

The work of Diocletian was cut out for him. He was thirty-eight years old, at the height of his vital energy; by his portraits a plain, small-featured man with a close-cropped head and a mild expression. We meet with the type often enough in daily life—usually fair, and usually well-fleshed, and rather pale of complexion. . . . His first action, that spring, after the battle of Margus, was to clean up on the Danube, where he found himself. In virtue of his campaign against raiding tribesmen from over the river he assumed the imposing title of Germanicus Maximus. . . . Thus early he rubbed one fact well into the consciousness of the Roman world

Diocletian sets to work

---

[1] Eutropius, IX, 26. He was interested in sculpture. See the story of the stonemasons of Sirmium; Mason, *Persecution of Diocletian*, p.259 *et seq.* The epistle of St. Theonas shows that he was interested in his library (*ibid.*, p. 348, *et seq.; vide*, § VII). As Mr. Mason says, he first comes before us with a quotation from Virgil on his lips. His building activities are famous. Spalatro used to be quoted by the zealots as the first definite sign of the coming medieval architecture.

—that it now had an exceedingly great and mighty emperor, and the sooner it realized that fact, the better. This attitude on Diocletian's part was for the benefit of the man in the street. He was not, in private life, quite so exceedingly great and mighty as he induced the latter to believe. He had not been in office six months before he began to develop the theme which was to be his most remarkable contribution to the theory of imperial monarchy. By giving his friend Maximian the status of Cæsar, he took the first step towards transforming the monarchy into a board of emperors.

There had been Cæsars before, ever since the days of Lucius Ælius, and it was not at first sight evident that the new dignity would be more than that which Ælius had held. But a year after the battle of Margus the difference began to grow visible. Not only was Maximian an amazingly different man—a fierce, active, virile fellow of irrepressible energy and abounding hope—but he was now created Augustus, and was taken into full and equal association as a partner emperor. . . . They called themselves "Jovius" and "Herculius." Diocletian was "Jovius" and Maximian was "Herculius." . . . Above all the other features of this step shone its surprising mingling of humility and confidence. . . . Diocletian was quite sure that no man single-handed could govern the empire. He had the faith and the self-assurance, in the teeth of history, to share his throne with another man. . . . If he had no other title to fame, he deserves immortality for that.

Before this book is finished, the reader will freely and honourably acquit Maximian of any of the more narrow-minded virtues. Never at any time did he qualify

The
Board of
Empire

for wings. But he played the game with Diocletian as honestly and as squarely as if he had not been the intolerant, ambitious man he was. Not only could Diocletian share a throne, but—a much more wonderful **Maximian** thing to do—he could even hypnotize his partner into playing fair.

His object in making this arrangement was to secure for himself some amount of peace and leisure in which to think out plans and policies, while Maximian shouldered the burden of activity upon the frontiers.

V

Reduced to its briefest terms, the problem before him was that of defending the empire at a cost within the ability of the empire to bear. . . . Neither then nor since has any one seriously suggested that the task could have been avoided. If it were impossible to make the defence adequate at a reasonable cost, then nothing was left but to retire from the contest and to surrender all hope of maintaining civilization against the barbarian. The whole trend of the tale so far seemed to indicate that there was no reason for doubt. Civilization, as such, is richer than barbarism, and has infinitely greater resources. It has nothing to fear from a struggle. . . . At least, it has nothing to fear from its foes. It may have something to fear from itself, and the folly and ignorance of its supporters. But Diocletian could take up the work secure in one certitude: it was a work which could be carried to practical success, if men at large so desired.

His solution was a mobile central reserve or striking

force. . . . Little by little the legions of Augustus had degenerated into territorial regiments recruited from the provinces which they garrisoned. They had become, therefore, very local in their interests and composition. Being chiefly recruited from the small land-owners and lease-holders of the frontier regions, they were growing to be limited by the peasant's social outlook as well as by his local interests. They lacked some of that coherence and unity which, through their common membership of Italian urban communities, the legions of the late republic had possessed. Any advantage in the provincial patriotism of the legions in Diocletian's day was counterbalanced by the fact that to concentrate large forces against invasion meant stripping one frontier to supply another; and the time had come when, with Persians on the Syrian border, Goths on the Danube, Franks and Alamanni on the Rhine and revolt in Mauretania, this was no longer possible. All the frontiers must be held; and a mobile reserve, to strike where needed, was the cheapest and most effective expedient. Such a reserve could, furthermore, be given just that unity, common training, common outlook, common opinion, which the old Augustan army had possessed. It would be an imperial army free from local interests or class prejudices—the freer, the better. Like the emperor himself, it would think of the good of the whole; it would watch the main trend, the large lines.

VI

The Imperial Reserve Force of Diocletian involved something like doubling the army; and this in turn

meant effective steps for finding the money. The reaction of this idea of the Imperial Reserve upon the
imperial office itself was peculiar and noteworthy. A
fresh circle of men, inspired by new ideas, began to surround the emperor. It was no longer quite so necessary for him to canvass the good will of the old provincial legions. Something of the seclusion which began
to mark his person, the difficulty of gaining access to
him, the awful majesty of his presence, arose from the
very practical need of guarding him from angry men
who did not like the new system. A great deal too many
of Diocletian's predecessors—Probus and Aurelian
among them—had been victims of the assassin's blade.
The only way to preserve him from illegitimate pressure—or even to give him freedom of judgment un-
hampered by undue persuasion and argument—was to
insulate him from the public at large. It is probable
that Diocletian himself was conscious that his judgment
might suffer if disturbed by undue persuasion. He
knew the art himself. . . . Hence were built up the
first courses of that wall of etiquette and ceremonial
which ultimately came to surround the sacred person
of Augustus. . . . The first Augustus, sitting in his
comfortable old clothes in his study at the top of the
house, might—had he known—have pitied the gorgeous
array of his successor. But then his own taxation had
been light.

Secondary effects of the Central Reserve

Seclusion of the emperor

VII

The new imperial idea had another consequence.
Diocletian seems to have felt that even the city of Rome
itself unduly localized the spiritual Rome, the world-

state, the sacred empire. As an Illyrian, not, perhaps, educated quite up to the standards which would have satisfied Cicero, or even Quintillian, he had no very great interest in Rome. Like Athens, Rome was a memento of past glories rather than an embodiment of present powers. . . . He never lived in the city of Cæsar and Augustus. When Maximian shared power with him, Diocletian took the eastern provinces under his own particular care, and settled at Nicomedia. Maximian, whose principal task was to watch the Rhine frontier, made Milan his headquarters. The distinction between Italy and the provinces was abolished, and with it the privileged position of Rome. . . . From these measures of Diocletian we may date the day when Rome finally ceased to be a conquering Italian city ruling an empire which she had won. She became now one city among the many which constituted the world state. Her career as a city-state was definitely ended. Rome submitted to the discipline which for five hundred years past she had imposed, for their good, on the people of the Mediterranean.

Privilege of Rome abolished

The need of very high war taxation made it necessary in fact to impose upon the empire a discipline such as it had never before endured. Diocletian proceeded to tighten the bonds of civil obedience. The old imperial organization which had plunged into the turmoil of the reign of Gallienus emerged, under Diocletian's hand, strangely changed in pattern and colouring.

The secret of the transformation lay in the fact that the old urban commercial life which, since the days of the Greek and Phœnician adventurers, had been the heart and soul of civilization, was dying. With the denarius down to a small fraction of its value, and prices soaring, and gold vanished from circulation,[1] it had become almost impossible to collect taxes in money— and quite impossible to collect the larger proportion of them in that form. The disappearance of the great financial corporations, and all that was involved in the collapse of commerce, made it impracticable to defer taxation by means of a loan. One form or another of loan, giving the taxpayer respite until he had found his feet, might have changed the course of history; but no power any longer existed capable of lending the money or the credit.

Causes of the change

With such a problem to solve, Diocletian's first step was the natural one of abolishing all privilege and all unnecessary exceptions. The whole empire had to fare alike. Saving a few cases indicated by particular expedience or ancient sentiment, he reorganized the empire with uniform system. There were no longer imperial and senatorial provinces. All were imperial. These were now grouped together in larger units called Dioceses, each governed by a vicar. The dioceses in turn were grouped into four great divisions, according to the natural geographical indications by which the empire fell into the Britanno-Gallic group, the Italo-African, the Illyrian, and the Asiatic. Four such groups seemed to imply four emperors. And this was very

---

[1] The mines yielded less; hoarding was taking place (and not private hoarding only; see Ch. IV, § XI) concurrently with the export of gold to the east in exchange for commodities. Apparently there was not much that the east wanted from the west in the early years of the Christian era, and a drain of gold resulted. Bury, *op. cit.*, I, 54. This probably had its share in creating the financial crisis. According to Sir Alfred Chatterton in the *Times* of March 20, 1930, the same process of absorbing gold is at work in India today. Some of the results of governmental hoarding are illustrated in Dr. Pant's *Commercial Policy of the Moguls* (1930).

nearly Diocletian's plan. The four great divisions were further grouped in two pairs, each under an Augustus. Each of the two Augusti then chose, and formally adopted, a successor and lieutenant, called a Cæsar, who in due time should step into his shoes. . . . A Roman of the old time, who had seen the Roman dominion struggle into existence in a hundred different ways, would have opened his eyes very wide at this symmetry and uniformity. . . . Most natural objects, from algæ to empires, have a somewhat irregular growth. Only now and then in human history do the occasion and the man so come together that these great symmetrical schemes are possible. The instinct of most men is to fear that such system as this is a Birkenhead Drill— the grace and discipline amid which a state goes down with all on board.

Whether it were to be so in this case, time would try.

The new
system

VIII

The system of grouping which Diocletian thus imposed upon the empire he duplicated from top to bottom. Every given area was at once an area of military command and an area of civil government. The military and civil authorities had, officially at least, little or no connection with one another, and their relationship was principally through the central government. The task of the military hierarchy was to defend the empire. The task of the civil hierarchy was to administer the law and assess and collect the taxes. Some such distinction between the military and the civil sides of life had been growing steadily for generations. Diocletian ratified and rationalized it.

He fulfilled more than one purpose by so doing. He governed the empire through men who had qualified themselves for the task; not by wealthy amateurs whose claims to omniscience were demonstrated at the public cost. And he built firm and effective barriers against military revolt. The men and the money would never again, as long as his system endured, be wielded by the same hands. Those two powers, whose conjunction had been so formidable, could now, in separation, be controlled by a small group of men who possessed the legal authority.

This symmetrical system was not, however, merely ornamental. It had a practical objective—it was an oiled and effective engine for collecting and dealing with taxes which were paid in kind. The old system had been impossible for such a task. The nature of these taxes and the mode of assessment employed illustrate several facts about Diocletian and his age. Perhaps he had come to the front just for the very reason that he actually was close in touch by birth and tradition with the country life, and understood to the full that natural agricultural economy which was now the standard economy. His friends and his allies likewise were most of them peasant-bred men. We distinctly see that we are in a country era. The city and the market and the banker's office are fading; barn and rickyard and storehouse are becoming all in all.

IX

Diocletian invented or applied several remarkable expedients for the purpose of running an empire upon peasant economy. It is perhaps more probable that he applied ideas which he had learnt from some other source, than that he invented them. This source was most likely the east—those countries which once, long ago, had been part of the Persian empire, and which today we know as Turkey, Syria and Egypt. His own interests had always been eastern, as we can see from his choice of the eastern provinces for his own government, and his selection of an Asiatic town—Nicomedia—as his seat. Asia had long been a peasant country. Even though it had been urbanized by the Greeks, it tended to slip back into a world of fields and vineyards and spaces and silence and seasonal activities. The power and influence of the Persian had receded before the town-dwelling commercial Greek; but if it were a question of organizing an empire of peasants, the Persian had much to say, and long practical experience to go upon.

Diocletian took one year's food for a soldier as his unit: the grain, wine, meat, oil and salt necessary to his keep for twelve months. This was called an annona.[1] An officer, according to his rank, was paid several annonæ. The materials were collected from the tax-payer and distributed to the soldier in the due proportion. As

Method of taxation

The tax in kind

[1] The annona was an old tax, which had been imposed occasionally in exceptional circumstances. During the Anarchy it had, for lack of ready money, been imposed with increasing frequency. What Diocletian did was to turn it from the exception to the rule. He systematized the expedient, and created a definite unit of taxation.

the requirements of the army were not every year the same, the emperor every year fixed the total amount that would have to be raised. This proceeding was called an Indiction.

A complete survey of the empire, revised every five years, formed the basis on which these taxes were assessed. Not the acreage but the productive value of the land was the thing taxed.[1] The peasant was thus not obliged to obtain money for his produce in a competitive market, in order to be able to pay his tax. He paid with what he grew. . . . This was a producer's paradise. It is a comment upon the innate wickedness of the human heart that even so the producer did not seem to want to pay any taxes.

Every five years, however, the army received a bonus in cash. The money for this was found by the senatorial and commercial classes,[2] and it was characteristic of the age that the necessity for paying cash was felt as a particular hardship. The taxpayer made more noise about these money taxes than about all the taxes in kind.

The money tax

Some time after Diocletian's reign, every fifteen years became counted a cycle of indictions, and years were

[1] "Thus there was a unit (iugum) of arable land, and the number of acres in the unit might vary in different places according to the fertility of the soil; there were units for vineyards and for olives; and the tax was calculated on these units. The unit was supposed to represent the portion of land which an able-bodied peasant (caput) could cultivate and live on. Thus a property of one hundred iuga meant a property of a hundred labourers or capita, human heads." (Bury, *History of the Later Roman Empire*, I, p. 47. See his notes for further details.) Mr. W. E. Heitland thinks that such a system was impossible to carry out, and never was carried out, with justice. (*Agricola*, p. 388.) But obviously it was an attempt at justice.

[2] The *aurum oblaticum* by the senators; the *aurum coronarium* by the decurions; and the *chrysargyron* by the tradesmen of all kinds. A special property tax, the *collatio glebalis*, was paid by senators. It was popularly known as *follis* from the little bag of money used in making cash payments.

dated by their position in the cycle. . . . And even today, many centuries later, we need only to look into our almanack to discover that the year in which these lines are penned is the thirteenth of its indiction—so much a thing of our own modern era is the work of Diocletian.

x

Tradition has been strangely capricious and unreasonable in identifying the friends and the enemies of mankind. It is certain that among those who rank with the bitter taskmasters of humanity the name of Diocletian stands fairly high. And yet few men can have spent less upon that mere personal luxury which is so offensive to those who have to foot the bill. He kept no harem. He was a respectably married man with a family undistinguished by any scandals. He did not drink—though Maximian did. . . . All the money that was ground out by this wondrous mill of organization was spent upon the defence, the policing and the general government of the empire. The taxpayer certainly received value for his payments. Not in the times of Diocletian did the Goths foray into the heart of the empire, and, from among the ruins of Athens, make philosophical disquisitions upon the disadvantages of civilization. Men might plough and reap in peace while G. Aurelius Valerius Diocletianus watched the course of the state.

The revenue well employed

XI

It was certainly Persian custom which Diocletian introduced into the Roman world; though that ancient and famous race of soldiers, sportsmen and poets might claim that what is Persian could hardly be called either soft or unmanly. The cold and proud Augustus might wear his old clothes. The slave-born Diocletian felt the need of facing a hard world in silk and diamonds. He wore the diadem—a band of white silk embroidered with pearls. Cæsar had died, not for wearing it, but for giving cause for a suspicion that he wished to wear it. . . . Augustus had been the first among equals in the company of the wealthy and cultivated men who were his agents. He had joked with them, and had submitted to considerable freedom of speech in his turn. . . . But the herculean ploughmen and bull-dozers who, wondrous with tabs and medals, entered the presence of Diocletian, were constrained to kneel and do obeisance to the majesty of the divine sovran. . . . The court of Augustus had been only a somewhat magnified version of any educated Roman's household. The court of Diocletian was disciplined like an army headquarters, with its etiquette and its regulations and its discipline, and its meticulous adherence to red tape. To get through the crowd and reach the presence of the emperor, a man needed uncommonly secure knowledge and prompt address. No one could do it without a preliminary initiation into the details of procedure. The seclusion which guarded Diocletian was no affair of chance.

The new Court

We should do Diocletian an injustice if we took too seriously the imperial window-dressing which he designed to over-awe the senate and impress the man in the street. Even if he did borrow a little from the Persian, it was with no oriental motives. . . . He was a Roman and a realist; his motives were psychological. The old shirt-sleeved monarchy of Rome had had serious disadvantages. It had been too casual; and all that Augustus and his successors could do had failed to get rid of the atmosphere of the improvised and the adventurous. The "Log Cabin to White House" principle needs revision when it leads to congestion of the traffic at Washington. Diocletian merely proposed a little selection of the candidates, and a little decorum in approaching the person of Augustus. It was a misfortune that his prescription proved rather too complicated to be workable. . . . We may guess that the etiquette which ultimately came to surround the sacred person was not always intended for the benefit of the latter. . . . But nevertheless some change was necessary. The reigns of Valerian and Gallienus had proved that. More respect was wanted; and Diocletian depended upon one great law of human nature—to wit, that decorum and discipline often enough create the respect which they seem to involve.

The principle

XII

The absolute nature of this new monarchy is often exaggerated—at any rate, by implication. In actual practice the emperor was very little, if at all, more absolute than formerly he had been. The quality of despotic authority was more in ceremonial and in words than in facts. Diocletian had enforced obedience and even reverence for the dignity of the head of the state; but he had not established any new power either of legislation or of administration. The senate continued to sit, and to perform its customary services of discussion and advice.[1] If it failed in this respect, the reason is to be found more in the absence of the emperors from Rome, and their absorption in special work, than in any change of custom. In after years, two or three reigns later, we begin to see that the position of the senate had not greatly suffered. The change was rather in its members. Senators were no longer exclusively of the old type, men of the city and the exchange, but more and more men of the great provincial estates, semi-feudal landlords, ex-soldiers and ex-ministers, who were of the imperial party. The old classical senator, with his elaborate pagan culture, was indeed not extinct; but the new booted and baronial genus was growing in numbers.

The new empire

Diocletian increased rather than diminished the checks upon imperial autocracy. His consistorium, a council which resembled the Privy Council of an English king, or a Cabinet Council, was a much more effective organization than the old consilium from which it sprang. It was called a "consistorium" because the members stood in the presence of the sacred emperor instead of sitting;[2] but this was the end of its servile and dependent characteristics. In its operation it was a genuine council. Neither the emperor nor his chief ministers acted with arbitrary despotism. The consistorium determined most of the important questions on grounds of public policy, and advised the emperor. Not even the Antonines had been more constitutional in their practice than this.

[1] Such of its separate powers of government, coinage, etc., as had survived the Anarchy, were swept away; but this did not make the emperor more absolute; it only removed a meaningless anomaly. See Bury, *History of the Later Roman Empire*, I, p. 18; the whole of whose Ch. I, § 2, bears upon this point.

[2] This was probably a bit of traditional Illyrian custom—the tribal elders who stood in a circle for their conferences; and in its origin it may have had nothing to do with monarchy.

From all these signs and symptoms we may deduce that the task of administering the Roman dominion was a growing task, and the machinery was also growing in extent and complexity. Diocletian perhaps began more than he completed. He started ideas rather than gave them their finished and final form. He started ideas of systematic and scientific government which were a good deal in advance of his age—if that be any crime. Not all of them managed to maintain their ground. But taking them all together, he made probably the greatest contribution any single man ever made to the science of practical government. His inventions, for many a century to come, enabled other and often smaller men to grapple with tasks that might otherwise have been too great for their powers.

Diocletian as a statesman

XIII

While this new organization of the empire was in course of conception and execution, Maximian took in hand the immediate business which needed a man of action. He left for Gaul a few weeks after he had been invested with the full imperial authority of Augustus. He was needed; and he was the right man for the task. . . . In more recent times he might have enjoyed a successful career as a Cape Horn skipper. Wheresoever orders needed to be given in a loud and peremptory voice, and obedience promptly enforced, Maximian was at home.

Gaul was in a serious state. The Alamanni and the Burgundi had broken the frontier lines, and the whole country was in chaos. Maximian arrived at Mainz and

at once began organizing a better condition of affairs.
. . . We have already noticed that famous break-
through of the Franks thirty years before, in the reign
of Gallienus; when, unable to get home again, the raiders
wandered on through Gaul, through Spain, and over
the sea to Africa. Their deeds had the first result of
destroying the productivity and the trade of the Spanish
mines, which for centuries had represented the largest
mining interests in the empire. In consequence it became profitable to re-open the British tin mines, and
while the empire was plunged to the lips in economic disaster, Britain entered upon a flourishing period of prosperity.

Most things have their compensations and their
counterchecks. The increasing wealth of Britain attracted attention among the inhabitants of the Low
Countries. The Frisians and their neighbours were developing the sailing-ship to the point at which, by construction and size and sailing power, it could make the
North Sea passages more easily and cheaply than ever
before. They were, and always had been, keen traders.
To divert some of the produce of the re-opened British
mines to Frisian markets was no doubt a very profitable
speculation,[1] in no way damaged by the possibility of
diverting a mixed assortment of other articles at the
same time. From the year 275 onwards, therefore, a
series of piratical descents on the British coast began.
We know them as the "Saxon Raids," and no doubt they
were mostly conducted by seamen of Saxon tribes; but

Maximian on the Rhine

State of Britain

---

[1] Tin is a valuable metal today; it was much more valuable in A.D. 275, and
hardly any cargo except the precious metals would have been better worth running. For the identity of the pirates, see Gibbon, I, p. 357, note 26.

they were in all probability inspired and financed from Frisia. They had been proceeding for eleven years when Maximian took up his command in Gaul.

As bad as the Alamanni and the Saxons were the plundering bands which were wandering over the face of the country. The Gaul to which Maximian came was in something of the same state as France after the Hundred Years' War. . . .[1] Ruined men, despairing of any good from work or from conventional means of subsistence, went about in parties pillaging and wresting a living from their fellows. By degrees the disorder spread over Gaul, and a large part of the population took up a somewhat indefinite revolutionary attitude, and contemplated, but did not exactly obey, a ramshackle revolutionary organization that was more a dramatic gesture than a purposed intention.

Maximian promptly cleared the Rhineland of invaders, and chased back into Germany any that were slow in their movements. Revolution, the hardest thing in the world to repress when it is real, is the easiest when unreal. A few hangings and floggings had an electrical effect upon the Bagaudæ. They melted like snow. Maximian stamped out disorder and saw that the social and political machinery was set going again. His vigorous hand soon cleared away the jungle of confusion which fifty years of civil war and German invasion had left. He could not undo what had been done; but at any rate he could rough-hew the work of the future for more delicate hands to shape. . . . He had hardly completed these urgent tasks when the British problem assumed a much more serious form, and gave rise to

The Bagaudæ suppressed

[1] Gibbon, I, pp. 355-356.

events which will profoundly influence the story told in this book.

With the revolt of Carausius, Britain enters upon the stage of world-politics, and begins first to play a part in determining the future of civilization.

XIV

Carausius was what we should call a Belgian by birth —a Menapian from that land between the Lys and the North Sea in which Bruges and Ostend and Dunkirk now stand. Like many another Roman soldier he was a self-made man. He had risen by his own ability as a seaman to the command of the Roman squadron which had its headquarters at Boulogne. His task was to hunt Saxon raiders; a task not altogether unlike that which, some sixteen centuries later, Q boats and mystery ships undertook from the same ports. Carausius was not untouched by the spirit of his age and country. The reports made to Maximian were highly peculiar. Carausius, they said, had a habit of allowing the Saxons to leave harbour unmolested. On their homeward voyage, heavy-laden, he intercepted them. The prizes were then divided amongst Carausius and his crews, who were prospering on the stolen cargoes of Saxon pirates. . . . Maximian found that the prosperity at any rate was a proved fact; and with some impetuosity he signed a warrant for the arrest and execution of Carausius.

A little reflection might have counselled a gentler approach. Carausius was, after all, the man in possession, and he was a popular commander. As soon as he knew that the warrant was issued, he transferred his

Allegations against Carausius

headquarters across the Channel, and invited the British to support him.

XV

Whether the charges against Carausius were true, we have no means of judging. They may have been the slanders of interested rivals; or they may have had just enough truth to make them true in the letter without being true in the spirit. What a hot-head like Maximian thought is not evidence. He was the sort of man who would hang Carausius first and investigate the charges against him afterwards. Since he failed to hang Carausius first, he does not seem to have felt it necessary to investigate the charges at all. . . . The army in Britain displayed a similar spirit. It took a roseate view of the worth of a man who shared his profits without grudging, and it did not trouble to consider pedantic arguments concerning the ethics of the case. . . . Carausius notified the emperors that he too, by solemn election, was imperator, Augustus, and divine.

The loss of Britain was a serious matter. The British contribution to the imperial revenue was alone enough to give the country importance, while its strategic significance gave it meaning deeper yet. Worse even than this was the fact that the whole tin trade was now diverted to the Frisian markets. . . . Maximian had a fresh fleet ready by the following April. That it was badly defeated we may be fairly sure from the profound silence of the authorities. . . . The position of Carausius was henceforth assured. He not only held Britain, but retained Boulogne as a continental bridgehead, through which he could, at will, pour troops into Gaul.

Revolt of
Carausius

In these circumstances it was necessary to parley. The position of Maximian on the Rhine was quite sufficiently precarious as it was, without having British legions landed in his rear. Diocletian accepted Carausius (not, we may be sure, very willingly) as a third Augustus, and the schism was patched up.

Reign of Carausius in Britain

XVI

The British emperor showed good will and patriotic good sense, as well as a singularly acute perception of the situation in which he found himself. He remained a Roman emperor testifying to the unity of the empire, and claiming no more independent sovranty than Maximian claimed. As long as he was left alone, he did very little to which Diocletian could object. But he took good care to make himself a very dangerous person to meddle with.

The policy of Carausius was to keep Britain an integral part of the empire, while at the same time basing his power on a close friendship with the Franks. The latter were ready to court the alliance of a man who could make a great difference to their position. Many entered his service, and were trained in Roman methods of war. From Carausius they may have learnt something much more important than this—to wit, the strategical significance of Britain, and its relation to the Rhine frontier. He showed them that Britain could be held against invasion, and that it could turn the Roman frontier by means of its command of the short sea-passage. . . . It was no common man who could perceive and utilize these truths.

Importance of the British revolt

XVII

If they had not before been visible to Diocletian and Maximian, they became so now. It was necessary to bring Britain back into closer relations with the empire, and so to secure the island that by no means whatsoever could it be used as an instrument for loosening Roman control over the Rhineland. . . . The man who was chosen to undertake this task was M. Flavius Constantius. . . . Five years after the rise of Carausius, Diocletian was ready. He was prepared to complete his plans for the pacification and reorganization of the empire.

CHAPTER III

CONSTANTIUS, CONSTANTINE AND THE BEAST

I

THE identity of Constantius is bound up with the last of the great changes for which the name of Diocletian is famous. By the co-optation of two sub-emperors, or "Cæsars," who joined the imperial board as the adopted sons and intended successors of the two Augusti, the number of the directorate was brought up to four. Carausius, as an intruder, did not count. The Cæsars were not intended to possess legislative or financial power; they had no consistorium, and exercised no control over the civil service. They were junior or apprentice emperors, learning their profession as they went along; and perhaps one of the chief purposes they were intended to fulfil was that of military lieutenants to the senior emperors. Their future prospects were not intended to be hazy or problematical. Diocletian drew up a truly original scheme for the new imperial board. When the Augusti died or retired, they were to give place to the Cæsars, whose vacated posts were to be filled by fresh co-optations. This automatic promotion was an integral part of the conception of the quadruple directorate. At the end of ten years the situation was to be reviewed and, if necessary, revised.[1]

Appointment of the Cæsars, March 1, 293

---

[1] During the past thirty years the theory has prevailed that Diocletian arranged beforehand as part of his new system to abdicate in the twentieth year of his reign. This theory, always tenuous, has steadily faded, and recently Mr. Norman H. Baynes, one of the greatest living authorities on the period, attacked it with

The two men first chosen to fill the new posts were M. Flavius Valerius Constantius and G. Galerius Valerius Maximianus. Constantius, who became Cæsar to old Maximian Herculius, had for some time been Prætorian prefect to the latter. Of Galerius, who became Cæsar to Diocletian, we shall shortly hear more. The adopted sons, divorcing their wives, obediently married the daughters of their new fathers.[1] By this proceeding they all became, in theory, a united and happy family. The wife whom Constantius thus divorced was Helena. Their son Constantine[2] was twenty years old.

II

The marriage of Constantius with Helena presented difficulties and obscurities to the historians who first recorded his life; and they have not grown clearer with the passage of time. We may dismiss as due to the malice of partisan enmity the allegation that she was his mistress. The enthusiastic assertion of the British that she was the daughter of King Coel of Colchester[3] may be put down to the contrary cause of partisan admiration.

convincing arguments. (*Journal of Roman Studies*, Vol. XIX, 1929, Part 2, p. 227.) The explanation given above in the text is an attempt exactly to cover all the facts. Some importance, otherwise inexplicable, attached to the period of ten years for Diocletian, for Galerius, and even for Constantine. See below, Ch. III, § XVII and Ch. X, § VI.

[1] Theodora, whom Constantius married, was only the step-daughter of Maximian, whose own children apparently were hardly old enough.

[2] All the important evidence concerning the life of Constantine is collected and discussed in two excellent monographs, *Constantine and Christianity* by C. B. Coleman, and *The Establishment of Christianity* by Maude A. Huttmann. (Columbia University Studies in History, Vol. 60, 1914.)

[3] Needless to say, the fact that, in English nursery tradition, "Old King Cole was a merry old soul" is not the slightest reason against the possibility that his daughter married Constantius.

It is usual to accept the account given by an anonymous —but nearly contemporary—writer, that Constantine was born at Naissus, the great city on the high road from Byzantium to the Danube.

Later Greek tradition said that the son of Helena was born at Drepanum near Nicomedia, where Constantius stayed at her father's inn during an official journey to Persia. The Greek accounts concur that Helena was a person of obscure birth, though the exact weight we allow to the idea that she was the daughter of an inn-keeper depends upon our view of inns—especially of Roman inns. Constantius himself would in all probability have failed to achieve distinction as a fashionable hairdresser. He shared with his friends and colleagues certain peculiarities of the Illyrian peasant—a powerful, stout-built, rough and red-faced man,[1] with a shaggy white beard in his advanced age, fierce and fatherly. His virtues were not especially ornamental—but they wore well.

St. Helena

Constantius, as we shall see, was by the universal testimony of all who knew him a man of kindly and good-humoured ways; by the testimony of his own actions he was cool, keen and steady rather than clever—the kind of man who succeeds in governmental service. Some of the striking differences between him and his son may have been due to Helena. Constantine was tall and handsome, with an impetus and rapidity such as his father never showed; he knew how to wear clothes, and he liked wearing them—and he was cleverer and per-haps a good deal less shrewd than old Constantius. And

[1] "Chlorus," his alleged second name, has no contemporary authority.

in all this, possibly, we have a vague outline of the handsome chambermaid at the inn, upon whom red-faced Constantius smiled.[1]

III

The divorce of Helena was not allowed to work out to the detriment of her son. Jovius, at some uncertain date, but probably about this time, took Constantine into his own immediate household. The biographer who wrote the life of Constantine compares him with Moses at the court of Pharaoh; from which we may conclude that he was conscious of the important nature of the experience he gained, but did not feel very much at home.[2] . . . Precisely where lay the incompatibility we are not told. There was always a peculiar sympathy between father and son, and a likeness in their general views, which suggests that Constantine spent his early years in close companionship with his father, and that he now perceived with unusual clearness the divergence between the principles in which he had himself been brought up, and those prevalent at Nicomedia. If so, he was wise enough to hold his tongue.

Jovius evidently liked to have the young man with him. The feeling which had impelled him to make those marriage alliances between the colleagues now made him happy to know that he had the company of his friends' children. It made everything safer and more satisfactory. In the meantime he had the training of the

---

[1] This is partly illustrated in the two portraits in the frontispiece. The head of Constantius is from a gold medallion, that of Constantine from a gold double-solidus, both in the British Museum. For these, and the very fine head of Galerius, the author has to render thanks to Mr. Harold Mattingley.

[2] Euseb, *Vita C.*, I. 8.

young man whose education by him and whose relation to Constantius would in due time constitute a powerful double qualification for the Cæsarship. He would have given Maxentius, the son of old Herculius, similar priv- ileges—but Maxentius was more wayward and restless. The service of Constantine was unbroken by any coldness with the emperor. It lasted some twelve years; and perhaps the excellencies and the faults which Constantine showed in later years illuminate the character of the imperial household in which he served that long apprenticeship.

Constantine's special training

IV

Constantius had been created Cæsar in March. The sphere of activity destined for him was composed of Britain and Gaul, while Italy, Africa and Spain remained in the hands of Maximian. Constantius took over the work of dealing with the situation on the Rhine and the North Sea.

His first step was to capture Carausius' bridge-head at Boulogne. Great preparations to this end must have been made before he took over the command. During the summer he invested the town and blockaded the port by throwing a mole across the entrance to the harbour. . . . Apparently Carausius was taken by surprise, for he allowed the chief part of his fleet to be shut into the harbour, and the fall of the town, after a determined resistance, involved the capture of the original source of the British emperor's power.

The fall of Boulogne was promptly followed by an advance across the Scheldt northwards against the Franks. It was now impossible for Carausius to take

Lower Germany reoccupied

any steps to their aid. He could only look on while Constantius occupied the Frankish and Frisian lands between the Meuse and the Rhine mouth, the ancient Germania Inferior which had been the scene of the exploits of Drusus, but had slipped out of Roman control during the Anarchy. . . . How important a part the Franks and Frisians had played in the events of the last few years, how insignificant a part the Saxons, can be seen in the change brought about by these measures. The British tin had now no market. The piratic raids had stopped with the accession of Carausius and the establishment of a Frisian monopoly in the British trade. Now raids and monopoly both alike came to an end, and the British merchants might amuse themselves, if they could afford to do so, by accumulating stocks for the future benefit of the Gallic middlemen.

Constantius spent the next few years in reorganizing the province as the new Germania Secunda which now begins to appear in the provincial lists. Meanwhile, he began the building of a fleet. His work could be made permanent only by the reconquest of Britain. The hardest part was yet to come.

v

The effects of Constantius' work were nowhere better appreciated than in Britain. Almost the first visible result was the fall of Carausius. The mining rights of the empire were imperial crown property, and since the power of Carausius had been built up on the profits of the tin trade, its present paralysis meant practically his bankruptcy. He was assassinated by a conspiracy at

Death of
Carausius,
A.D. 293

whose head was his minister Allectus, and the latter stepped into his shoes.

What was in the meantime happening elsewhere had a very real effect upon the course of events in Britain. While Constantius was engaged in Gaul, Diocletian himself prepared to take an active part in the east. He left Nicomedia in March, 295. The trouble he had to deal with was of precisely the same kind that had confronted Constantius in Gaul. In the one case it had been the changes in the tin trade: in the other it was the decline and almost total extinction of the Indian trade. The connection between the two lay in the fact that tin was one of the few cargoes which India would accept in exchange for goods. Neither gold nor tin was available: and Alexandria and the Egyptian towns, as well as the African towns all the way along to Spain, were in a ferment of the kind, irrepressible and irrational, which follows economic disaster. People had all the strength that is given by honest indignation, and all the misplaced energy that is created by entire ignorance of how to remedy the trouble. . . . Two very insignificant persons, Achilleus and Julian, were elected at Alexandria and Carthage respectively. They had neither any real power of maintaining themselves nor any policy to guide them if they had. Nothing useful could be done with them except repress them.

Diocletian invested Alexandria in July. The vast city, the greatest and most populous in the world, justified its repute for fierceness and turbulence. For more than eight months it held out against Jovius and all the might of the empire. He cut off the water, and finally took Alexandria by storm. Busiris and Coptos were also

Siege of Alexandria, A.D. 295

subjected to severe punitive measures. The latter town was the chief market for Indian trade. One of the actions of Diocletian which has become famous illustrates the trouble that was eating at the heart of Egypt. He collected all the alchemical books treating of the transmutation of metals, and burnt them. . . . Egypt was starved for gold and, not being able to acquire it in the normal way, had been conducting experiments in its manufacture.

VI

Alexandria fell in early spring. Leaving Maximian to deal with the situation at Carthage and in western Africa, Diocletian, towards April, moved up to Antioch.

First Persian Campaign, A.D. 296

Maximian spent three years in Africa, where he was successful in suppressing Julian, repelling the invasion of the desert tribes, and settling the country. The success of Diocletian was slower to come. He had brought Galerius down from the Danube to take command against the Persians. Able though he was, Galerius suffered from a constitutional disinclination to adapt himself to circumstances. He was trapped by the Persian horse-archers, exactly as Crassus had been, and his army was cut up with heavy loss. What followed was famous. Diocletian had no use for unsuccessful subordinates. When he went to meet the returning army, he signalized his displeasure by allowing the choleric Galerius to walk before his carriage for more than a mile on foot. Galerius obeyed; but perhaps he did not forget.

Such measures were effective in persuading Galerius that obstacles should be surmounted, not defied. His second Persian campaign did far more justice to the military abilities which had lifted him to success. Advancing through Armenia, he was intercepted and brought to issue by the full force of the Persian king. Galerius stampeded the Persian horse by night; and the defeat which in consequence overwhelmed the Persian army induced the King of Kings to negotiate. Diocletian, all benign, arrived at Nisibis to admire the victory of Galerius and to control his temper.

Second Persian Campaign, A.D. 297

His presence was very necessary. Galerius showed a tendency to unjustifiable optimism which needed the guiding influence of a steadier mind. The Persian king was a skilful and vigorous statesman, who managed to spin out the negotiations until he had a new army behind him. He then flatly refused the most important of the demands Diocletian pressed upon him. He would not consent to accept Nisibis as the staple town for the Mesopotamian trade. He no doubt held the winning cards since in the decline of Egyptian prosperity, he controlled all the Indian land routes and therefore the whole of the remaining trade with India. The moderation which Diocletian was compelled to exercise, the emperor used to extract a spectacular success to cover his real failure. The Persian king was willing to concede territory rather than trading rights. Diocletian obtained the concession of five provinces. Such was the total upshot of the Persian campaign.

VII

Constantine was with Diocletian during these events, and may have known much more about them than he

The Recovery of Britain

ever told his biographer. It is easy to believe that he did not rise in the affections of Galerius; for while the latter was failing against the Persians and incurring the rebuke of Jovius, Constantius had been not only much more successful in re-opening the old trade channels of the west, but had effected the most spectacular *coup* of the age—the recovery of Britain.

If three years had elapsed since the occupation of Lower Germany, the interval had perhaps been designed for more purposes than the building of a fleet. It had allowed the treasury of Allectus to fall gradually lower, its replenishment to become gradually more unlikely, and his confidence to ebb in its company. From subsequent events, moreover, it seems likely that Allectus had to reduce his effective forces, from lack of means to pay them. His difficulty was that he did not know where Constantius intended to strike. To provide against all possible events, he stationed himself with a mobile striking force at London, whence he could move rapidly in any direction by military road. His fleet lay in the neighbourhood of the Isle of Wight—no doubt at Portus Magnus. . . . Constantius commanded the Roman fleet at Boulogne.

The blow came from the Seine mouth. The prefect Asclepiodotus, setting sail with what proved to be the main Roman expedition, managed in thick weather to slip the British fleet, which was on the watch for him.[1]

---

[1] We are told (a) that the Romans were proud of themselves for starting with a side wind in stormy weather; and (b) that they escaped the British fleet in a thick fog, subsequently landing in the west of England. If these facts are correctly reported, they indicate that the voyage was made in March, April or May, and that the Romans took advantage of a high barometer and an easterly wind (frequent enough in that season) which dropped, and ended in a calm with a sea-fret, during which they made westward under sweeps.

He landed at one of the westerly road-heads—but at which one is not certainly known.[1] As soon as he had the news, Allectus marched rapidly to find the enemy. So rapid was his march that he arrived exhausted and with depleted forces and was completely overthrown. His death laid Britain at the feet of Constantius. When the Cæsar crossed from Boulogne, not a hand was raised in resistance. Agricultural Britain was indifferent to the fate of a rebellion which had been the private speculation of a few men interested in her mining industry. *Death of Allectus, A.D. 296*

By the recovery of Britain, Constantius was placed in effective possession of the whole of the territory over which he had been given legal authority. He pacified and reorganized all the Roman north-west, from the wall of Hadrian to the Alps. The traces of his work still survive. So deeply did he impress the imagination of the peoples he ruled that he became almost as famous a name as his son; "l'empereur Constant" was a tradition in the Middle Ages when the name of Galerius had perished, or had joined those of Judas and Nero. A rough and genial humanity was the charm that worked the trick. He had the wisdom which does not waste upon men the sentiment they do not want, but gives them that thing which above all others they do want—liberty to think their own thoughts and work in their own ways.

VIII

The reorganization which was begun by Constantius gave Britain nearly seventy years of renewed prosperity.

[1] From the circumstances, it is highly probable that Asclepiodotus and his expedition landed at Poole. See the Ordnance Map of Roman Britain. Weymouth is also possible. Both routes would lead to Badbury.

The Saxon Shore

To his period, and perhaps to his policy, if not to his actual execution, belongs the fortification of the "Saxon Shore," from Brancaster in Norfolk to Portchester in Hampshire. This was the coast chiefly exposed to the Saxon raids. The new fortifications were no mere field works or stone-faced earthen banks, but were solid stone building, with walls ten to fourteen feet thick, bastioned for defence by mechanical artillery. Many of them can be seen to this day. Pevensey Castle, the citadel of old Roman Anderida, built to protect the iron mines, is almost complete. The western half of Richborough still stands on the edge of the low cliff that once was washed by the waters of Pegwell Bay, looking over towards Thanet.

These works were part of the general policy of reorganization and refortification which Diocletian and his colleagues put into execution along all the frontiers of the empire. The restoration of the Rhine frontier was the particular work of Constantius. After he had finished, it remained fast for many years. The Alamanni made two efforts to break the lines that were gradually excluding them from their old Tom Tiddler's ground in Gaul. He beat them at Langres and at Windisch near Basle, and followed it up by a punitive expedition across the Rhine. . . . The policy of the emperors, while it closed the frontier to armed enemies, accepted many peaceful immigrants, and they made a practice of settling their prisoners of war on vacant lands, especially in Gaul, where they became producers and potential sources of revenue.

War with Alamanni, A.D. 298-299

That such a policy had become possible and profitable was due to more causes than one. The slave dealers who

THE REALM OF CONSTANTIUS I.

ATLANTIC

OCEAN

Britain
York
London
Boulogne
Rouen

SAXONY
FRISIA
FRANKLAND
Cologne
Mainz
Treves
ALAMANNIA

Gaul · Langres
Vindonissa
Bordeaux · Lyons
Nimes
Saragossa · Arles
Toledo · Tarraco · Marseilles
MILAN

Spain
Cordova
Gades

ROME

Italy

Caesarea · Carthage

Africa

had followed the armies of Cæsar to buy up the prisoners of war were no longer in business. Their customers had dwindled in numbers and decreased in wealth; and the amount of capital they could invest in slaves was now small. Agriculture in western and central Europe had for long been growing more and more a skilled labour which needed long training and close personal application. There was no room in it for an unlimited number of unskilled persons. And then, in recent years there had been considerable contraction in the amount of ordinary produce raised for urban markets. From all these causes, it was a much better business proposition to settle prisoners of war upon land where they could support themselves. No one was going to do it for them. Settled, therefore, they were. Not all of them succeeded. Some of them, after trying and failing, once more came under the official notice of the government, with results embarrassing sometimes for one party and sometimes for the other.

Policy of Constantius to the invaders

Exactly how far the land and agricultural population of the empire in general, and of Gaul in particular, had suffered from the half century of anarchy, it is hard to say.[1] It is probably safe to assume that with the restoration of the frontier and the reorganization of the provinces, the population of Gaul rapidly recovered its numbers. The new colonists are not likely to have obtained the longest-cultivated or most valuable land. Their agricultural knowledge perhaps stopped at the simpler forms of arable and stock farming. There is no reason to suppose that Gaul would have lain derelict without

[1] Some think that the empire had increased rather than lost. (Bury, *History of the Later Roman Empire*, I, p. 62.) On the other hand, the German invaders were not so numerous as has been imagined. (*Ibid.*, pp. 104-105.)

them. The truth is most likely that room was made for them by extension of cultivation. . . . Certainly men like Constantius did not settle within the empire dangerous enemies whose presence was likely to be a menace to their neighbours.[1]

IX

Successful as the Board of Emperors had been in restoring government and the reign of law, in reorganizing the military frontiers and even the agricultural prosperity of the empire, it could not show quite such good results in the way of restored trade and credit. The very success of the government in basing its transactions upon a peasant economy and in giving prosperity to agriculture, tended to draw from the world a dull acquiescence in the existing situation. Money was still behaving in a fantastic manner. It was 2½ per cent of its nominal value; that is to say, prices were about forty times what they had normally been. Jovius and Herculius, with all their virtues, were not the right men to tackle such a problem. Delicate persuasion from Jovius, and the most peremptory orders from Herculius, might be equally useless. It needed some gift which neither of them possessed.

Diocletian and finance

Diocletian tried the methods which had been successful with agriculture. Finding that in spite of good harvests prices still rose, he issued for his own provinces a schedule of maximum prices and wages. His expedient may have had its use in preventing the unfair exploita-

---

[1] Gibbon, I, 362 . . . "multitudes of secret enemies . . . were introduced into the heart of the empire." Without doubting that the absorption of new settlers into citizenship needed time, we are not called upon to accept the view that these settlers held the full German Nationalist doctrine.

tion of his soldiers; and possibly this may have been the whole purpose it was intended to fulfil. The schedule lasted a few years and was forgotten. That it had no permanent effect upon the level of prices we may be quite sure. He also reformed the currency, and issued a true gold coinage. This may in the long run have been more successful in stabilizing prices; but even so, his triumphs in the sphere of finance were not brilliant.

x

Nineteen years had passed since the death of Numerian, when the reform and reorganization of the empire, the strengthening of her frontiers and the defeat of her enemies, were symbolized and signalized by the formal Triumph of Diocletian and Maximian. Along the route which Scipio and Cæsar and Augustus and Aurelian had ridden, Diocletian and Maximian, the son of the clerk and the son of the peasant, now rode; and no one knew that it was to be for the last time.

Triumph of Diocletian, A.D. 302

The list of conquests for which they triumphed is curious and formidable. It makes no mention of the African Wars, but enumerates British, German, Sarmatian, Armenian, Caspian, Adiabenic, Median and Persian victories. Diocletian and his colleagues had needed practically to re-conquer the empire which they had reorganized. They had faced a Britain far better armed and governed than the half-barbarous Britain which Claudius invaded; a Germany much more formidable than the old Germany which Drusus knew; a Persia stronger and more united than the Parthian power which had destroyed Crassus at Carrhæ and defied many

Success of his policy

Roman armies. Their successes had been no mean or meagre victories. . . . Even the Alexandria which Diocletian stormed, but for which he would not triumph, was a greater city than the one in which Cæsar met Cleopatra. Most of all, their reorganization was a wonder to contemplate. No man before them had smoothed out the irregularities and varieties of the provinces, and subjected them to one uniform system.

Their work was to last; but it was to last under conditions so strange and unexpected that they themselves could not have foreseen them. Constantine, we need not doubt, rode in the procession—the last Roman Triumph. He, too, could not have foreseen the part he was to play in subjecting the empire to those new conditions—a revolution which would change its nature and transform its spirit.

XI

Neither Constantius nor Galerius took part in the Triumph. The next winter, however, Galerius spent some time with Diocletian at Nicomedia.

His very presence at Nicomedia was a mystery which the subsequent centuries have done nothing to elucidate. On what errand he had the right to be there at all, why he should have chosen that time, and why he should have chosen a particular subject for discussion, no historian recorded. We shall be better prepared to form an opinion of our own upon these subjects if we first glance at Galerius himself, the man.

Galerius at Nicomedia

The Christian writer, Lactantius, attributes a great deal of the character of Galerius to his trans-Danubian origin. His forbears came from the lands which in later centuries produced Haynau and Suvaroff; and he shows us the original model from which those milder and more civilized copies were made. A stalwart man he was, of immense height and girth. His portraits show that slight, indefinable touch of the Mongol which hovers so elusively about some eastern Europeans—a parchment in his skin, a lankness and blackness in his hair, an expression in his mouth. He certainly had the Mongol touch in his temper. To some sorts of feeling he was entirely obtuse. He ruled by terrorism. Lactantius can hardly write his name. To him he is "The Beast": a bully, a brute, a tyrant whom his servants feared and his soldiers hated. . . . This is a portrait by an enemy: but the course of events seems to prove it tolerably true to life.

Why had he come to Nicomedia? And what was he discussing with Jovius? There were men near the person of Jovius who were prepared to pass the word quietly to their friends outside the gates. He had come to talk about the Christian religion.

The Christians were quite ready to believe that Galerius was inspired by a pure and disinterested hatred of their philosophy. But was he? He never showed any other sign of interest in any sort of philosophy. **Objects of Galerius** We shall be exercising prudence if in all that follows we bear in mind the existence of Constantius, and the prospect that when Jovius and Herculius resigned, he would be their most powerful and popular successor. . . . The Beast might need to go round about very circumspectly to prevent this consummation; but he prepared to do so, and he began by talking about the Christian religion.

XII

It was not very difficult for him to find a series of entirely impersonal and impartial arguments; and those which he could not think of himself, cunning brains among his counsellors could supply.

So far, the issues involved in the work of reorganization had been simple. They had involved non-controversial questions such as the repulse of invasions and the repression of disorder, the institution of new methods of local government, and new systems of collecting the revenue. If there were any need for argument, it was argument over facts. There had been no controversy over principles, or ideas. . . . This was where Galerius started his new hare. He came to Nicomedia to tell Jovius that their work was not yet finished. Not all the foes of order and good government had been suppressed. He instanced, of course, the Christian Church.

Problem of the Christian Church

It is interesting to reflect that there was a time when the Christian Church could be instanced as a foe of law and order, and an enemy of good government and social safety. From all that we can now make out, Jovius was not convinced, and did not welcome these views with enthusiasm. Even the Christian apologists, while denouncing him and predicting for him a warm and unpleasant future fate, admitted that he was dragged unwillingly into evil ways by the violence of the Beast.

But the arguments of Galerius, up to a point, were incontrovertible. There was no disputing the power of a party within the state which had no legal rights and no legal responsibility. In theory—or at any rate in principle—the Church had not even the right to exist. It was an illegal body, whose creed had only to be stated in order to demonstrate its unlawful nature. It acted as a corporation, though it was no corporation. It owned money and other chattels: it exercised power and influence: it was an alien and intrusive body, an imperium in imperio, counteracting the legal influence of properly constituted authorities, drawing away the obedience of citizens to a code of conduct and a scheme of ideas not endorsed by the government—imposing a law in supersession of the constitutionally valid law of the sovran state. It was a seditious body. It was a conspiracy, a treason and a revolution.

Views of Diocletian

Jovius in vain expressed his conviction that the best plan was to let well alone, and to avoid unnecessary interference. He himself was surrounded by men of the Christian faith, and had little to complain of. But the case against the Church involved at least one argument which Diocletian could not avoid or abate. He had made the Divine Monarch the corner-stone of his new and reorganized empire. The Church was the one power in the world which very particularly, and on principle, declined to recognize the divinity of the monarch. She had never recognized it, but had from the very first made a point of denying it. . . . Hence the Church was the one power which stood out against the whole scheme which Diocletian had brought to the verge of success. And the Church was a very powerful organization, with ramifications which spread throughout the empire. Outside the army it was by far the strongest single force in the Roman world.

Hunted from pillar to post by the tireless conversation of the Beast, the reluctant Diocletian was induced

to refer the whole question to a Consistorium. The
Beast had already taken steps to secure the necessary
votes; he had no difficulty in getting his own way, and
Diocletian was committed, against his better judgment,
to the task of suppressing a force of whose origin and
nature he had but an imperfect idea.

XIII

The resistance of Diocletian had the effect of directing the persecution along lines that were perhaps not all
that Galerius wanted. The Beast wanted something
that would stampede public opinion, confuse all the
issues, and throw all reputations into the melting pot.
He very nearly got it. Jovius, however, ensured that
the procedure should be regular and legal, and should
be aimed at cutting off the supply of recruits to the
church rather than at extinguishing its present membership. His share in the arrangements was far more dangerous to the existence of the Church than all the sound
and fury of Galerius.

On the twenty-third of February, A.D. 303, the
church at Nicomedia was seized and demolished, and
the Scriptures cast into the fire. It was the festival of
the Terminalia, that ancient holy-day when the peasants
beat the bounds, and celebrated, with immemorial ritual,
the division of the fields. By a strange irony this festival
was selected for the beginning of a contest which ended
the supremacy of the pagan religions.

The next day, the Christian faith was "proclaimed."
The edict was posted publicly at Nicomedia, in the presence of both emperors. It was instantly torn down by

a Christian whom we know as Saint George, and who became in later ages the patron saint of England. What followed was a struggle of which we need not expect the events to be described by the sufferers with calm scientific impartiality. This much may be said for the government—or at any rate, for Diocletian—that no one seems to have been ill treated who was willing to obey the law. Probably thousands—perhaps the vast majority—of Christians shrank from the contest and gave in: and these were unharmed. But proportionately bitter and savage was the wrestle which began between the government and the men who formed the heart and core of the church. The man George was roasted to death without any satisfactory apology being extracted from him.

The Church "Proclaimed" February, A.D. 303

Even though the Beast had failed to obtain all he wanted, he was successful at this point in hurling Jovius himself into the maëlstrom. Within a fortnight, fire twice broke out in the palace of Nicomedia. On the second occasion Diocletian's own bed-chamber was involved. The chamberlains were examined; they were Christians, and by the new law they were liable to the torture. No incriminating admission could be got from them. Neither the lash nor the fire succeeded in forcing any confession. The bishop of Nicomedia—Athenius—was arrested, with numerous members of his church. Nothing could be discovered. Some were beheaded, some burnt; the prisons were crowded with suspects: and Galerius left in a hurry, swearing that his life was not safe from the Christians. . . . But the Christians were convinced that he had fled from Nicomedia in order to escape investigation. He, and not

Allegations against Galerius

the Christians, had caused the fires; and he had involved Jovius personally in deeds which, though done by process of law, were little likely to be forgotten or forgiven by a powerful party of his subjects.

XIV

The contest spread. Just before Easter, the edict of prohibition was issued in Syria; by June it had been published throughout the dominions of Maximian, and Constantius had an opportunity of perusing the document the fruits of which his son had just seen at Nicomedia. . . . It was closely followed by a second edict, ordering the arrest of all Christian priests. The prisons were soon crowded. Espionage, arrest, torture and terrorism were the order of the day. Much of it was outwardly successful; but the timidity of hundreds of ordinary people was counteracted by the sensational martyrdoms of a few.

The spotlight was crowded with eager candidates for fame. Those men, consumed with zeal, who preferred with passion to face and suffer death rather than to abate one jot or tittle of their faith; those who saw the possibility of saving in one way the souls they had endangered in another; the difficult men who found even martyrdom easier than work; all these were prepared to suffer—and not by any means in silence. The death of the saints proceeded to the accompaniment of a torrent of protest, and a flood of impassioned rhetoric.

Resistance of the Christians

The reason why Christianity could command so many men and women who were willing to die for it is simple. It was much the most interesting feature of the day.

It was indeed one of the few serious subjects on which it was possible to talk with perfect freedom and at unlimited length. Generally speaking, men will gravitate towards those things and ideas which give them excitement. In the Roman world, the average sensual man crowded the racing-ring and the theatre because there were the thrills to be got which his modern equivalent gets on the race-course or at the Pictures. That Roman world looked with growing apathy upon the cut and dried doings of its official pagan religions, with their formal gaiety, their standardized emotions, their bright unmeaningness. They did not even distribute gifts. Christianity offered a very different and far more interesting programme—real and violent emotions, flaming passion, hideous danger; actual racks and thumbscrews; genuine martyrs being burned at the stake. A religion which can offer these sensational attractions is sure of a large public. We may add to these that it distributed loaves and fishes freely, when there were any to give; and even when there were not, it promised righteous judgment and eternal life.

XV

This year—A.D. 303—was the Vicennalia, the twentieth year of Diocletian's reign. It was celebrated with great festivities at Rome. It afforded Jovius and Herculius an opportunity of meeting to discuss the subject of the church. Maximian was warmly in favour of the policy of Galerius. What Diocletian thought of his motives we cannot be sure; but it is fairly sure that he induced Maximian to swear an oath that he would re-

The Vicennalia, Summer, A. D. 303

sign his imperial rank at any time when Diocletian did so.

Among the subjects which they discussed may have been the attitude of Constantius, who had begun that peculiar policy of silence and pro-Christianity which he maintained to the end. The sympathies of Galerius were well known. He cultivated the old idols of the Roman populares—those heavenly twins, the Peasant and the Proletarian. Nothing would be more natural than for a rival to seek support among the classes touched by commercial traditions and Christian ideas: and this is exactly what Constantius did. The bishops recognized him as a friend, though they could not quote any definite words he had ever uttered to prove it.

Attitude of Constantius

Christianity had expanded and grown powerful in the towns of the Roman empire. It was a religion which, finding its first opportunity in the free communication and busy traffic of Mediterranean commerce, had gathered power in those centres where ideas circulated most freely, and where the enquiring spirit of the Greek mind most exercised its influence. Christianity had never hitherto been a peasant religion, although there were in it influences derived from the peasant life of nearer Asia which some day might enable it to appeal to an agricultural population. At this stage it drew most of its supporters from a world which manufactured and traded, and knew the use of money and the laws of finance.

That proverbial tendency of birds of a feather to flock together must not be forgotten. Seen from one point of view, the laws and commandments of Christianity were only the laws of civilized social life, somewhat sublimated in an elaborately thought-out theology, and given a sanction in the will of an eternal and benevolent God. No statesman who saw them in this light would feel any enthusiasm for victimizing the holders of such ideas.

XVI

In accordance with an ancient tradition of humanity, the celebration of the Vicennalia saw all the prison doors thrown open wide. Murderers and thieves went free to cheer for Diocletian and Maximian. Bishops, priests, and others imprisoned for the deeper crime of Christianity, were interviewed before they were allowed to go. In their case, freedom was conditional. They must first sacrifice to the Lord and God Cæsar Augustus. Governors had been notified that if a little suitable persuasion would induce the Christians to fulfil this requirement, it might be used. This was the "Third Edict." The "Third Edict," Summer, A.D. 303

Throughout the summer, therefore, the battle raged. The prisons rapidly emptied of the weaker brethren; while the men who were prepared to endure to the end once more faced every form of bribery and terrorism that might induce them to sacrifice. The prison authorities were not always particular. Sometimes humanity on the part of the magistrates, and sometimes orders from the Treasury, which was worried over the expense incurred, led to regrettable scenes in which Christians, violently protesting, were hauled into court, were declared to have satisfied the law, and were ejected (not always with perfect gentleness) by the police and military. The real die-hards returned, in a considerably battered state, to their dungeons, there to pray fervently until the next time came. . . . And while these men held out, the government had not won.

XVII

Thirteen days before he was due to leave Rome, Diocletian, driven by some devil, abruptly left the city and began his journey home. Before he reached Ravenna he had developed a chill: and although his household carried him by slow and easy stages, he was, by the time he arrived at Nicomedia, a sick man. The Christians did not fail to underline the fact that with the beginning of the persecution, the luck of Diocletian had stopped. With the Third Edict, it crashed.

He was not seen again until, on the first of March, 304, he emerged from his retirement, weak and wasted, a man who had been touched by the finger of God, and whose active life was over.

Diocletian had always dated his reign from the day of the death of Carus in the year 283. Ten years later, he had co-opted the Cæsars. The twentieth anniversary had passed, and he had not further reviewed his position. September 17, 304, was the twentieth anniversary of his election at Chalcedon. That day came; but still he had not reconsidered his position and showed no sign of doing so. Since the beginning of his illness an event had happened which made Diocletian less eager to loosen his hold on office. This event was the publication of the Fourth Edict, at some time in March while he was still no more than convalescent. By this edict, the policy of Diocletian was reversed, and Christianity was suppressed under the penalty of death. Maximian was the person directly responsible for its promulgation.

Diocletian had now to face the fact that slowly but surely Galerius was obtaining a free hand and practical supremacy. The attempt to restrain him had failed. Jovius began to discern the cataract ahead.

Galerius arrived at Nicomedia. He had already extracted from Maximian a renewed promise to resign when Diocletian did so; and now he faced the latter. After a long and fruitless discussion, the veiled threat of force compelled Diocletian, a sick man, and now politically isolated, to give way. The appearance of Galerius at Nicomedia was, indeed, a *coup d'état*. Not merely did he compel Diocletian to abdicate, but he gained for his own nominees the imperial positions that fell vacant.

His triumph was complete. Constantius, the person most nearly concerned, was far away, and was curiously silent.

The resignation of Diocletian and Maximian involved the promotion of Constantius and Galerius to the rank of Augusti. The plan had been that Maxentius, the son of Maximian, and Constantine, the son of Constantius, should in due time become the new Cæsars. Galerius insisted that Maxentius was a man he could not work with: and to Constantine he simply objected. He wanted men who could be relied upon to carry out his policy. In response to the surprised enquiry of Jovius, he named the men he wanted: one of his officers, Severus, and his nephew, Maximin Daia. He adhered to these names in the face of protest; and to them Diocletian,

Victory of Galerius

solemnly washing his hands of all responsibility, consented.[1]

Diocletian indeed had no choice: but he knew by now that his famous scheme for a Board of Emperors had not avoided the dangers of a disputed succession. The main problem still remained to be faced.

To the Christian church, the decision was a sentence of death.

XVIII

They did not wait for September 17. On the first day of May, 305, Diocletian abdicated. The ceremony was formal and public. At a solemn assembly of the army outside Nicomedia, Diocletian gave his last public address.

He referred to his own ill-health, and to his need for rest. He resigned the empire into hands better able to grapple with the labours it involved. . . . To his audience, the identity of the new Augusti and Cæsars was a matter of course. Everyone knew beforehand the names he was about to read out. When, therefore, he proceeded to nominate Severus and Maximin Daia as the new Cæsars, the assembly at first was merely puzzled. Some supposed that Constantine—who was actually standing at Diocletian's elbow—must have received the new name of "Maximin" on his appointment. . . . When Galerius pushed Constantine aside and presented to the Assembly a person who was to most of them an entire stranger, the surprise grew still deeper. No voice was raised in objection. Discussion was not part of the order of the day. But that fact was more dangerous to

Resignation of Diocletian and Maximian, May 1, A.D. 305

---

[1] Lactantius, *De M.P.*, xviii.

Galerius than to Constantine, for it is imprudent to surprise a large body of men who have no opportunity of answering back.

XIX

Having invested Maximin with his own imperial robe, Diocletian descended from the platform, simple Diocles again, and drove through the streets of Nicomedia on his way to Salona in his native Dalmatia. Men are often restored to health by the air in which they grew up; and Jovius was to spend many years yet in peaceful retirement.

At the same time Maximian, in Milan, having executed a similar act of resignation, retired to his villa in Lucania, leaving the new Cæsar Severus in charge.

XX

So the position stood, but not for long.

CHAPTER IV

THE START FROM YORK

I

THROUGHOUT the proceedings at Nicomedia, Constantius had remained silent. He could not, at the moment, effectively challenge the actions of Galerius; and the serious question indeed remained whether he himself, under any circumstances, would ever be able to do so. His own health was giving way. . . . Galerius counted on this. For the moment the Beast occupied an absolutely triumphant position. Old Constantius would die before very long. Constantine was at the Court of Nicomedia, impotent for harm. As soon as Constantius died, Galerius would step into an unquestionable supremacy such as no emperor before him had ever held. The stakes were vast, and Galerius all but had his hand upon them. . . . Could any power prevent him from success?

II

The first step was to disentangle Constantine. The tearful letters which Constantius began to address to Nicomedia, imploring that he might be allowed the comfort of his beloved child's presence at his death-bed, the Beast treated with cheery contempt. Nothing was less likely than that he would allow Constantine to escape alive. Even as it was, great caution was necessary. One of those mishaps which sometimes occur to inconvenient

persons might at any moment chance to Constantine. First steps
There are said to have been "accidents" in the hunting
field. The future history of Europe hung upon a hair
at Nicomedia in the days just after the resignation of
Diocletian.

Since no open breach had happened between the two
Augusti, Galerius could not give a point-blank refusal
to repeated requests. It was necessary at least to return
an outward and verbal consent to the departure of Constantine. . . . Galerius gave it late in the evening, ac-
companying it with the necessary authority to set out.
He then went to bed and proceeded to sleep over the
question. Constantine would not start without report-
ing himself. The emperor could then, upon some excuse, either revoke the permission or send word ahead
along the route. He would not need to be too explicit.
. . . He had not yet made up his mind which of these
courses to follow.

The next morning he was still undecided. After pur-
posely remaining in his room until noon, he ultimately
sent for Constantine.

III

What Galerius had decided to say to Constantine will
never be known, for his officers explained that Constantine had walked straight out the previous evening, with
the authority given him, and was now some fifteen hours
ahead on the postal roads. . . . The fury of Galerius
was far from being unjustified. To his instant orders
for pursuit, the reply was brought back that the roads Constan-
tine's ride
had been cleared of post-horses. The Beast almost wept

with rage. He had reason to do so before the tale was ended.

Most men, probably, with Galerius behind them, went fast. Constantine emerges into history as, like Dick Turpin, the hero of a famous ride to York, which began beyond the Bosphorus, crossed the Straits, threaded the mountains past Naissus to the Danube, made its way through descending Alpine passes, and finished over the great plains of Champagne and the territory of Picardy. They say he hamstrung the post-horses behind him at each relay, as he rode; [1] and no doubt it was necessary to stop at nothing to get away safe from Nicomedia. But the chase must have been growing remote before he passed Hadrianople, and his ride through Naissus was through a home country. As soon as he was past the Illyrian frontier, he was in lands where his father's writ ran without fail, and he could slacken his pace. Sixteen hundred and odd miles is no trifle for the most hardened rider; and the going had been varied. He rode into Boulogne just as his father was preparing to cross the Channel to Britain, and according to all the traditions, Constantius welcomed his handsome travel-stained son with emotion and joy. [2]

His arrival at Boulogne

The first point had been scored by Constantius. His hostage was safe out of the hands of the Beast, and secure among loyal and devoted men. Events might now march.

---

[1] So Zozimus says. Objection has been raised to the statement (by Gibbon, Vol. I, p. 398); but men who were riding for life and death were not likely to hesitate over a few horses. Without the fresh remounts a pursuit was useless, and Constantine was in front of any possible warrant for his arrest.

[2] Lactantius, *De M.P.*, xxiv.

IV

Constantius and Constantine had about a year together. While we cannot fix the date on which Constantine joined his father, we may reasonably conjecture
that it was a month or two after the resignation of Diocletian. The months of June or July would fit the
visit of Constantius to Britain. He was now growing
old; and the east winds in Britain usually last into early
June, and are not idly to be challenged by elderly men.
The date cannot be much later, for his expedition took
him into Caledonia, for which the middle months of
summer are indicated. In autumn, apparently, he settled at that Caer Ebrauc which Roman pronunciation
lengthened into Eburacum, and English clipped into
York. There he tarried the winter through.

The vale of York today probably does not differ
much, in its main aspects, from the land Constantius
knew. It was so obviously adapted for an agricultural
people, that from the earliest time it was cultivated from
the Humber, if not up to the Tees, at any rate as far as
the neighbourhood of Catterick. A man who rides
down it, whether on horseback as then, or on a railway
train today, can see its whole breadth, bounded between York
the Hambleton Hills on the east, and on the west the
fells which rise slowly to culminate in that gigantic knot
at Hawes, whence so many rivers take their rise. This
great vale of York, watered by the Ouse and the Derwent, has always been the dominating fact of the political geography of Middle Britain. In later times it was
Edwin's Saxon kingdom of Deira, Olaf Kuaran's Danish
kingdom of York, and Duke Richard's English duchy,

whence a new dynasty of kings arose; but in these early times it was the tribal land of the Brigantes, who occupied all the country, from the North Sea to the Irish Sea, up to the Wall. *Brigantes* was the caste name of the governing kindred. As for the people themselves, they were in all likelihood identical in type with those who now dwell there.

V

Isurium (Aldborough) was the original centre of the Brigantes. Some fifteen miles southeast the Romans built their own fortress; and there, under the protection of its walls, arose Eburacum. As far as advantages went, it might have continued to be the centre of government and administration as long as Britain endured. In agricultural wealth it was inferior to no other part of Britain. It touched, northward and westward, the lead-mines of Wolsingham Moor and of Swaledale, and the **Position** coal-mines of the Tyne Valley. On the south, it faced **and wealth** **of York** that estuary of the Humber into which fell not only Derwent and Ouse, and tributary Swale and Ure, but also Wharfe and Aire and Don and Trent, draining a good half of the richest central portion of Britain, and bearing its water-borne commerce. Hence Eburacum commanded the eastern water-gate of Britain, and the routes north, and south and west. It received by sea the German trade from the Rhine Valley,[1] as against the Gallic connections of London and the south. When the first Roman governors built the northern road system, all the roads were laid in such a way that the city became the point of support for every other point in

[1] Charlesworth, *Roman Trade Routes and Commerce,* p. 219.

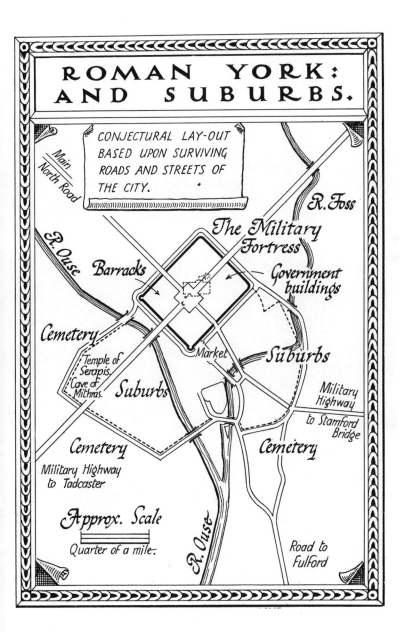

ROMAN YORK: AND SUBURBS.

CONJECTURAL LAY-OUT BASED UPON SURVIVING ROADS AND STREETS OF THE CITY.

Main North Road

R. Foss

The Military Fortress

R. Ouse

Barracks

Government buildings

Cemetery

Market

Suburbs

Temple of Serapis

Cave of Mithras

Suburbs

Military Highway to Stamford Bridge

Cemetery

Cemetery

Military Highway to Tadcaster

Approx. Scale

Quarter of a mile.

R. Ouse

Road to Fulford

middle Britain.[1] Military highways linked it with the
frontier fortress of Carlisle on the Caledonian border,
and that of Chester on the Cymric border, where rose-
red Luguvallium looked over the Solway flats, and
crimson Deva watched the hills of Mold. This was the
strategic triangle which held middle Britain.

If we are to judge by the extent of the old Roman
cemetery, the city of Eburacum must have been large.
The fortified wall—of which one multangular tower
and traces of the artillery platforms still survive—enclosed only the buildings of the military fortress, small
in area compared with suburbs which spread across the
river and along the main roads. . . . The walls of
mediæval Chester were built exactly on the walls of The city
Roman Deva, and of nearly the same though a softer
and therefore a cheaper stone. But the walls of mediæval York enclosed a very much greater area than those
of Roman Eburacum. The southern and eastern walls
of the Roman city were allowed to disappear, while the
north and west walls were maintained and extended into
the circuit of the mediæval city. . . . It is very possible that the larger size of mediæval York merely meant
that the old Roman wall was extended to embrace the
unfortified Roman suburbs. If traces of those suburbs

[1] In this respect it formed a duplicate of London. The origin of London is
uncertain. Its position as a road junction renders very hard of belief the opinion
(of which Professor Haverfield was the chief exponent) that it was a purely
Roman foundation. (See J. S. Reid, *Municipalities of the Roman Empire*, pp.
228-229.) The importance and position of London depend upon peculiar circumstances which existed long before the Romans, as they existed long after.
Eburacum was a military fortress in a sense in which London never was, and in
the days of Constantius the military centre of gravity was still in the north.
Gibbon's idea that the inhabitants of Caledonia and Ireland were "naked savages"
is an interesting illustration of the way in which ideas have changed. Carlisle and
Chester were certainly not built against naked savages!

have vanished, we may remember that even the buildings within the Roman wall, most of them very substantial, have disappeared, and that a thousand years of re-digging foundations and re-building houses in a prosperous city is not likely to leave much intact. If we think of the mediæval wall of York as the limit of the Roman suburbs, we shall at least see why the cemeteries begin just outside those limits. Such was the Roman custom, at Rome as well as at York.

VI

Eburacum was a *colonia*—that is to say, a self-governing city with the kind of city-government which originally had been arranged for colonies of Roman citizens. In the days of Constantius the word had become a technical term with a wider meaning. It still denoted a city corporation of Roman citizens— but they were very seldom men born in the city of Rome, or even descendants of such men. They were men of any and every part of Europe, citizens of the Roman empire; and whether a Roman citizen had been born in Britain or Syria or Morocco was politically of rather less importance than whether an American citizen of today was born in Maine or Montana. One place was as good as another, as far as that went.

The city government

The city corporation was organized on the model of the old Roman city-government. It consisted of two orders—on the one hand, those inhabitants who possessed a certain property qualification; on the other hand, the "plebs," the peasants, artisans, tradesmen and members of authorized societies. Unskilled and low-skilled occupations were chiefly followed by slaves, who did not count. The higher or senatorial order, the decurions or curial class ("aldermen" as we might call them), were eligible for municipal office. Their qualification was not enormously or invidiously high. In the days of Constantius, seventeen acres of land, or a capital of less than eight hundred pounds (four thousand dollars American) were probably enough to place the proud candidate among the more distinguished section of humanity. He would not, it is true, be able to move in quite the same circles as the senatorial landlords in Italy or Spain whose yearly income topped the fifty or the hundred thousand; but the making of great fortunes demands time, and they had been at it longer in Spain and Italy. It gave them, at least, the status which enabled them to deal with one another on equal terms; and we need not doubt that the first call upon the profitable business which passed through the *colonia* was shared among the decurions, the duumvirs who were their chairmen, and the honorati who had passed through office.

The decurions

Heavy liabilities adjusted the balance. The magistrates of a Roman city produced from their own private pockets the financial resources by which most of the city services were supplied. Their fellow-citizens did not expect them to study an undignified economy. As long as Roman civilization endured, public opinion smiled upon those local patriots whose pride in their city led them, whether in or out of office, to dip into their own purses for the benefit of others. When those rich men died out, the self-governing Roman city died out too.

Although the decurions of Eburacum—and for that matter, those of other British cities—probably left us accounts of their names, lives and work, in the hope that we might remember them with applause, nevertheless no record has survived. We know, however, a little about at least one of the local dignitaries of York.

The commercial community

He was Marcus Verecundus Diogenes; not (presumably) a landowner, not a senator, not a Briton at all, but a Gaul from the middle Loire, who probably was one of the York representatives of the Gallic silvering and gilding industry. He bore the dignity of a Sevir Augustalis—a fraternity which kept alive the memory of the first and most famous Augustus, and ranked next in status to the decurions. Eburacum as a commercial centre might not class with Alexandria or Antioch, but its trade was nevertheless sufficient to attract men from other parts of the empire, and to give them, if not great fortunes, yet a reasonable prosperity and competence. The exquisite glass, which can still be seen in the Yorkshire Museum, with its wonderful colours and lovely shapes, came from southern Gaul, where the industry succeeded direct to that Carthaginian glass-making which derived from Tyre and Sidon. It also, no doubt, had its agents and representatives in Eburacum. The same is true of the pottery. The yellow-brown, highly glazed ware which is found in abundance was as good a quality of its kind as Britain was to know for many a century to come. Most artists would prefer it for colour and shape and texture to modern mould-made china. It came from Gaul, and needed its salesmen and depôt managers in Eburacum.

VII

How numerous and important were the foreign influences in Eburacum we can see from other evidence   Foreign
than this.   One of the Gallic commercial agents, prob-   influences
ably, was responsible for the altar to the Deo Arciacon
that has puzzled archæologists.   The exact identity of
that divinity, who was doubtless of distinguished consideration in his own locality, has never been established.
Some have thought that he presided over the destinies
of Artiaca, which nowadays is Arcis sur Aube in the
region of the upper Seine: and that is no great way
from Langres, where Constantius settled the Alamanni. . . . But there were worships in Eburacum more
recondite and strange than that of simple clod-hopping
Arciacon from Arcis.   There was a temple of Egyptian
Serapis near the railway station.   Not far away some
one, when digging, turned up a little gold plaque, curiously inscribed with Gnostic letters, profoundly caba-
listic and esoteric—no doubt concealing from the vulgar,
under mysterious veils, some of those elementary moral
truths which the vulgar never trouble about until
hidden from them. . . . Whosoever this Gnostic may
have been, he was no simple or rustic person, and he
came from much further afield than Arcis sur Aube.

A chapel of Mithras certainly existed at York. We   Sun-
might have expected as much from the military char-   worship
acter of the city.   The Asiatic cult of Mithras [1] was

---

[1] Mithraism was descended from the old Persian religion prior to its reformation by Zarathustra. Moulton, *Early Religious Poetry of Persia*, 1911, p. 79 and
p. 135 *et seq.* The latter passage will show why Mithraism should be a soldier's
religion. See the full description in Sir Samuel Dill's *Roman Society in the Last
Century of the Western Empire*, p. 80 *et seq.* . . . . There are many unlikelier
things than that Constantius himself attended the Mithraistic "Cave" at York.

probably more strongly represented in the army than any other. Where it differed from such formal, official cults as that of Augustus, which M. Verecundus Diogenes no doubt ably represented, was that Mithraism formed a thoroughly live and systematically organized religion, with a genuine fraternity and a symbolism all its own. It was a club and a benefit-society and a church with moral uplift and inspiring ideals. It probably appealed to soldiers more than the mother-worship of Serapis. The youth with the Phrygian cap, the Bull-slayer, is still familiar to us on the monuments and tomb-stones. His churches were called "Caves" in remembrance of the story of his life; and the blood-bath, the "Taurobolium," which consummated the initiation into his mysteries, was a ceremony not suitable for old ladies or people with weak hearts. The stout aspirant, however, rose from it (in theory, at least) renovated, purified, and a perfected man.

VIII

The horrors—or at any rate the terrors—of the blood-bath of Mithraism must not give us exaggerated ideas concerning the character of those who dwelt in Roman York. They were in most respects as decorous, as evangelistic, even as sentimental, as any who dwell in York today. That a portrait of the reigning monarch decorated their living rooms we may assume without question. Possibly M. Verecundus Diogenes or one of his colleagues imported such articles in bulk. Nothing of the domestic architecture of Eburacum has survived. What the Pict and the Gael left, the wear and tear of

centuries has destroyed by slower but even more effective means. . . . York, like other British towns, was
probably distinguished from the corresponding towns
of the Continent by less density of building. That
fondness for possessing a garden which is so marked a
characteristic in the modern Briton seems already to
have made its appearance. We possess one fairly complete example of a Roman town in Britain—Calleva
Atrebatum. By the kind offices of its Irish visitors
(though probably much against the will of its proprie-
tors) it was left permanently uninhabited, and its
ground plan survives for our inspection. It was what
we nowadays call a Garden City; and although York
was no doubt a busier centre, and less model in its arrangements, the same tendency probably marked it.
For the most part its streets were lined with houses of
the villa type, rather than with solid blocks of building. The
What the villa type was, in Britain, can be judged by "Garden City"
the remains of the country houses which are scattered
plentifully over the land. Roman Britain had a style
of building peculiarly its own—modified and adapted
to suit its climate—charming, airy, red-tiled and ram-
bling, built in wood and brick, more like certain kinds
of modern American building than anything which
followed it upon the same ground. They had mosaic
floors, baths, and central heating by means of hot-air
flues. Probably they had the plastered and painted
walls which Roman houses usually possessed. . . . A
good deal of the charm of those old villas was due to
their spread-eagle open building, which the *pax Romana*
rendered possible. It was followed by over a thousand

years of dark, cramped and fortified building from which the old spirit had utterly fled.

One thing taken with another, the York of that era probably needed to make very little apology to succeeding ages. Only within very recent years has European civilization regained the standard of material life which Eburacum could have shown in the days of Constantius: the planning, the building, the style—meant for the intercourse of merchants, officials and citizens—the central heating, the baths, the shops, the public buildings, the roads; the perhaps too conventional, too respectable citizens, with too much vague humanitarianism' and tender ineffectualness. Some earlier Dempsey or Hackenschmidt from the northwestern frontier may have stood, ponderously looking on, while the funeral procession passed, and may have seen *in situ* those stones which now we inspect in the Museum, with their singularly touching and domestic inscriptions, which tell us, among other things, that human affection, human loss, human pain were then, as they are now, things equally urgent and puzzling, and that in Roman Eburacum the questions were asked which still trouble humanity. The world—at York, as much as elsewhere—was eagerly awaiting an answer.

High standard of Roman town life

IX

If we need to see what manner of man dwelt in the civil side of York in those days, let us cast our eyes upon that noble memorial stone of Julia Velva [1]—whether

---

[1] Raine, *Two New Roman Memorial Stones*, reprinted from the Annual Report of the Yorkshire Philosophical Society, 1922.

Mrs. or Miss the inscription does not tell us. There, upon a couch of honour, lies Julia—a little battered, but perhaps, at the age of fifty, she was not so young as she had been. At the head of the couch sits the donor of the memorial, her heir, Aurelius Mercurialis. . . . No rough Bohemian, no shaggy-trousered fellow from the frontier, this. Regard his carefully tutored whisker, his correct, well-tended beard, his perfect grooming. His toga is minutely shown—no doubt at his personal direction, and by his attendance at the stone-yard to superintend—folded in the demure knot which was the style of the really well-dressed man in the York of his age. . . . A thoroughly civilized, conventional, elegant, sophisticated fellow, fully moralized; by his looks, he diligently read in his Marcus Aurelius, and understood that external events should be indifferent to the true philosopher—or at all events, that the true philosopher should try to be indifferent to them. . . . He would have received us with courtesy, inwardly in silence noting that our toga was not correctly disposed.

A citizen of Roman York

Such were the men who were carried on the overhead charges of the fields of York and the Rhineland commerce. No doubt Aurelius Mercurialis himself, far from being an idler, attended to the business of estates which, originally Julia's, became in time his own. He, too, was probably, like Julia, British in blood, descended from the Brigantian tribesmen who from time immemorial had possessed the land of Britannia Superior.

He may have been an *honoratus* in his time, classing with the past Lord Mayors of York: we do not know. He may have been *duumvir*, presiding over the senate of Eburacum as Camillus or Cicero presided over that of

Rome. He was almost quite certainly *decurio*. Whether he was, or not, we may, when we try to imagine what these words meant, safely think of Aurelius Mercurialis with his precise grooming and his fashionable toga. Prosperity, safety, education and social order are the forces that breed such men. They are fine flowers grown in glass-houses. They were rendered possible, and fenced from adversity, by the legions. . . . In Gaul, in Spain, and especially in Illyria, the contemporaries of Aurelius were suffering from depressed trade and the collapse of the currency. Aurelius himself was up to the present more fortunate. What was the look and guise of that other half of the Roman world—the military?

X

We need not look away from York itself to find some record of the military men who passed through it and dwelt in it. Among the sculptured stones in the Museum is one that is famous, not for any particular detail it gives, but for the illumination it throws upon the human quality and character of the age: the "Sleeping Soldier." [1] In some of its features it forms a link with those ancient religions of Asia Minor which trace back to the Hittite empire. It is a figure of the mourning Attis, with Hittite hat, curled over to become a Phrygian cap; but the rough-handed, big-hearted man who hewed the figure out knew, probably, very little of Attis, and nothing at all of Phrygia or the Hittites, and accordingly he has transmogrified the conventional figure into an unmistakable Roman soldier, with tunic,

The "Sleeping Soldier"

[1] Raine, *Proceedings of the Yorkshire Philosophical Society*, 1929, p. 7.

and cloak, and fur hood, resting his elbow upon his shield and his chin upon his hand, as many a Roman soldier, then and later, stood and gazed from the towers of Eburacum over the vale of York. . . . There he stands, fixed in stone for ever—a man of whom we can see the like amongst us plentifully to this day: a large, somewhat full-fleshed man, with a straight neutral nose, lips a little full, and a mild ox-eye. His modern descendants have most commonly a pink complexion and a tendency to chubbiness. . . . An amenable, equable, good-tempered man, not very sensitive, and inclined to an amiable materialism; physically powerful but somewhat lethargic when left to his own resources; very easily disciplined; a sociable, clubbable man, with nothing particular to tell us. He is a frequent species on modern golf-links, where his play is good and his conversation indifferent. To encounter a whole legion of such men, stripped and prepared for battle, with its officers placed and its commander looking on, would be a work for which no one would feel any needless enthusiasm. But the effectiveness of such men is wholly social; taken one by one, as individuals, their power is gone.

Eburacum, almost from its first foundation (and at this date it was perhaps not very much more than a century old) had been the headquarters of the IXth legion [1] and afterwards of the VIth. (Victrix.) These, recruiting themselves gradually more and more from the British population, as Roman citizenship and Roman education extended themselves among the inhabitants

The Garrison

---

[1] For some earlier history of Legio IX (Hispana), see the present author's *Tiberius Cæsar*, Chapter VII.

of the island, had become, we may fairly believe, in the time of Constantius, predominantly British. To a great extent, the same process had been at work all along the frontiers of the empire. But the new army, the Striking Force "in sacro comitatu," had no such local affiliations. It was a picked force, composed of men of all countries, chosen solely for their military excellence, and (since they might have to fight anywhere) for their adaptability to all climates. Not only so, but non-Roman auxiliaries—"foederati" they would have been called a century later—were present with Constantius in Britain: Chrocho and his Alamanni. These last had felt the weight of Constantius' hand, and knew what it was. Their relation to him was a special one. As mercenary soldiers serving under a definite contract, they had a more personal tie with the old emperor. As foreigners, they had no prejudices or convictions in matters of domestic Roman politics. The man they admired and respected was the man who handed out their monthly pay.

XI

Constantius at York

It is not likely that the influences which were at work during that winter in York were sudden; it is not likely that they were slight. Still less were they entirely the creation of Constantius and his friends. One or two little pronouncements of policy from Constantius may have set the ball rolling. He was known to be a believer in low taxation [1] and in religious toleration. The

---

[1] Diocletian (as Lactantius tells us, De M.P., vii) kept a large gold reserve against eventualities, and insisted on his colleagues doing the same. Constantius, who was opposed to this policy, is said to have whipped up a "gold reserve" by voluntary contributions, which, when the inspectors had gone, were returned to

reaction of these beliefs no doubt brought to him the passive support and the positive encouragement of many men. Along the coasts of Britain and Gaul there was still an active trade, which would benefit from his views of taxation. Spain, though she did not come under his jurisdiction, was for the same reason likely to entertain feelings of sympathy. Constantius, as the man who had restored the British trade to the Gallic routes, was popular with the traders and customers of inland Gaul. They liked his principles and his methods.

With this trading community, Christianity was deeply intertwined. Christianity had first spread through the facilities for intercourse created by the commercial system of the empire. It was so far a religion of commercial civilization rather than of country life, and it was connected with all that scheme of law, and internationalism and universality which were peculiar characteristics of the commercial civilization. It had arisen in the deeply commercialized and industrialized east. The comparatively low stage of economic development which marked Britain was reflected in the slight degree to which Britain was touched by the persecution. The real struggle was being waged in the east, while in Britain mere tolerance was for the time being a policy sufficiently active to fulfil all purposes.

His interests

Britain could boast of only one important martyr—Alban: though two citizens of Chester and "many more of both sexes" are named among the more obscure suf-

the donors. (Euseb., *Vita C.*, I, 10.) This question of the gold reserve was evidently a subject of warm dispute at the time. The enemies of Diocletian believed that its existence forced up prices, and was the cause of his famous Tariff of Maximum Prices, which failed to stop the rise. An interesting and amusing account of this Tariff will be found in Prof. F. F. Abbott's *Common People of Ancient Rome*, Chapter V.

ferers. Scanty as these details are, they seem to indicate that the British persecution was not connected with York. Even the historians who recount with careful detail the abominable deeds of the pagans agree in attributing a humane and tolerant spirit to Constantius. We may infer that he softened and suppressed, wheresoever his authority penetrated, the too zealous action of individual magistrates. . . . But the death of Alban had one feature of even greater significance. The military executioner refused to carry out the sentence, and preferred to die for the crime of military mutiny. Upon the man who actually performed the execution, some peculiar fate descended. Whether or not it is accurately recorded by the Christian propagandists, we may probably deduce with accuracy that the execution of Christians was not popular in the army, and that those who took part in it were regarded with disapproval.

Martyrdom of St. Alban

XII

Constantius himself might have found some difficulty in distinguishing cause and effect in this matter. The views of the army and the views of its chief may have had a certain amount of mutual interaction not always possible to measure with exactitude. A ruler, feeling along the line of least resistance in order to detect the trend of public opinion, is liable to increase that trend; though he only increases that which already was there. . . . All the circumstances combined to press Constantius along a certain line of policy, by which he gained first the sympathy and then the active support of all the parties and classes under his government. He

can hardly have been unconscious either of the appeal
of the policy he had to offer, or of the gradual turning
of opinion and expectation towards himself. Personal
ambition does not seem much to have moved him. He
was playing his game very steadily and patiently, without the possibility of taking his winnings; and with that
impersonal patience he played it out to the end.

Plans
formed
at York

Constantine had arrived none too soon. The legend
that he only reached his father to find the old man on
his death-bed is probably based on some misunder-
stood remark of his own, that when he reached
Boulogne, Constantius was already dying. The year
which they spent together was a time during which
many momentous designs were planned. Constantius
possessed the carefully built up influence, the long-won
confidence of men; he had the ideas, the tradition, the
plans for the future. Constantine possessed the youth,
the physical power and moral energy. The old man had
forged the weapon; the young man was able to use it:
and during their conversations that year Constantius
must have inducted his son into its arrangements and
purposes, its system and operation. A year is not too
long a time in which to introduce a comparative
stranger to matters so delicate.

What was schemed, probably in detail, at York that
year was the conquest of an empire, the refounding of
its policies, and the institution of new principles which
should last a thousand years. . . . Galerius could sit
and gnaw his thumb-nail if he liked. He could not
reach them at York in Britain: he could not find out
their plans or purposes, where, behind that silver ditch
of the Channel, they sat among their soldiers—with,

perhaps, Aurelius Mercurialis brushing his whiskers in the background.

As often happens to men who have divested themselves of personal ambition, Constantius was singularly favoured by luck. Nothing any longer mattered to him, and as if that fact were a powerful spell all things **Death** worked together for good to him. When he died at **of Con-** York,[1] on July 25, A.D. 306, after a reign of thirteen **stantius** years, he had reigned just long enough to give his son an assured position and a prosperous realm. He died just on the verge of great changes with which he was not fitted to deal. Constantine stepped into his shoes just when the necessities arose which he was particularly competent to deal with. All things considered, Constantius could have asked little better of fate than the life and death fate gave him.

XIII

Constantine was not the only watcher by the bedside. Constantius had a family by his marriage with Maximian's step-daughter; and the old patriarch was just the man to entertain a sincere and even a sentimental affection for the three daughters and three sons of Theodora. Their names—Constantia, Anastasia, Eu-**The** tropia, Delmatius, Julius Constantius and Hannibal-**family** ianus [2]—are prophetic and significant. They indicate that a new type—perhaps a new race—had appeared

---

[1] The "imperial palace" of Gibbon never existed. Constantius no doubt had a house at York. He would hardly live in the military headquarters. But whether this house were large or small, and whether within or without the walls, we do not know.

[2] Gibbon, I, p. 206, f.n. 8 with Bury's annotation.

upon the scene. Such names were to succeed those of
Fabius, Marius, Lucullus and Crassus as those of the
rulers of the Roman dominion.

Their bearers may have been more, but not very much
more, than children. The eldest can scarcely have been
older than eighteen or twenty years of age. . . . Constantine was a man of thirty-two. He took them under
his protection, and this family of young half-brothers
and sisters had very little to complain of with respect
to the treatment they received from him. We must
bear their existence in mind. They were to count, later
on.

XIV

The burial place of Constantius is unknown; his
epitaph, however, survives. Infinitely greater, as a memorial, than any tomb, was the man he had provided to
take up his task and follow in his footsteps. Before the
death of Constantius all the necessary measures had been
so carefully taken that only the last and crowning step
was required. . . . Would the army accept Constantine as Augustus? . . . While the suffrages of that
fierce incalculable electorate were being canvassed, he
remained invisible, and apparently unconscious of what
was happening. His seclusion was a prudent provision
not against failure but against success.

He had no alternative. To sink back into a private
station was impossible. The temper and policy of
Galerius produced efforts which we, at this distance
of time, can see to be absolutely necessary and inevitable, although to their astonished owner no doubt they
seemed to have no such necessity. They compelled Con-

Constan-
tine com-
pelled to
become a
candidate
for empire

stantine to fight for his own safety, to grasp at the sanctuary of the imperial crown, and to make a bid for the support of all the powers hostile to Galerius. It was the presentation to Constantine of this dilemma which forced him to act as he acted, and to think as he thought. It was not so much that the world was destined to be cast in the mould of Constantine, as that it was forced to take the shape in reverse of Galerius. All this is typical of a certain sort of irony which runs deep in human life.

Constantine made no overt appeal. If he were to succeed, the memory that once he had asked for the empire would be damaging to the kind of dignity with which he intended to surround the imperial throne.[1] He must already, before his election, have foreseen at least the main lines of his later policy, for his conduct at York is only explicable on these grounds.

Under-currents

XV

In the short precedent period, while he and his father were together in Britain, hints of strange and revolutionary change had flitted across the face of the world. Tides of opinion and of passion were mounting to their maximum; ideas were silently passing away, and others were arising. At York, Constantine was in a position to study the shifts and trends of public feeling, and he must have been aware of the multiplicity and complexity of the forces which were urging him and beck-

[1] Euseb., *Vita C.*, I, 18. "On purpose . . . that no man might glory in electing Constantine to be emperour." See also the letter to the Governors of Palestine, *Vita. C.* II. 25 *et seq.* (esp. 28 and 29) which purports to be Constantine's own statement.

oning him. If he shrank from taking time by the fore-lock, others were awaiting the opportunity. He himself, the man Constantine, was a straw in the wind, an index to the direction of the storms and cyclonic systems of human feeling which he did not make and hardly could alter, but only registered. The army no doubt knew that if it made certain choices it could rely upon the backing of powerful civilian interests. The problem resolved itself therefore into the question, what the army really wanted.

It had two points of view. As the largest professional organization of its day, it needed to be satisfied of the financial benefits likely to accrue to its members. As the greatest political organization in the Roman world, it needed to be convinced that the policies of Britain and Gaul deserved to be backed against the remainder of the empire. . . . Both these points were satisfied. Constantine was accepted as the leader best qualified to express those policies. . . .

The army backs Constantine

XVI

So it began, as beginnings so often do: somewhat hastily, somewhat obscurely, a little before anyone was quite ready, some time before anyone was in a position to note down the events: everyone full of assumed confidence and private trepidation, all resolved to push for all they were worth, but not knowing what the morrow would bring. . . . Not everyone realized the full extent of all that was being done. It is quite obvious that Constantine had begun with an epoch-making precedent. He did not admit that he had been elected—that is, given his dignity and rank from its original owners, the Roman people. His theory was that he was appointed by God, nominated by his father, the senior Augustus, and accepted by the Roman people (that is to say, by the army) which witnessed the act of God. . . . But this in all probability was a good deal over the heads of the majority of the troops.

The first practical step was to secure the whole dominion that had belonged to Constantius. This involved a southern front. Between July and October (when the great series of events began which we shall shortly need to note) the whole north-western Striking Force, with all available auxiliaries and supply organization complete, was transferred from Britain to the Rhone mouth and the Alpine frontiers of Gaul. . . . No small or ragged army set out from York. Never again, probably, until August, 1914, did such an army leave the shores of Britain. The reconcentration was probably effected before the summer was over. After the equinox, weather in the Channel is no longer reliable.

Any Briton who stood, that summer, by the Pharos of Dover, where the light then burned which has been extinct these many centuries now, could have seen, day after day and week after week, the passage of that army on its way to make history: the movement of the detachments down the military highways, through London and Canterbury—men from Gloucester and Chester and Carlisle as well as from York; men from special camps, picturesque German auxiliaries, Rhineland cavalry, Asiatic bowmen whose bows no European of those days could bend—a panorama of Roman might and world-dominion. All these, as they came, were

Reconcentration in Gaul

taken over by Roman embarkation officers, and ferried across the level shimmering straits to Boulogne, whence they started on their long march south-east.

Probably it was not altogether unlike more modern troop movements, with its delays, congestions and confusions; men sitting on their packs by the roadside, wondering why some more favoured legion went by; columns halted and diverted to make room for high-bred trotting post-horses which whirled along spider-wheeled cars carrying the armed messengers with the mail for distant lands—possibly for Nicomedia where Galerius Augustus sat, waiting for news. The army moves

XVII

Constantine wrote to Galerius, informing him of the death of Constantius, and of the approval of his own candidature by the army in Britain. He sent his portrait, showing himself duly crowned; and while he expressed his regret that he had not been able to consult the wishes of Galerius beforehand, he pointed out his own reasonable claims to succeed his father.

The Beast glowered and growled. He did not see the reasonableness, and at first was for ordering the portrait and its bearer to be put on the fire together. This, however, was only his way of expressing annoyance, and after he had heard the views of his advisers, he accepted the facts of the case. He was strictly within the recognized conventions when he promoted Severus in order of seniority to the dignity of Augustus, rendered vacant by the death of Constantius, and when he caused Constantine to enter upon the lowest rung as Cæsar. Attitude of Galerius

At the moment, Galerius was not prepared to make any move. For a power based upon south-eastern Europe to invade and subdue north-western Europe is a proposition which needs long and careful thought. Galerius accordingly proceeded to think over it very long and very carefully, and he had not finished his thinking when events abruptly wrenched the decision altogether out of his hands.

XVIII

It was upon the October of the year 306 A.D. that events converged as upon a crucial date. The military considerations, though highly important, were only a small part of all that needed to be taken into account by the guiding spirits. The Roman world was drifting rapidly into a situation in which critical decisions would need to be taken. Such policies in war, in government, in trade, in religion, in the general views and spiritual orientation of men as were then adopted, would settle the fate of Europe one way or another for ever.

Crisis approaches

Typically enough, just at this moment the candle of history goes out. At the moment of crisis we are left groping in a twilight in which nothing is perfectly clear. We can judge the actors only by their actions; and in some cases we can suspect their actions only by noting where they are when the lights go up again. . . . One thing is certain. Men did not drift fatuously into that crisis. As the darkness comes down there were whisperings, conferences, alliances unknown to us, communications we cannot trace, help passed, betrayals arranged, and all the many provisions which mankind is best pleased to settle in obscurity. It was brief, but it was

a twilight of the gods: it was the death of what we know
as classical civilization.

XIX

If the spirit of the great emperor ever revisits York,
and passes again over the spots he knew in life, perhaps
he re-enacts his departure on the journey the issue of
which was to be so incalculable and so momentous. All
is changed: but not to his eye. . . . He issues from a
ghostly headquarters near the south porch of the cathedral. Perhaps beside that very porch he mounts his
horse and rides down the Stonegate, the old South Street.
Terry's restaurant, fronting the old south-western gate
of the citadel, he leaves on his right; he rides through
the Guildhall, where the broad highway lies fair before
him, and over a stone-built bridge whose masonry has
long ago mouldered to dust. At Trinity Street he
emerges into the modern Micklegate; at Micklegate Bar
he leaves the suburbs of Eburacum behind him, and in
Blossom Street, where the omnibuses thunder and the
electric street-cars whirl by with a roar and a spark of
blue flame, he sets his face for the long wearying journey
by the straight road to Tadcaster and the South.[1]

Constantine leaves York

[1] According to the latest discoveries the southeast wall of the Roman city ran
across Aldwalk and Bedern. Hence, drawing in this new line of wall on the six-
inch Ordnance Map, we see that the Minster is pretty nearly on the site of the
Prætorium. The south porch evidently fronts upon it. Stonegate represents the
old South Street. Terry's restaurant must stand almost upon the site of one of the
guard-rooms of the South gate. High and Low Petergate are approximately the
cross streets, though probably they are slightly too far south to represent them
exactly. The road represented by Stonegate, and continuing through Micklegate,
was the main military highway to Tadcaster. On both sides of the city this
road, according to the Roman custom, was lined with tombs. That to the south,
near Micklegate, was apparently the more important. From it came the Sleeping
Soldier, the stone to Julia Velva, and the stone to Bebius Crescens discussed by
Mr. Platnauer in *Report of the Yorkshire Philosophical Society*, 1911. See *Proceedings* Y. P. S., 1925.

CHAPTER V

THE SECOND CAREER OF MAXIMIAN
HERCULIUS

I

**Revolt
of Rome,
October,
A.D. 306**

Up to this point, all had been preface. In October the real story began. The revolt of Rome against the Roman empire was a magnificent symbol of all that was impending. Constantine's successful action had set men thinking and talking. The further he came southward, the warmer was the heat in his face. In Britain, toleration and neutrality had been an advanced policy. At Arles, it was time to revise this view.

According to Bishop Eusebius of Cæsarea, Constantine himself told the curious story that has often been repeated, concerning the circumstances under which he began to take a particular and personal interest in Christianity. It was, in all probability, in Britain, during his journey south from York, that he saw the gigantic cross figured in the sky. All his men who were with him saw it. It was a little past noon when the prodigy appeared. . . . By the testimony of Constantine, there was an inscription on the cross—IN HOC VINCES: conquer through this.[1]

**The
vision
of Con-
stantine**

This is one of the most famous visions of history—if indeed it were a vision. The very strong likelihood is that it was no vision, but an objective fact. Far from contending that it was a revelation vouchsafed to him-

---

[1] Eusebius, *Vita C.*, I, 22.

self alone, the emperor appealed to witnesses who saw
it in his company; and such an appeal is at any rate
proof that he himself regarded it as objective. . . .
How far it might be to him a message from the most
high God, and a sign of wonderful fortune, Constantine alone is the sole judge. But as a visible phenom-
enon, it involves no great strain on our credence. . . .[1]
It is not difficult to believe that there were markings
upon the Cross sufficiently near the words to suggest
the phrase: for if it were late September in a fine, cold
autumn, few who are familiar with the skies of Britain
would doubt the possibility: and Constantine would by
that time possess news from Italy which would fill his
mind with thoughts of the importance of the faith it
symbolized, and the possibility of conquering through
its influence.

What was the news that could exercise so profound an
effect upon Constantine, and suggest so much to his
mind? It was the approaching Revolt of Rome, and
the accession of Maxentius.

II

Throughout the summer, while Constantine was re-
concentrating the Striking Force in southern Gaul,
Galerius had remained inactive. There was reason for
his passivity. The condition of affairs in Italy was such
that he could safely strike neither at Constantine nor
at his Italian enemies. That Constantine knew all that

[1] Such occurrences are fairly frequent. In the spring of 1929 a number of
correspondents wrote to the *Times* to report the figure of a wonderful cross in
the sky; several others kindly wrote to explain how it was caused. There is not
the slightest evidence that the vision of Constantine took place in Italy.

was happening, and was hand in glove with them, is
probable, if not certain. The power behind the unrest
was the Christian church in Italy.

The more the drift of events against Galerius became
visible, the more its Christian character grew plain: and
even when there were other elements, very far from
religious, mixed up with it, these tended more and more
to take shelter under the wing of the bishops, and to
allow their case to be grouped with the Christian. . . .
Constantine must have been well aware of the main
facts long before they came to light: and he must have
seen the force that lay—at least in Italy and Africa—
behind the bishops. It was a force which every statesman who desired to be successful must take into account, and to which he must adapt himself. The closer
he came to Italy, the more he perceived these truths.
Neutrality was not enough. He must take a definite
side in the contest.[1]

III

Such considerations as these added weight to the
moral impression made upon him by the sign in the sky.
They suggested ideas and interpretations. . . . His own
statement is that the night after he saw the sign, Christ
appeared to him in a dream, and commanded him to
adopt it as his cognizance. The next morning he ordered
the cognizance to be made. It was the famous Labarum; and in after years he showed it to Eusebius.[2]

[1] Eusebius, *Vita C.*, I, 20-21.
[2] Eusebius, *Vita C.*, I, 24. From the order of Eusebius' narrative, it is obvious
that the vision happened before the rise of Maxentius to importance. A good
deal of uncertainty seems to exist concerning the mascot of Constantine. It

This was the beginning of the Labarum, which was a jewel, like the insignia of an order of knighthood, and not a banner—though later on a representation of it came to be borne upon the banners of the army. . . . Just how far all this was literal and sober earnest, and how far it was inspired imagination, we have no means of judging: but handsome is as handsome does, and a gift which convulses worlds and changes empires is not made or unmade by the name we call it.

IV

On the 27th of October, A.D. 306, the revolt of Rome and the accession of Maxentius took the world by surprise. At one stroke Italy, Africa and Spain, the remaining half of the west, were lost to Galerius, and started on a separate existence of their own.

The whole political world was convulsed by an event which had more than one aspect of the utmost importance. Constantine's election might have been an accident, or the natural result of the claims which could be put forward by the son of Constantius. But the election of Maxentius showed that the process at work was a political one, and involved a complete "landslide" in public opinion. Still more important, from some points of view, was the method by which this result had been achieved. The revolt against Galerius was taking the shape of a legitimist revolt, a rebellion of hereditary successors against the method of co-optation

Election of Maxentius

was probably one variety of a pattern which had several forms. That it was a solar emblem which Constantine turned into a monogram of Christ, seems probable.

and adoption which had been employed by Diocletian, and was as old as Augustus.

The election of Maxentius was, however, distinguished from that of Constantine by one very important feature—old Maximian was by no means dead. He was very much alive. The first serious hint of trouble in Italy had brought him out of retirement like a bolt from a bow. As he had never really understood the remarkable proceedings of his old friend Jovius in resigning the empire, he hastened to point out that evidently it had been a mistake; they were still wanted, and he urged upon Diocletian that duty, if not pleasure, pressed upon them the task of taking over once more the direction of affairs. His disgust and disappointment were great when Jovius gently repeated his own determination to enjoy a quiet life. Taking Maximian's representatives for a walk in his kitchen-garden at Salona, Diocletian indicated the cabbages that grew there.

Diocletian refuses to help

"Am I," he asked, "to waste my time upon empires when I have cabbages like these to occupy it?"

The reply of Maximian is not upon record. He most probably thought Jovius as mad as a hatter. But Jovius was yet to prove himself once more an extremely wise man.

Failing Diocletian, Maximian turned to his own son Maxentius. If Italy was to march, then he must lead: for the one thing unendurable to Maximian was to be out of the procession. . . . Maxentius was quite willing. His tastes were of the expensive sort; and empire is certainly an expensive luxury.

There is reason to suppose that Maximian had a complete and convincing alibi ready, in the event of any unfortunate disaster overtaking their plans. It was not needed. When he pulled the strings, the principal representatives of Italian unrest called upon Maxentius. They proved to be two officers of the Prætorian Guard and a Quartermaster General. . . . An agreement was reached. The son and legitimate successor of their old Augustus was to place himself at the head of an Italian revolt. On the 27th of October, as we have seen, this agreement was executed. Rome became once more the home of a Cæsar.

V

Galerius, of course, was not free from blame. He seemed to think that possession of an imperial crown entitled him to display all the less exalted characteristics of human intelligence as well as all the less endearing characteristics of human temper. He knew perfectly well that Rome was restive under the knowledge that the seat of imperial government was permanently trans- Behaviour ferred to Milan. A French government which pro- of Galerius posed to abandon Paris and set up at Lyons or Marseilles, or a British government which wished to leave Westminster for Liverpool, would have fewer obstacles of sentiment to over-ride than had Diocletian, when he appointed Milan to be the new capital of the western empire. Galerius was called upon to display at least tact; and it is an unfortunate truth that tact is almost the only human quality which Galerius never displayed. He chose this time to enforce with extraordinary severity the new assessments of taxation in Italy. Rome had been exempt from taxation for many centuries past. It might be just that the privilege should cease; but it is hardly a reasonable expectation to fancy that men long free from taxes will be particularly amenable when they are at last imposed.

All the smouldering discontent was given direction by two influences. The Prætorian Guards, once the most important power in the empire, were faced with the prospect of being transformed into a superior police force. But the skill and courage brought into the movement by this agency was only implemented by the immensely more widespread popular influence of the Christian church.

Unity of Italy

VI

The emperor Severus, hastening to Rome as rapidly as speed would take him, unmasked in succession a number of dramatic and terrifying facts. Galerius had secured the obedience of his immediate subordinates by appointing weaklings, and he had then been mad enough to send one of these weaklings into Italy with a veteran army which had at one time been long under the personal command of Maximian himself. The imminence of danger obliged Maximian to take the lead in person; and the instant he entered the fray, the difference between the painted lathe and the true-forged metal became evident. Whatsoever the old man was, he was no fool, and he was no weakling. The troops went over to him in a body, and Severus bolted again as fast as he could to Ravenna. After they had cheered jolly old Herculius till they were hoarse, the army invested Ravenna and blockaded Severus inside.

Constantine and his men, at Arles, watched the play

unfold: whether tragedy or comedy, none yet could tell.

Ravenna, surrounded by marshes, and lying upon the sea, was a fortress very nearly impregnable to ordinary methods of attack. Even to get at the walls was diffi- cult, while to cut off the entry of supplies and rein- forcements by sea was impossible without a fleet such as Maximian did not possess. But although the walls of Ravenna were strong, the mind of Severus was weak. Old Herculius did not err upon the side of subtlety, and it was probably Italian-born brains which devised the successful plot to get Severus out of Ravenna.

Commissioners were sent in directed to talk the ordi- nary diplomatic commonplaces, but, as friends, secretly to reveal to Severus the hideous truth that he was being betrayed by his own colleagues. . . . It is significant that Severus found no difficulty in believing the allega- tion. He did not seem to find much difficulty in believ- ing the word of Maximian when the latter swore to protect his life if he would surrender Ravenna and re- sign the empire. Accordingly Severus did surrender Ravenna. . . . Galerius watched with horrified amaze- ment while the tool he had trusted broke in his hand. Constantine and his friends at Arles must have laughed a good deal in private. So far, it was certainly comedy.

Severus in Ravenna

VII

The fall of Ravenna was an event of crucial im- portance, which determined the course of history. Had Severus held out a little while longer, the Illyrian army, advancing into Italy under the personal command of

Galerius, might have raised the siege, crushed Maximian, and re-taken Rome. It was a very different condition of affairs which Galerius actually met in Italy. The great strongholds were garrisoned and ready. Maximian, thoroughly in his element, contested every inch of the way with all his accustomed skill and energy. By the time that Galerius, basing himself upon Fanum Fortunæ, had reached Narnia on the road to Rome, it had become evident that, unless an accommodation could be reached, the Illyrian army might sacrifice its leader. Galerius, in these circumstances, became surprisingly moderate and genial. He invited a conference. He suggested that Maxentius would obtain far more by a peaceful agreement than by fighting to a finish. When all his proposals were rejected, he showed the real state of the case by a rapid retreat which only his utmost exertions prevented from becoming a rout. His unfortunate army provided for itself during the retirement at the expense of the still more unfortunate Italian peasantry. The whole episode conspicuously failed to add to the prestige or the popularity of Galerius.

But his failure was not by any means his downfall. His power remained intact. He made a second appeal for a conference. It was easy to say that nothing but his own policy ever rendered any conference necessary at all; the fact remained that some kind of formal arrangement would have to be made. By a master stroke of diplomacy he induced Diocletian to emerge from retirement to preside over the congress. The parties met at Carnuntum. Italy was represented by Maximian.

The Congress of Carnuntum had much greater success than some of its modern analogues which could be mentioned. Diocletian achieved his last and possibly his most sensational success in the field of diplomacy when he persuaded Maximian to resign a second time, and to retire once more into private life. How he did it, history has not revealed to us. Whether Maximian melted before the tender pathos of Jovius, or was persuaded by his artful wiles, or won over by a bold appeal to his self-interest, we cannot guess. The only thing we may be sure of is that he was not convinced by an appeal to his reason, nor terrified by an appeal to his fears.

The success won by Galerius at the Congress of Carnuntum went further than this. The safe-conduct given by Maximian to Severus had been violated by Maxentius, who gave the ex-emperor the choice of his own death. At Carnuntum, Maxentius was excluded from the succession, and Valerius Licinianus Licinius was appointed as the legitimate successor of Severus.

VIII

Wide and astonishing as was the victory of Galerius at Carnuntum, it had one defect which is not uncommonly fatal to treaties—it could not be implemented. Maxentius, at Rome, showed not the slightest disposition to get out. Constantine and his men at Arles were probably smiling still more broadly at the course of the play—by this time unmistakably a comedy. . . . Maximian, as soon as he was away from the hypnotizing presence of his old friend and colleague, seemed to find some difficulty in comprehending how he had ever consented to resign, and to give away the claims of his

Result
of the
Congress

son. Finally, he went to Gaul and visited Constantine.

His visit shows that he was beginning to perceive the necessity of a general alliance of the western powers if they were to hold their own. With this view Constantine evidently agreed—at any rate, agreed sufficiently to enable him to meet Maximian's advances halfway. Any treaty they might make would be, in effect, a pact of common defence, the spoils ultimately to go to that one of the two who could take them. Maximian was an experienced, a successful and a confident man. He probably anticipated very little serious difficulty when the day of division came.

Marriage of Constantine to Fausta

The agreement was sealed by a marriage between Constantine and Fausta, the daughter of Maximian, which took place at Arles in December, a month after the Congress of Carnuntum. This marriage, which did much to settle the fate of Constantine and the destiny of Europe, was not his first. He had been married before—childlessly; and he had one natural son by his mistress Minervina. But it was his marriage to Fausta which constituted his true entry into the social heritage left him by his father. He married the daughter of an emperor. . . . Maximian, who did not dislike the idea of having an emperor for a son-in-law, at the same time publicly and solemnly recognized Constantine by the official title of Augustus.

IX

In all this Maximian without doubt acted in good faith. Possibly it had not occurred to him that any objection could be raised to his proceedings. But Maxentius seems to have raised very strong objections indeed. He had ample cause for assuming such an attitude. The actions of Maximian had been highly temperamental. After organizing the Italian revolt, and making his son emperor, he had, without consulting his son, resigned and allowed the claims of the latter to be overridden. He had then made an alliance with Constantine and recognized him as Augustus. . . . Such a catalogue of actions only needs to be rehearsed in order to show how much ground for objection it might afford Maxentius. Not only had Maximian been extremely arbitrary, but he had acted as if he were an irresponsible despot, entitled to override other men's wishes and interests as he thought fit.

Split between Maximian and Maxentius

All the participants in the Congress of Carnuntum had missed one very important point. When the world at large is indifferent and uninterested, statesmen may distribute the earth and the fulness thereof pretty much as they please. But when the world is passionately interested in the result, the actions of statesmen have to conform to the expectations of public opinion. A starfish stranded by a spring tide is no more helpless than the statesman who has lost touch with the demands of his public. The fatal weakness of Maximian Herculius was his inability to realize that he was a servant of the people he ruled, and must in the long run fit his actions to their wishes. Galerius and Diocletian, before they ended their careers, must have recognized to some extent this truth; but Maximian never recognized it.

Maxentius had been thrown up to empire by a real force—a genuine movement of feeling and opinion. He himself partly realized as much. He knew that in

Strong position of Maxentius some way the backing behind him was real and reliable, and that he would have to answer to it for his actions; though his understanding of this truth may not have been quite perfect. At least, he knew better than to handle it as if he possessed unlimited power. He would not last a day if Italian opinion thought that he was playing false. As long as it trusted him, he could not be overthrown.

All this was totally invisible to his father. Maximian fretted and fumed, and could not imagine why his son seemed to exercise more power than he did himself. He was so confident of his own rightness that he appealed to the decisive tribunal—an assembly of the army. The case was heard in due form, and the verdict went decisively for Maxentius. The stout old man, who had always been so practical and so successful, had to give way to the idle and gilded youth who had not one single virtue beyond the crucial one of recognizing facts. . . . But how great a virtue that can be! . . . Maximian could not understand it. He, Maximian Herculius, found it necessary to leave Italy and take refuge in Illyricum. Galerius did not want him there. He hastily left Illyricum, and crossed the border into Gaul.

X

Freed from the embarrassment of his father's assistance, Maxentius took the bold step of claiming the sole and exclusive sovranty of all the Roman dominions. **Claims of Maxentius** It may be that in so doing he did not very greatly alarm his rivals, nor create in their breasts any keen anticipation that he would make good the ambitious claim; but all must have recognized the significance of the step. So far as Italy was concerned, it destroyed the agreement into which Maximian had entered with Constantine, and it asserted both the ancient supremacy of Rome in the Roman empire, and the absolute and uncompromising nature of the claims put forward by the Italians. The future would show what meaning the claims might bear in actual fact; but the important thing is that they were made.

They implied, of course, that the division in the Roman world would not be settled by agreement and mutual concession, but only by the victory of one of the parties. Above all, they were a repudiation by Italy of the politics and principles entertained by the old gang, that Board of Emperors which Diocletian had founded. Not only were the claims of Galerius and Diocletian and their tool Licinius repudiated and refused, but those made by Maximian also. The Congress of Carnuntum was abrogated, and the gage thrown down.

XI

Constantine and Fausta made Maximian welcome. **Maximian in Gaul** The latter, convinced that he had sinned, but probably with very indefinite ideas as to the precise nature of his sin, was in the mood for repentance and humiliation. He surrendered all his imperial rights. He would be good. His daughter and son-in-law sympathized without, perhaps, taking his professions too literally. They were wise.

In all his relations with Maximian, Constantine showed a certain amount of tenderness towards the peculiarities of a somewhat difficult old man. It suited him to play with these pretensions and powers of Maximian: but for all that, very deep lines of division and distinction separated their interests. Constantine understood and shared that sense of vocation, that passion for the work of government, which compelled Maximian to haunt the scenes of his old success. He understood, however, something else which Maximian did not understand—and that was the extent to which a statesman depends upon the public opinion of those he rules. Constantine was separated from the old gang by his readiness to consult the trend of opinion. He was separated from Maxentius by his power of apprehending what that trend was.

Maxentius had some of the defects of his parentage. The weaknesses of Maximian sprang ultimately out of his conviction that beliefs, ideas, thoughts did not matter. The very fact that frequently they do not matter only involved him deeper in the slough. Maxentius had avoided this error; he knew that beliefs did matter, but he did not quite know which were the important beliefs. He had enough contact with reality to induce him to pay considerable respect to bishops, and to the church they governed. He realized that the influence they exercised might be decisive. But he did not realize that his own habits might be as deep an affront to the moral discipline of the church as any disrespect he could show to doctrine.[1] A modern man, looking about him, may be at a loss to identify in his own experience those particular charms about other men's wives which induced Maxentius to risk his career and his life. But it is un-

Constantine and Maxentius

---

[1] Euseb., *Hist. Eccl.*, VIII, 14.

doubted that he did offend the church generally as well as the small select coterie of wealthy families which constituted the social world of Rome. The Christian writers enlarge, with consternation, upon the shocking facts. As these do not seem materially to differ from scandals familiar to us today, we may perhaps deduce that sinners, as well as saints, have changed remarkably little during the intervening centuries.

XII

Old Herculius could not settle down. An irreducible minimum of misplaced self-confidence made it impossible for him really to doubt his own importance. He could not really, when he came to face his own soul, doubt that the supremacy of Maximian Herculius was the most pressing necessity of the universe. He really was not able to believe that the world could exist without him. Temptation overcame him by fits and starts. He could not help meddling with the dangerous machinery of war, revolution and government. Earnestly as he fought the weakness, a little indulgence in political conspiracy was too sweet to be resisted. . . . Lion-cubs are sometimes charming pets; but the court of Arles in these days must too often have felt some of the sensations of a household with a full-grown and occasionally forgetful lion loose in it.

This restlessness was bound to culminate in trouble. A temperament which his son had found intolerable was not likely to be much more endurable to a son-in-law. . . . Constantine kept his temper for eighteen

Difficulties with Maximian

months. When at last he lost it, it was for reasons which most men would have thought ample excuse.

XIII

Constantine's government in Gaul

The years during which Constantine was giving his direct personal attention to the government of Britain and Gaul were years of prosperity for them. They formed, moreover, the advertisement which gave publicity throughout the empire to the benefits of Constantine's rule. Bishops "on the run" and priests hiding from the Cheka of Galerius are not likely to have failed to point out to their flocks the shining example of good government which lent glory to mankind beyond the Alps. Constantine was not called to any hurried or urgent action. Quite as good as any action was this waiting and preparation, during which public opinion was gradually influenced in his favour, and public expectation was turned towards him.

We gather hints that his military organization was kept keyed by the necessary work of the German frontier. None of this work was of the first importance. It practised the troops without incurring serious loss or expense. We should never have heard of the German campaign of A.D. 309 but for the proceedings of Maximian in connection with it. Constantine himself went up north during the summer, taking with him the Striking Force "in sacro comitatu"—or at any rate a substantial part.

XIV

The season wore, and direct touch between Constan- Maximian
dreams
dreams
tine and Arles was interrupted. Whether old Hercu-
lius was dreaming dreams, or whether he had some
substantial ground to go upon, we do not know; the
strong probability is that he let his temperament and
imagination get the better of him. He grew persuaded
that Constantine's delay was unduly protracted. At
last he grew convinced that Constantine was lost, and
would never come back. Herculius was once more
called upon to save a world which too long had lacked
the privilege of being directed by him.

Who could doubt the result? Herculius, breathing
energy and noble self-sacrifice, hurled himself into the
fray. He at once seized the treasury at Arles. Some
of the troops were evidently influenced by his beliefs.
He was, after all, a man of dominating character. With
the financial resources of Gaul, and the pay of the
troops at his disposal, he began to organize his position.
He sent to inform Maxentius of the change in the state
of affairs. . . . Had his information and inferences
been correct—had Constantine really been lost—his
conduct would have gone down to history among the
great deeds of wise and foreseeing men. In what he
supposed to be a pressing emergency he showed every
virtue except the wisdom of verifying his data.

Unfortunately for him, he was mistaken. Constan- Flight of
Maximian
tine was not lost. The man who had ridden from
Nicomedia to Boulogne could get from the Rhine-head
to the Rhone-mouth faster than any messenger could
carry the news of his coming: and in the midst of his

self-sacrificing proceedings Herculius was surprised by the return of Constantine. He had only time to gallop to Marseilles. Pursuit was hard upon his heels, and the investment was instantly closed around the city. The first assault failed: the ladders were too short: and men could recover their breath and look about them.

As soon as Constantine had heard the news of Maximian's proceedings, the Striking Force had crossed rapidly from the Rhine to the Saône valley, embarked at Chalon, turned into the Rhone at Lyons, and come downstream straight to Arles. Marseilles is some forty-five miles on by road, southeastward. Once in that ancient and famous city, Maximian was safe, for Striking Forces cannot carry heavy siege trains with them. . . . He would have held out, for the idea that the world did not passionately yearn to be ruled by him was one which penetrated with difficulty to his intelligence. But at this point an unexpected force intervened.

Maximian
arrested

The troops who followed Maximian had evidently done so in good faith. They had not the slightest wish to fight Constantine or to repudiate his authority. They had believed it to be the fact that he was lost or dead. His return wholly changed the situation. Taking matters into their own hands, they promptly surrendered the city and Maximian Herculius with it.

Serious as the case was, Constantine did not forget that he had married Maximian's daughter, and possibly he could understand Maximian's side of the story. He made it officially clear to all concerned that Maximian had no authority and no imperial status; and he addressed personally to the old gentleman some home truths which the latter found it hard to forgive. With these actions the affair terminated.

XV

But nothing ever terminated with Maximian. Shut off now from every other resource, he sternly resolved upon a One-Man Revolution.[1] Had he carried out his project consistently, he might have succeeded. He made the mistake of seeking a helper: he consulted his daughter Fausta. Evidently he could not conceive that she was not boiling with anger at the insults levelled at him by her husband. The idea was, that Fausta should see that he could get into Constantine's room on a night to be fixed. The revolution would then happen. . . . Fausta, however, privately entertained ideas totally different from those credited to her by her father. She preferred to be an empress rather than merely an emperor's daughter: and she told Constantine the whole story.

The One-man revolution

She might have held her tongue, but moral instances are not often simple. If her story was true, old Maximian was a highly dangerous person; and there was no room for him and Constantine together in the same world. None the less, even her word was not blindly accepted.

The trap to catch Herculius was therefore laid with care and completeness. In the darkness of the appointed night he came quietly towards Constantine's bedroom.

---

[1] This story is related by Lactantius, *De M.P.*, 29, 30. Gibbon, I, 410, f.n. 41, disbelieves it; but apparently only because he does not wish Constantine to have any excuse for the execution of Maximian. Lactantius was high in court circles, and the ultimate source of the tale is probably Constantine himself.

The sentries had been reduced in number to encourage him; but Maximian spoke to them, revealed his identity, and was allowed to proceed—confident, probably, that he had but to make himself known in order to command the homage of any soldier. He reached the room. Quietly entering, he stabbed to the heart the recumbent figure on Constantine's bed; and we have no reason to suppose that he was not an expert at the job. Thus the One-Man Revolution was accomplished.

Or nearly. . . . The lights went up; the door was opened; and Herculius walked into the hands of Constantine and his guardsmen. . . . The proof was absolute and indisputable. The man on the bed was one of the palace chamberlains; and his fate proved the fate intended for Constantine. No answer could be made, and no excuse pleaded.

Death of Maximian

Maximian was notified that he was at liberty to make his own way out of life. Whether he intended any symbolism by his choice is perhaps doubtful; at any rate he hanged himself.

So at last he terminated something.

XVI

But there was something he had not terminated. Old, betrayed and alone, he left implanted in Fausta the seed of a deadly revenge—his own character. In due time it would ripen. . . . We shall see what came to pass when it did.

XVII

Maximian's death marked the end of an era. The turn-
over came slowly, but unmistakably. The first of the
persecutors had come to a tragic end. The second
passed away a year and a quarter later, in the person of
Galerius; with whom perished Diocletian's scheme of the
quadruple Board of Empire.

Since the Congress of Carnuntum he had begun
slowly to perceive that he had failed: his policy could
not be implemented, and effective power was passing
into the hands of his rivals. It all dated from that evening when he had gone to bed, leaving Constantine to
walk straight out of the palace at Nicomedia. . . . His
last years were clouded. He spent his time in reclaim-
ing waste land in Pannonia, and he drank too much. . . .
As a result, the unhappy Beast fell into bad health. He
died of some dreadful form of cancer or gangrene; and
the Christians pointed impressively to him as the second
example of what the world might expect to see in the
deaths of the persecutors. The Beast, however, had no
apologies to offer.

Galerius recognizes failure

The April before his death, he joined with Constantine and Licinius in putting his signature to an edict of
toleration, by which the Christians were no longer to
be directly penalized for their religion. He added to it
a request that the Christians would pray for him, for
themselves, and for the safety of the republic. . . .[1]

[1] Euseb., *H.E.*, VIII, 17. Gibbon, II, 132-133. The request did not necessarily mean that Galerius was personally uneasy; it was a request that the Christians would voluntarily pay that homage to the state which had been intended
by the obnoxious rite of burning incense to the divine monarch. They had no
objection, if they were allowed to select the form and method themselves. The

The Edict
of Tolera-
tion, April,
A.D. 311

Maximin Daia was not one of the signatories; but a little while afterwards the local magistrates in his dominions were directed quietly to drop the action taken against Christianity. Many Christians were released from prison in consequence; for it was in Maximin's dominions that the persecution had been most severe.

In this edict of Galerius, no particulars were specified. He remarked that he was issuing, under separate cover, his instructions to the magistrates concerning the interpretation to be put upon the laws in question. What these instructions were, no one now knows. Only by arguing back from a number of scattered and obscure facts is it possible to divine the truth.[1] Galerius was neither giving the Christians an unconditional toleration, nor was he making good the damage done to their organization. To make good the damage done to individuals was of course impossible, and need not be thought of. . . . The edict of toleration only sought to produce by a change of method the same results as before intended. The Christian churches were to become legally collegia, guilds: corporate bodies with rights and liabilities defined by the law. In these days (as we shall presently see) the guilds were rapidly becoming closed hereditary corporations. Christianity also would become a closed hereditary corporation. It would be one of many, all sanctioned and protected by the state.[2]

compromise so made has lasted ever since—at any rate in southern and western Europe.

[1] Mason, *Persecution of Diocletian*, pp. 301 and f.n. 329-333. Mr. Mason thought the instructions probably confidential, and that the Christians only found out what they were by suffering the consequences.

[2] Hardy, *Christianity and the Roman Government*, Chapter IX, on "Christianity and the Collegia" reviews the connection between the two. It will easily be seen by how natural a transition Galerius could systematize the status of the churches as collegia.

The Christians were remarkably slow to respond with enthusiasm. After a short time, it became fairly clear that they did not accept this kind of toleration. The long-drawn-out battle began afresh. The Church refused to be a collection of collegia; it declined to be hereditary; it would not be closed. It planted its standard for freedom of organization and universality of membership, and for the supreme authority and the divine foundation of its teaching. . . . In doing this, in the teeth of torture and terrorism, it did what no other section of the Roman world did, or could do. It prevented the completion of the deadly circle of stereotyped institutions which was closing round the empire. It secured that the future of Europe should ultimately be one of free political association, not of hereditary caste.

Galerius died at Sardica. Maximim Daia now became Senior Augustus. The Cæsar Licinius took over the government of Illyria.

Death of Galerius, May, A.D. 311

XVIII

The disappearance of Galerius meant a regrouping of the powers—now reduced to four. Constantine and Licinius (who had both signed the edict of toleration) took part in significantly friendly overtures. Maximin Daia and Maxentius were much further apart, had little in common, and found few serious opportunities of helping one another, but they did what they could to embarrass a common foe. They clearly occupied the weaker position.

Where the situation might be expected to break was in the relation between Constantine and Maxentius.

The new situation

The policy of the latter was an aggressive one. He intended—as he had shown in his claims to the title of sole Augustus—to rationalize his position by seizing the whole empire. An onlooker, weighing the chances and the necessities of Maxentius, could not ignore certain conditions of instability in his position. He could not stand still. To save himself he must keep moving. In what direction would he move?

His secret programme would almost certainly include a war. This narrowed the issue to a struggle with either Licinius or Constantine: for at present there would be neither purpose nor possibility in a war with Maximin Daia. Now, it was much easier to strike at Constantine, while holding Licinius, than the other way about. All the indications were thus in favour of a preliminary contest between Constantine and Maxentius.

The death of Maximian Herculius helped to determine this particular issue. Even though Maxentius had no particular reason for regretting the fierce and ambitious old soldier, he found the opportunity a convenient one for propaganda. It was a great advantage to be able to appeal to universal human sentiment rather than to the cold logic of political advantage. War seemed so much more moral when founded upon the outraged emotions of a devoted son. Public opinion in Italy was a little uncertain. As far as it could be stampeded, it moved for a programme of filial affection and abhorrence of the selfish arrogance of the idle rich. . . . Maxentius was quite ready to lead the crusade against the class of which he had hitherto been a distinguished adornment. To Tax the Rich and Sup-

Aggressive Italy

press the Murderer of Maximian was the warm-hearted human slogan which he finally adopted.

Italy did not rally quite so well as he hoped. The historians suggest that he devoted too little time to business. It is an elementary truth that business and pleasure are both of them whole-time jobs which are not conveniently mixed. Constantine, giving his whole attention to the former, was ready first.

The Idle Rich had lost no time in sending urgent deputations to the Murderer of Maximian. They implored him to save Italy. The facts which they had to communicate were of the highest interest. A revolt in Africa had been suppressed by Maxentius in a way which suggested that the confiscation of property in favour of the imperial treasury had been a principal object. In Italy, Maxentius had put pressure (not always exclusively moral) upon his wealthier subjects with the aim of inducing them to make contributions to the treasury outside the legal and guarded processes of taxation. He may have needed the money; but unfortunately for himself, he gave the impression that he employed it as much for personal as for political purposes. Most men are far more willing to see their money wasted upon the ambitions than upon the pleasures of a statesman. . . . The results therefore were not what Maxentius had doubtless reckoned upon. His policy of Taxing the Rich only drove the outraged non-Christian landlords into the same camp as the scandalized Christian moralists: and the two parties together could probably sway a very large proportion of public opinion in Italy, Africa and Spain. The conversations seem to have

Maxentius and Italian opinion

satisfied Constantine that the ground was ready for him, and that he could act without fear of undue haste.

XIX

It was therefore Constantine who chose the time and the place and the strategy and the terms of the contest. For some time it had been approaching; and now he stepped to meet it.

CHAPTER VI

THE CONQUEST OF ITALY

I

SPEED in war is in direct ratio to the preparation which has made it possible. Six years had passed since Constantine left York. If we need any evidence that his Italian campaign had been long foreseen and carefully provided for, we can find it in the rapidity of his actions now. As soon as the political events had made war inevitable, he could call upon an army which did not need to halt or look behind.

The month was September—the same month in which Capture of Hannibal, some five centuries before, had made his passage of the Alps. The Striking Force of Constantine, A.D. 312 crossing from Arles by the great road which, since Hannibal's time, had been built through the Mont Génèvre pass, seized and took Segusio on the Italian side of the watershed almost before the defenders realized their advent. The Italian army, standing off to watch the passes, closed immediately; but it had not got past Turin on its march before it was met by the rapid advance of the Striking Force. Maxentius had embodied in his army the latest military improvements evolved on the eastern frontiers. His "spear head" was a division of Asiatic heavy cavalry, such as a couple of centuries later carried all before it. But the dazzle-tactics of Scipio and Cæsar were still able to deal with such troops. Before the discipline and the swift evolutions of the Striking Force, these cavalry were soon in retirement; then in retreat; and at last in rout. Turin shut her gates just in time to prevent the pursuers entering with the pursued. It was a prudent if harsh measure. After the army of Maxentius had been cut up and dispersed before Turin, the city negotiated terms for herself. They were favourable. . . . Milan, the political capital of Italy, then surrendered. Almost before it was known in Rome that he had crossed the Alps, Constantine was dining in the imperial palace of Milan.

II

By destroying the field army of Maxentius, the battle before Turin threw into Constantine's hands the whole of Italy between the Alps and Padus—all that had once been Cisalpine Gaul. It would remain his until another army appeared to dispute its possession with him. He had no intention of waiting on that event.

Maxentius had all the material advantages of numbers and supplies. The core of the Italian army was the renowned Prætorian Guard, which, with other Italian units, made up a force of eighty thousand men. Forty thousand more had been raised from the north African fighting tribes: and what kind of material they are, the ancient Phœnicians and the modern French have shown us. Another sixty-eight thousand were believed to be available if required. This gave a total of a hundred and eighty-eight thousand men, who were equipped and supplied from stores which for years past Maxentius had been busily accumulating.

But the whole of this army could not be put into

the field at the same time or in the same place. Constantine's aim was to use the superior speed and discipline of his Striking Force to destroy the army of Maxentius in detail, so that he never should meet the whole of it at once. He had nearly a hundred thousand men, all taken together; but of these more than half were the garrison troops and frontier guards of Britain and the Rhine. His famous Striking Force, even when reinforced by all the available frontiersmen, was only about forty thousand strong; but it was a carefully picked and highly trained army. A large part of its power lay in its speed.

Plans of Constantine

III

Before Constantine could prudently advance upon Rome it was necessary to deal with the army which lay in Venetia, with its headquarters at Verona, under Ruricius Pompeianus. Continuing north-east through Milan, he turned into the south-eastward highway at Bergamo; at Brescia he met the cavalry outposts of the enemy, who retreated before him upon Verona.

The fortress of Verona lay in a narrow loop of the river. It was accessible only from one side; and by its bridge it had free communication with Venetia on the opposite bank. Blockade was impossible as well as inexpedient. The place had to be taken by force, and it had to be taken swiftly.

The Adige at Verona is a dangerous torrent in a difficult ravine. Even the men of Constantine's Striking Force were at first held up by the impossibility of crossing; but the crossing had to be made, in the teeth of possibility or probability, and in their teeth it was made.

Siege of Verona (October)

Verona was invested and cut off. A sally by the besieged was repulsed. The leaguer was drawn tight. Ruricius thereupon made his way through the blockade and began to organize a relief force. He collected an army large enough to fight Constantine upon level terms. Constantine did not wait for it. Leaving his main body to continue the siege of Verona he moved out with a picked corps to intercept the army of relief.

At first Ruricius declined a field action, intending to use his army rather for the purpose of raiding, intercepting and worrying the besiegers. The whole interest of Constantine was concentrated upon the task of forcing the issue with the utmost rapidity. In order to entice Ruricius into action, he caused his men to take the narrowest possible space. This device ultimately succeeded. Towards evening the army of relief **Battle of Verona** decided to fight. As soon as it had irrevocably committed itself, and could not withdraw, Constantine wheeled out wings from the rear ranks of his force. Since, in this way, they held the entire strength of the relieving army, Constantine's men could not be outflanked or enveloped, and the battle which began at sundown was a hand-to-hand soldiers' battle in which individual training counted for everything.

The battle lasted the whole night. When morning dawned, it was over a field covered with Italian dead, among whom lay Ruricius Pompeianus himself. Verona surrendered. The way was now open southward. Constantine wasted very little time in putting the Striking Force again upon the road.

CONSTANTINE'S ITALIAN CAMPAIGN, A.D. 312.

Aquileia

Bergamo Brescia
MILAN Verona
Segusio Hostilia
Mt. Genevre Turin Placentia
Pass
Bologna

Ariminum
Fanum

Narnia
Saxa Rubra
ROME

Saxa
Rubra

R. Tiber

Constantinians

Maxentians

IV

From Verona the great military highway runs almost due south. It is a little less than thirty miles to the crossing of the Padus at Hostilia. Once over the river, it is some forty miles to Bologna. Here is the junction with the main Æmilian-Lepidan road, which runs straight along the north-eastern edge of the Apennines from Placentia to Ariminum. At this point Constantine turned.

Although he had crossed the Alps by a road identical with that which Hannibal intended to take and like the Carthaginian wizard had fought his first action near Turin, the subsequent route of Constantine had been entirely different from that of Hannibal. As he was destined to be swiftly and completely successful, where Hannibal failed, it is worth noticing what he did. For thirty-nine miles from Bologna down the Æmilian-Lepidan way his road coincided with Hannibal's. At Forli, the Carthaginian had turned aside for the pass to Etruria and Lake Trasumennus. Constantine, however, continued steadily on to the sea at Ariminum, sixty-eight miles from Bologna. Thence he proceeded by the coast road to Fanum Fortunæ, another twenty-seven miles or so. Here, turning into the southwesterly road, he was on the famous winding highway, the Flaminian Way, which was the Grand Trunk road to Rome.

The rapidity of his march was disconcerting to the plans of the defenders of Italy. It was more: it was morally intimidating. Maxentius himself was not sufficiently experienced in war to realize the portent implied in those giant strides with which the Striking

The advance upon Rome

Force came up to Fanum Fortunæ; and there was hesitation among his officers—no one caring to be the first to admit that they had been out-generalled and outdone. At last they agreed upon an unanimous report which aroused Maxentius to the full truth. Every effort was now made to prepare for Constantine's approach. Fresh troops were concentrated north of Rome. The third battle which the Striking Force would need to fight would be by far the hardest of the three: the Prætorian Guard itself would form the core of the defensive army which covered Rome.

Maxentius notified of the danger

V

A little uncertainty and confusion marked the period during which the plans of the defence were taking shape. The principal risk faced by Constantine was the possibility that Maxentius might adopt the Fabian tactics, shut himself up in Rome, and leave the Striking Force to amuse itself as it liked. In such a case, it might be impossible to get him out, and the fate of Constantine would be the fate of Hannibal.

There are signs that Maxentius intended to follow this plan. Here, however, several very important factors helped to determine the issue. Constantine possessed friends in Rome who were ready to help in any way possible, and there was a distinct trend in public opinion upon which they could profitably work. The unpopularity of Maxentius made it additionally hard for him to venture upon some steps. He could not order the devastation of the countryside. He could not quite safely ignore the landowners who pointed out the danger

Pressure upon Maxentius

to their property, and who demanded protection. When the man in the street (whose genuine signature in such matters is always unmistakable) began to take part in the discussion by urging Maxentius to go and fight, and contrasting him in a painful way with Constantine, Maxentius had to go. Certain forms of popular pressure are not easily to be defied. He therefore took the crucial step of deciding to make a stand at Saxa Rubra, some nine miles outside the city.

This decision staked the issue on a field battle, which Constantine was eager to fight, instead of upon a siege which he might have found beyond his powers. Hannibal never had the luck of Constantine. The element of luck was something which Constantine and his friends fully admitted. All they said was, that it was miraculous and supernatural luck, too good to be the ordinary, every-day luck of human life. It was the hand of God.

VI

Just south of Saxa Rubra, two little rivers fall into the Tiber. One of them is the Cremera, which flows past Veii. Above the river lies Fidenæ. A few miles further up the Tiber is the Allia; and rising northward is Mount Soracte. It is classic and sacred ground to the lover of Roman history. The map is dotted with those wonderful names which seem to belong to a world of legend rather than to the world of reality. Between Veii and Fidenæ the commanders of Maxentius took ground. It is flat and low-lying plain, rising slowly up towards Soracte, and it was probably chosen as being suitable for the armoured cavalry, the "cataphracti,"

The Italians prepare to fight

and the Moorish light horse. Apparently the army was drawn up somewhat obliquely, so that it crossed the road at an angle; its right wing rested on the Tiber, while it would not be altogether untrue to say that the whole army backed upon the river. Upon the road itself the Italian infantry was drawn up, with the Prætorians in reserve. The cataphracti formed the left wing; the Moorish light horse, the right.

The Striking Force, coming in column down the road from Falerii, was led by the cavalry under the personal command of Constantine. The whole action must have developed at a run, the cavalry leaving the road and deploying into line until it closed with the cataphracti, while the infantry marched straight on against the Italian centre, changing their formation as they went.

The whole line began to swing, the Moorish horse coming forward so that Constantine's rear-guard had little more to do than to ride off the road to meet it. In this state of affairs all was touch and go; for a very slight success would have brought the Moorish horse round to the rear of the Striking Force, and have tied the latter up ready for destruction. But the luck held. Constantine's headlong charge broke the ranks of the cataphracti, and hurled them back in disorder. The Africans were at the same time driven before the rear-guard; many were chased into the torrent of the Tiber, and the wings of the Italian infantry centre were thus stripped away. Nipped between assault on three fronts, the Italian infantry of Maxentius broke and fled. Only the Prætorians held fast. They neither gave nor broke, but fought with steady and resolute courage until they fell where they stood.

The
Attack
at Saxa
Rubra

It is nine miles from the Cremera to Rome. While the infantry were wrestling with the Prætorians on the field of Saxa Rubra, the cavalry pursued the mounted men who were pouring back into Rome. The Mulvian bridge, carrying the Flaminian highway over the Tiber into the city, was choked with fugitives. Maxentius himself was among them when the bridge (a bridge of boats, never intended to bear such weight) began to collapse. . . . There grew up a legend afterwards that *The breaking of the Mulvian bridge* Maxentius had laid a trap for Constantine, and had fallen into it himself. Whether this be so or not, the bridge certainly gave way. Long and careful search was subsequently made at Constantine's order, and the magnificently attired body of Maxentius, covered with mud, was brought up from the depth of the Tiber. He had been drowned through the weight of that splendid armour.

VII

Less than two months, therefore, from the day of his passage of the Alps, Constantine made his triumphant entry into Rome. He was welcomed as a deliverer rather than acclaimed as a victor. The speed and success of his campaign might well seem miraculous to the ordinary onlooker; and yet if there were miracle mingled in it, it was the miracle of supremely wise planning and complete foresight. He had taken care to be wanted. Small wonder then that he was a welcome guest.

The whole character of his entry showed that it was friendly and peaceable. No proscription stained it. According to the custom of most ages until our own, the family of Maxentius, which was capable of transmitting a claim to the empire, and possibly a few of his friends, were executed; [1] but no other bloodshed marked the accession of Constantine. With the fall of the Prætorians and the dispersal of Maxentius' army, practically all his opponents were disposed of. The great senatorial landowners of Italy, the bishops who led the public opinion of the church, and such merchants, bankers and shipowners as survived, all alike welcomed Constantine. The whole of the west accepted him as representative of their wishes. [2] No enemies were left who needed his attention.

It remained to reward his friends. Here questions of profound policy arose, and it is plain that Constantine had thought out clearly beforehand the implications of all his actions. There is no sign of any hurried improvisation since some unexpected vision at Saxa Rubra. Not long after his arrival in Rome he occupied the rightful place of Augustus in the senate. In addressing the house, he went over his own past acts, and indicated the views and policies that had inspired them. He expressed his respect for the august body to which he was speaking, and his intention of upholding it as the grand council of empire which from the first had been its chief characteristic.

While this was not an attitude which would have satisfied the senate of earlier days, it came as a gratifying announcement to the senate which had been neglected by Maximian and bullied by Maxentius. Warmly

Constantine's entry into Rome

The senate

---

[1] Zozimus, a hostile witness, speaks of a few supporters being executed. Everyone, however, agrees that there was no reign of terror.

[2] Euseb., *H.E.*, IX, 9; *Vita C.*, 32, 34. Constantine restored confiscated land, recalled exiles, and set free political prisoners.

appreciative of the prospect of still being respected and consulted, the flattered senate proceeded to use its revived power in order to support its benefactor. It conferred upon him the ancient honours and dignities which the senate had always possessed the privilege of bestowing: and it passed a resolution that Constantine should be regarded as the first of the three Augusti who now ruled the empire.

Maximin Daia, who was, in point of fact, the senior Augustus, was hardly likely to relish this. Little as a resolution of the senate might count when made in the teeth of a united army, it counted a great deal when made on behalf of a man who was at the head of the most efficient and successful military force which for centuries Rome had seen, and who governed one-half of the Roman world. It gave Constantine just that prestige and signature which he needed to put the final touch upon his actual power.

VIII

To the bishops, Constantine had even more welcome announcements to make, although these did not receive their final form till some months later. He had almost certainly, before he left Arles, discussed the heads of an agreement with the bishops and with Licinius. Its ratification would naturally depend upon the results of the Italian campaign. He could now announce that the terms would be carried out as soon as the details were finally agreed upon.

From the time of his arrival in Rome, the bishops became a regular court party, with free access to Con-

The bishops

stantine's presence. There was usually a group of churchmen at court, whom he consulted.[1] It was probably very soon after his arrival in Rome that the discussions began which were to bear fruit five months later in the Edict of Milan.

The legal suppression of a body like the Christian Church cannot be carried out without a great deal of material damage. Owing to his father's policy, and to the comparatively small numbers of Christians in Gaul and Britain, Constantine had not hitherto encountered this problem in a pressing form. At Rome he came face to face with it. If Christianity were no longer a crime, and if it were not now punishable, Christians ought not continuously to suffer a penalty for what was not illegal. The destruction of Christian property by order of the state ought to be made good, on exactly the same principle as that on which Christians were discharged from prison after the edict of toleration. On no possible argument could it be right to abolish a crime and continue the punishment.

The Roman government may have had its failings, but it was always legal. Constantine evidently saw and appreciated the logic in the argument of the bishops, and it may have been by his advice that they did not press him for immediate action. It was a matter which he could take up with Licinius, and possibly he could secure the restoration of church property not only in the west, but throughout the empire. This was the plan adopted.

Question of
church
property

In the meantime he was especially friendly to the Christian leaders, and was sufficiently well-informed to

[1] Euseb., *Vita C.*, I, 35.

betray no surprise when occasionally these turned out to be formidable ascetics with inflexible wills and unconventional clothes—the kind of man who has become familiar to us since, but was not so common then.[1] He rebuilt churches that had been destroyed during the persecution, and gave money to charities which may not have been far from the same connection. Eusebius tells us that he made a practice of systematic benevolence to the neglected poor, as well as to those who had fallen into poverty from good stations in life—to widows and orphan girls in particular, whom he provided with dowries.[2] This was not altogether a new policy on the part of the empire. A generous care for the unfortunate was as old almost as the principate itself. Constantine's action implied not so much any novelty as a definite return to stable conditions and traditional customs, after an age of confusion and emergency. It especially commended him to men amongst whom benevolence and charity were essential virtues.

IX

The suppression of the Prætorian Guards was a measure which he carried through for his own ends. With the new military organization which Diocletian had begun and Constantine was perfecting, there was no room for the guards, who had been a centre of rebellion and unrest. Had the senate and the bishops been consulted, they would probably have been puzzled to know whether their interests were well or ill served by

Prætorian Guards suppressed

---

[1] *Ibid.*, I, 35. At this date, Stoicism had long been conventional, and Cynicism was extinct.
[2] *Ibid.*, I, 36.

the abolition of the Prætorians. The latter had, on more than one occasion, secured for Rome the principal voice in the election of emperors and the decision of policy; but they had been from their first beginning the instrument of the military emperors; their concentration at Rome had been a sign of that masked civil war which Tiberius had waged against the senate; they had been the principal means by which the influence of the senate had been neutralized and its power controlled; and their abolition was destined, in the long run, to restore to Rome her independence. That independence was not all that Rome imagined or hoped, and it did not restore either the great days of Cincinnatus or the great days of Verres. But it was to be of no less importance, even if it was less obvious in character; and the spiritual independence of Rome, her ability to take a strong part once more in the counsels of the world, dates from the day when the Prætorians were disbanded. If the church, rather than the senate, picked up the dropped thread of power, that perhaps was a case of the survival of the fittest.

Meaning of the measure

Constantine remained only a short time—perhaps a couple of months—in Rome; and he was destined rarely to revisit it. That short period, however, was of extraordinary importance. The old senatorial Rome did not fail to celebrate his triumph by the due appointment of games and holidays. Some of the buildings erected by Maxentius were dedicated instead to Constantine: and since classical Rome was now too poor and too unskilled to build a Triumphal Arch for even the greatest of her soldiers, she pulled to pieces the arch of Trajan to make an arch for Constantine. It was all she could do. But while the senate in which Camillus had once spoken paid these feeble and halting compliments, the Church of which St. Gregory and Innocent the Third were some day to be members sought to represent Constantine as a Christian warrior, the peer of Charlemagne and St. Louis. The arch of Constantine remains as a testimony to the death of classical art. No trace remains of those statues which are said to have been set up at the same time, showing Constantine bearing the cross. But the thousand years which followed are a gigantic testimony to the inward and spiritual truth of the thought.

The transference of power from the senate to the Church was an unnoticed process, and it was not a definitely intentional one: but it was a real revolution, and the two months' stay of Constantine at Rome marks the moment when the spark passed from one to the other.

The new power in Rome

From one point of view, no doubt, the growth of Christianity and its struggle with the state are a subject for the theologian and the religious historian. But the student of politics has a view of his own, into which neither theology nor religion need enter. To him, the Church is a political organization, and, as such, one of the most interesting that have ever been formed. Its conflict with the state was a battle between two organizations founded upon different models. The power of the Church lay in its central principles. The power of the state lay in its external discipline. It was rigid, because it had no principle of coherence, but was held together by the pressure of compulsion. . . . The changeover from the senate to the Church was a change from the conception of law to the conception of principle.

X

Constantine returns to Milan

Constantine returned from Rome to Milan. Let us consider a little more closely some of the features of that Church, the brief for which he carried with him, and was about to discuss with Licinius.

XI

In all the proceedings connected with the measures taken by Diocletian to suppress the Church, there is very little trace of any mass of pagan public opinion hostile to the Christians. The persecution was almost entirely an official one, conducted by the government; and in such tales as those of St. Alban there are signs that it was none too popular with the man in the street. . . . However humorous the ordinary sensual man might find the spectacle of Germans being devoured by lions in the circus, we must not forget that the Germans in question had frequently burnt his house and murdered his family. No such reasons inspired him with pleasure at the sight of a bishop being roasted to death, or even subjected to the lighter forms of penalty under the anti-Christian laws. The bishop was often connected with him by the pleasant intimacy of having rebuked his habits and looked after his poor relations. The coals-and-blankets aspect of Christianity has sometimes come in for adverse criticism. But the Christian habit of giving away things, instead of seeking to acquire them, was certainly among the novelties which im-

Influence of the Church

pressed the public opinion of the Roman age. In this, the Church managed to give a striking turn to a secular Roman tradition.

It had long been a Roman custom that rich men should be pretty free in their gifts for public purposes. They had given for political and social reasons; and since men and women usually respond most readily to things that give them pleasure, the most profitable course was to devote such public gifts to entertainments of various kinds. The Church, on the other hand, had concentrated upon the idea of giving with the purpose of doing good to the recipients. The Roman of humble station was quite accustomed to render suitable returns to his beneficiaries. While the Church no doubt amused some and bewildered others, she certainly impressed a good many by asking only for moral returns—a certain amount of respect for the ten commandments, and as much belief as people could manage to show in the doctrines of the faith. Thus, although the serious Christians may have been a small minority, there was a very much larger fringe of sympathetic and interested onlookers, who tended to grow steadily in numbers. This, in fact, is the normal method by which Christianity has spread; and the process can still be seen in full operation in most of the considerable towns of Europe and America.

The persecution, then, was political; and it turned on a definite issue:—Was the ultimate faith of a man due to his religion or to his government? There is nothing unreasonable about this issue; it might arise again, and it does tend to arise even now. The hostility of the Soviet Government to religion of all kinds is probably

Its relation to the state

based not so much upon any difference of opinion on philosophical subjects as upon the fact that even a small and humble religion is in the habit of claiming the last word and the final loyalty of its believers. If we hold that a man must obey the command of the secular magistrate even if it violate the moral law of his religion—then we are siding with Galerius and Diocletian. If we hold that the authority of the moral law is greater than that of the magistrate—then we are siding with the Christians.

We have not yet really solved this problem, as antivaccinators and conscientious objectors of various sorts are liable to find out to their cost. We have not even solved it in principle or in theory. Possibly it is insoluble, and in every age we must take our chance of temporary and approximate solutions near enough for the exigencies of practical life. Later ages merely burked it by the method of making the magistrate Christian. Constantine himself did not even go as far as this. He only suspended the question.

Policy of Diocletian a failure

We must therefore not falsify history by fancying that the purposes of Diocletian and Galerius were merely foolish and irrational: nor even that they were indulging in the luxury of sitting in judgment upon ideas which they were too little educated to understand. Diocletian made the greatest effort that ever was made to restore the authority of the Roman state to a pitch at which it was capable of keeping control of an empire stretching from Carlisle to the Tigris. If he failed, it is important for us to understand the nature and causes of his failure. He ran against a problem which the utmost wisdom of humanity has not yet sufficed satisfactorily to settle.

XII

Even more important principles underlay the difficulty experienced by the imperial government in suppressing Christianity. We may dismiss at once the quite
groundless belief of many modern people that there is
something automatically self-defeating about persecution—that, indeed, to persecute an idea is almost enough
to make it successful. The prohibition of any action by
law, and the enforcement of the prohibition by punishment, are processes which can be completely and permanently successful. The fact that some prohibited actions survive prohibition is due to the existence of special
causes.

Early Christian tradition never for a moment attributed the survival of the Church to the human supe- Philosophy
riority of its members. It attributed its survival to the of prohi-
miraculous grace granted the martyrs, by which they bition
were enabled to endure things not normally endurable.
The survival of the Church was, by its own evidence,
due to causes outside its human structure. But not all
men admit the reality of supernatural help, and in any
case there were other special causes operating. Of these,
some were certainly political.

By removing the discussion and decision of political
questions away from the mass of men, the empire had
removed from them also any great interest in political
subjects. The average man no longer worried about
political right or wrong; he had ceased even to think
about it. It is probable that large sections of the population of the empire, whose ancestors had dwelt in tribes,
not in city-states, never had thought much about it, and

did not care. Winning horses and champion gladiators were their real public interest. The result was that Diocletian had no such public for his ideas as the bishops had. He could not appeal to public opinion; it did not exist. But the bishops could appeal, and did; for them there was a large public and an enthusiastic public opinion.

They possessed this advantage over the government because the tradition of free discussion, which had been lost in politics, survived elsewhere. The Fathers of the Church were talkers. There are good reasons for the occasional tremendous supremacy of the talker and for the world-shaking results of his talk. A good talker— either the man who gets his effect round a table, or he who gets it from a platform—is usually a man who thinks aloud; and to reveal thought is the first step towards harmonizing it. It is talk that distinguishes man from the beasts, and enables mankind to achieve those extraordinary feats of agreement which set a million persons marching together for one end. Silence may be prudent. It is certainly easy. Even brick walls and logs of wood are good at it. But talk is the creative thing that calls down fire from heaven and sets men alight. A talker is always adjusting his mind to things and events. That is the definition of talk. It is the noise made by the human brain at work.

Agreement is the only thing ever produced by talk; but when we see the results of agreement, we may grant their magnitude. It had built up the Roman state, and then the Roman empire. The minds, the tempers and the wills which had once created the republic were not going to sit down into the meek retirement of petty

The appeal
to public
opinion

senatorial politics under the empire. The spiritual de- Character of the bishops
scendants of Camillus and Fabius, rejecting with
vehemence this mockery of human life, flung themselves into the task of hammering out the power of the
Church. The spirit of the old senate and assembly had
come to dwell in the synod and ecclesia, where men still
talked at great length, and with impassioned energy, and
where minds were still formed and finished by the hammer and anvil of controversy. . . . If we are ever surprised at the assertion of historians, that Constantine
welcomed the presence of the leaders of the Church, and
was seldom without a group in his company, we may
remember that the conversation of half-a-dozen bishops,
most of them prepared to be burned at the stake for
their opinions, probably had a freedom and novelty not
without charm to a man brought up amid the more
limited conversation of camps and courts.

XIII

To realize some characteristics of the early Fathers it
is necessary to read their works—or at least, parts of
them. They loved words with a deep and abiding passion. Their writings are incredibly voluminous. Their
conversation, public and private, seems to have been
similarly interminable. They talked and talked, and
wrote and wrote, with an immensity that has something Freedom of speech
Homeric about it. They swept paganism away in a tor-
rent of words. They talked the strong, silent men of
imperial Rome down, out and into limbo for ever. The
rack, the fire and the arena could not silence early Christian bishops. Though burned at the stake and boiled in

oil and eaten by lions, they would not hold their tongues. Their last dying speeches and testaments shook Jove off the throne of this world—and it is very possible that they shook off Jovius too. Whatsoever else they may have upheld, they certainly upheld the right of mankind to talk as much as it likes.

Distance and ignorance perhaps make us exaggerate the charm of the orators of ancient Greece and Rome. Most of the speakers in senate or assembly were no doubt as dull as any modern politicians. But that which had been true under the republican city-state proved true under the monarchial world-state, and perhaps will always and everywhere be true: the earth and the fulness thereof are the reward of the men who talk the hardest.

If the writings and speech of the Fathers were not invariably distinguished by the characteristics which mark the scientific investigator, the reason is plain. They derived their tradition as much from the political as from the philosophical side of things. They conceived that the true use of words was not to express an idea but to mould a mood in those who heard them. Good words were those which made for edification— that is, for construction, or creativeness.

Young men who start their lives with the faith that language was meant to enshrine intellectual truths are liable to have a rude awakening from their dream. Language was made, and is carried on, by men who use it as a gesture or as a blow; who use it to manipulate the minds of other men as the potter uses his hand to model the clay.

To mould a mood

XIV

Some instinctive perception of all these things lay behind Constantine's interest in the Church. The existence of deliberative assemblies and popular conferences is not in all cases valued solely for the benefit of the governed, although incidentally it may benefit them. Very often it is valued quite as much for the benefit of the governor. There were precedents for that peculiar form of political discernment which induced Edward Plantagenet regularly to consult parliament. Constantine was guided by the same discernment when he consulted the Church: for by means of this Church he was enabled to gain touch with and hold upon social elements which had been out of the control of earlier emperors.

The Church, far more than the senate, embodied the experience and the ambitions of the people of the empire. It represented, as the senate did not, a certain organized and agreed set of ideas concerning the essentials of human life; it was capable of producing, as the senate was not, a coherent political philosophy applicable to contemporary conditions. We shall see, presently, in detail, more of the exact nature of this political philosophy. The weakness of the pagan religion was that it was incoherent, parochial and undeveloped. The fatal defect of the senate was that its politics were antiquarian, and were applicable only to old and long-vanished conditions which the world would never see again. It could advise the emperor concerning the state of agriculture in Italy and Africa, and the condition of the agricultural population: and no doubt its views on taxation deserved noting. But it could no longer thresh out

The representative quality of the Church

great principles, or put forward great politics; above all, it could no longer form the training ground of those vivid and violent personalities who originate action.

Constantine, on his way back to Milan, carried with him something more than the terms of an agreement with a religious society. He had charge of the interests of the body which preserved the experience of the past and held the hope of the future. He had long ago perceived the expedience of standing well with the Church. He now began to understand that he had come into contact with something vital, which bore the spirit of life in it.

Constantine's new religious policy

Statesmen—especially when they are also soldiers—seldom feel any great passion for the weak and feeble things of the world. It is unlikely that Constantine admired the Church because it seemed helpless and persecuted. He admired it because it was remarkably strong and unusually dangerous to meddle with. It claimed to be under the direct care of the power which created the thunderbolt, the hurricane and the earthquake. No one could fail to see that while Galerius, Maximian and Maxentius had come to unfortunate ends, the friend of the Church had been just as noticeably fortunate in all that he had undertaken. Granting all the care and all the foresight of which human nature is capable, there is, as every experienced man knows, a margin of luck impossible to expunge. Just there, where his care and foresight could do nothing, and his precautions were of no effect—just there his luck had run at its strongest. Not Cæsar's self, when he crossed the Rubicon, had had such fortune as Constantine since he crossed the Alps.

Completion of the Italian Campaign

XV

Less than sixty days since he entered Italy, he came back to Milan, master of the west. Few men have ever enjoyed sixty days so crowded with events.

CHAPTER VII

THE ILLYRIAN CAMPAIGN

I

In the spring after the conquest of Italy, Licinius came to Milan. His presence there was, if nothing else, a testimony to his confidence in Constantine's good faith. He came ostensibly to marry Constantia, the young half-sister of Constantine. Other business of a diplomatic nature was also transacted in the intervals of leisure which they managed to find. Quite possibly it was about the same time, and at the same place, that Constantia's sister Anastasia married the patrician Bassianus; and Licinius may have made the acquaintance of his fellow-bridegroom.

Conference at Milan, March, A.D. 313

Licinius deserves a little attention. He was by no means a cipher. He belonged, perhaps, to the old school of Illyrian soldier—the school of Aurelian and Carus. He was a self-made man, who had risen from the ranks by his own ability; a man not perhaps very highly educated, but certainly a man of character. His rise had been due largely to Galerius, whose intimate friend he had been. Licinius, therefore, may be accepted as a quite sincere and a perfectly honest man, of some vigour and decision, but not of any especial discernment. His views and opinions were gathered from the general consensus of those around him, rather than from any profound penetration of his own. He was an excellent representative man. He represented the views of that most formidable element—the Illyrian army. The head of the Illyrian legions had in all ages been a man whom it was necessary to take very seriously indeed.

So far, the relations of Constantine and Licinius had been cordial. They were both frontiersmen, who with thoughts of their own kept watch upon the more civilized south. If we examine the moves in the diplomatic game between the two emperors, we shall see that interesting deductions can be drawn from them. It is clear that Constantine had particularly wanted to secure the benevolent neutrality of Licinius, who possessed the power to paralyze at any moment the possibility of an Italian campaign. A friendship between Licinius and Maxentius would have kept Constantine still a minor monarch of Britain and Gaul. . . . Hence, Constantine offered Licinius what practically amounted to the reversion of the western empire. The fact that the marriage of Licinius with Constantia was arranged to take place after the conquest of Italy shows that the offer of the reversion was contingent upon Constantine's success. The fact that Licinius came to Milan for the marriage shows that he had absolute confidence that Constantine would play a straight game. After the marriage was effected the situation took the form that Constantine had a natural son, Crispus, thirteen years old, and no other heir. If any accident should chance to him, therefore, Licinius, as the husband of the eldest daughter of Constantius, would obviously be the man marked out for the succession. This, of course, was putting a good deal of temptation in the way of Licinius, and whether he was absolutely proof against it we shall presently see.

Constantine and Licinius

Position of Licinius

But in any event, it was a substantial consideration in return for his neutrality.

It was just this substantial quality in the consideration which rendered it possible for Constantine to extract from Licinius in addition the support he wanted for his terms with the bishops. The document known as the Edict of Milan was probably drawn up during the preceding winter. Licinius may have scrutinized it and discussed it; but he is not likely to have taken a very active part in framing its terms.

Another person also, we may believe, saw the draft of the Edict before it was agreed to and promulgated. Diocletian received an invitation to Milan [1]—nominally to attend the wedding, but much more probably to lend the weight of his name to the Edict. But he could not bring himself to go. He had a good excuse in the state of his health and the season of the year, which was not suitable for an invalid to travel in.

The purpose of the invitation becomes all the more probable when we learn that Constantine was by no means pleased at the refusal. He wrote somewhat warmly in answer, objecting to the support which Diocletian had given to such men as Maximin Daia and Maxentius. It is possible that Diocletian would have stood better with later ages if he could have brought himself, as Galerius did, to admit himself wrong and to retract his policy. He had not been the principal or the fiercest persecutor. Yet while Galerius swallowed the pill and essayed at least some kind of recantation, the gentler Diocletian could not bring himself to apologize to men whom he regarded as wilful law breakers, still

Diocletian's refusal to attend

---

[1] Aurelius Victor *Epit.*, 39. Gibbon, I, 425.

less to compensate them. . . . And, as we shall presently see, it is possible that he had other motives of which neither Constantius nor Licinius knew. So the matter remained. After all, his excuse was sound. But the excuses of Diocletian were always sound.

II

The document, to which Licinius gave his endorsement, declared the complete liberty of Christian worship, and extended a similar liberty to the followers of every other religion. It did not merely extend to Christianity a liberty already enjoyed by other religions; it created a liberty for Christianity in the first place, and allowed other religions to participate in this liberty. And since this liberty was supposed always to have existed in former times, and only by accident to have been denied to Christianity, full compensation was to be paid to the Church for all property, of every kind, that had been confiscated by order of the state during the late regrettable misunderstandings. Directions are given concerning the proper quarter in which to lodge applications for compensation.

The Edict of Milan changed the Christian Church from a more or less seditious conspiracy barely tolerated by the state—and of late years strictly forbidden—to a legally authorized corporation recognized as holding corporate property.[1] The feelings of the bishops are no

---

[1] During the year, Constantine developed the policy of the Edict. He exempted the clergy from taxation (Eusebius, H.E., X, 7. Gibbon (Bury), II, 567): a step which in 319 was extended to the other provinces which he had acquired. Later on, in 320-321, the Church was placed in a legally favourable position as regards testamentary benefactions.

doubt only faintly represented by the psalms of praise and the ecstatic panegyrics of Constantine which have found their way into the histories. It is unreasonable to profess surprise that a high view of Constantine's character, and a favourable belief in his prospects of eternal salvation, should be entertained by men who now, for the first time for many years past, could look a policeman in the face.

Licinius affixed his signature to the Edict of Milan with all the more readiness since he would not be called upon to foot the bill. The Church in Illyria was neither rich nor numerous, and the compensation he was undertaking to pay was accordingly moderate. Constantine would need to shoulder the more serious moiety of expense. . . . They were still in the midst of the wedding festivities when they were scattered as if by a bolt from the blue. Maximin Daia crossed the Straits in force and proceeded to strike a lightning blow against the dominions of Licinius. . . . This was the pagan answer to the Edict of Milan: for if it came to the question of compensating the Christian Church, Maximin was the man who would have to sell his shirt.

The bolt from the blue

III

Maximin Daia was so typical a person, and did one or two things of such interest, that it is well worth while to dwell on the circumstances of this sudden assault upon Licinius. Not without cause had Constantine coupled together the names of Maximin and Maxentius. . . . Certain resemblances existed between the two men which made their names a hint, almost a charge, stinging and disturbing to the mild Diocletian. This, it seemed to say, was whither the policy of Diocletian led. We have already noted that the first edict of toleration, issued under the names of Galerius, Licinius and Constantine, was not subscribed by Maximin Daia. His Prætorian prefect, Sabinus, circularized the provincial magistrates in his department, directing them to take no further action against members of the Christian Church. This was as far as Maximin would go.[1]

It is from the subsequent actions of Maximin that we gain the clearest idea of some of the issues at stake in the religious contest. The strife in Asia was in many respects more bitter, and exemplified in a more noteworthy form the extreme characteristics of both sides, than the strife in Europe. In wealthy and industrial Asia the old pagan religions had long become wealthy vested interests. They bore very little resemblance to the Idylls of Theocritus. They were trusts which combined the exploitation of the public faith in spiritualism, divination and sorcery with a Red Light interest which was all the more vicious because mixed with religion. Modern social reformers hardly meet these various things in the same combination: and they are certainly saved from the need to attack religion in the name of morals. The early Christian, faced with this difficulty, had no hesitation. He condemned every religion but his own; and he has suffered under the reputation of bigotry ever since.

These powerful interests refused to go down without a fight. Late in the year 311, or early in 312, an agitation began to bring pressure to bear upon Maximin.

Maximin Daia

---

[1] Eusebius, *H.E.*, IX, 1.

The leader of this movement was Theotecnus of Antioch. An appeal was made to Maximin for the expulsion of all Christians from his dominions.

The Christians believed that the appeal was secretly engineered by Maximin himself; and although we are not called upon to believe the accusation, it is probable that they based it upon their inner knowledge that any real public opinion behind the agitation was lacking.

Character of Maximin

Maximin received the various petitions and requests with pleasure. The Christian historian [1] has drawn a vivid and pungent sketch of him: a man almost paralyzed by the belief in omens and portents—unable to eat or breathe until he had ascertained by divination whether he ought to or not. His religion did not, however, place any restrictions upon his freedom with wine and women. He was liable, when drunk, to issue orders of which he repented when sober. His table was famous; and he entertained at it the corrupt and extortionate officials whom he employed and protected. As for women, he did what he liked; and no one, except the Christians, dared to withstand him in any of these things. . . . And, in fact, Maximin and Maxentius arrived, by different paths, at the same goal.

IV

Maximin's reply to the petition from Tyre has been preserved.[2] He reviews the high and respected position held in the religious world by that city, grants the petition, and points out the excellent seasons and general

[1] Eusebius, *H.E.*, VIII, 15.
[2] *Ibid.*, IX, 7.

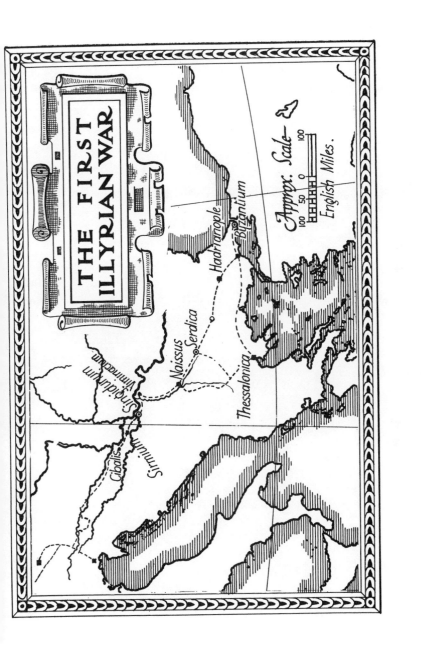

THE FIRST
ILLYRIAN WAR

Approx. Scale—

100 50 0   100
English Miles.

Singidunum
Viminacium
Naissus
Serdica
Sirmium
Cibalis
Hadrianople
Byzantium
Thessalonica

prosperity which they are all experiencing. This (says Maximin, beerily) is a result of careful observance of the old worships. . . . Authorization having thus been given, the trouble for the Christians began. They may be excused for pointing, with a yell of triumph, to the drought, famine and plague which smote Asia that summer. Maximin had appealed to the test of success; and by it he was answered.[1]

Maximin and the Christians

The fall of Maxentius, which followed within a very few months, left Maximin isolated before the ominous coalition of Constantine and Licinius. When he received from them a notification of the intentions which they were preparing to embody in the Edict of Milan and a request that he would join in them, he was struck with consternation. He ordered Sabinus again to suspend operations against the Church. The Christians did not trust his intentions. The published edict did not expressly permit the holding of synods, or the full public activities of the Church, and they thought it imprudent to go beyond the strict letter of the law. The action against them was only in suspense. Maximin was far from having accepted the idea of joining in the Edict of Milan.[2]

Brought to pause on this side, Maximin and his advisers tried another line. During the autumn they framed a scheme intended to reorganize paganism and to place it on an equal footing with Christianity. The old religion had hitherto been local and isolated; there had been no framework of organization including in one body all the various temples and priesthoods. They

Consolidation of paganism

[1] *Ibid.*, IX, 8.
[2] *Ibid.*, IX, 9.

proposed to revolutionize the situation by organizing a regular hierarchy like the Christian, with its succession of grades, its subordination of authority, its discipline, and its exact placing of individual detail in the general unity. . . . The hierarchy was appointed. The leaders of the new non-Christian church were carefully selected to compete with Christian bishops on their own ground.[1]

It is a very curious side-light upon the growing power of Christianity that such a scheme as this should ever have been projected. Evidently it was time, no longer merely to repress a peculiar form of religion, but to defend the established cults from a rapidly expanding rival who was becoming a master. A very few years before, no such idea could have been thought of.

Although Maximin had suspended his action against the Christians, he had done so rather as a diplomatic move than anything else. It is probable that the invitation he had received to join in the Edict of Milan included an invitation to be present at the conference. Whether this be so or not, he evidently knew the date on which Licinius would be in Italy. Maximin's amenability convinced Licinius that he could safely go. . . . Mobilizing his Striking Force during the winter, Maximin crossed Asia Minor by a succession of forced marches which strewed his route behind him with stragglers and store wagons. Byzantium, on the Straits, fell after a siege of eleven days, and Maximin set foot on the soil of Europe.

This was the news that scattered the conference of Milan.

Maximin invades Europe

[1] Eusebius, *H.E.*, VIII, 15. Gibbon, II, 134.

V

Maximin had done his best to emulate Constantine. The swiftness of his movements was hardly less remarkable. But the siege of Byzantium, and the more prolonged resistance of Heraclea, delayed him just long enough to enable Licinius to receive information, recross the Alps, and take the long high-road through Naissus. Old he might be, but he was still vigorous enough to beat Maximin Daia at this game. He met Maximin much nearer to Byzantium than to Milan. Parleying brought no result. At the battle of Heraclea the Illyrians of Licinius beat twice their number of Asiatic troops; and the most famous episode of the battle was the flight of Maximin, who rode a hundred and sixty miles in twenty-four hours.[1]

Battle of Heraclea, April 30, 313

The mode of life which Maximin had made his own was hardly the best training for violent exertions of this kind. Asia could have produced another army; but she had difficulty in producing another general. Maximin arrived home in a tumult of mingled feelings. He felt that he had been deceived by his prophets and diviners, and some of them experienced the unpleasant consequences of this conviction on his part. Whatever his motives may have been, he issued an edict of toleration, including in its provisions compensation to the extent of restoring to the Church all property that was retained by the imperial treasuries.[2]

He was too late. He died shortly after the issue of the edict. Exactly how he died is uncertain; vexation,

Death of Maximin, July or August, 313

[1] Gibbon, I, 426. Eusebius, *H.E.*, IX, 10; *Vita C.*, I, 51.
[2] Eusebius, *H.E.*, IX, 10.

a thunderbolt, and the judgment by God are all mentioned by awe-stricken Christian authorities. Overexertion is a probable cause. He seems to have collapsed in health, and to have become blind. . . . He was not very greatly regretted.

VI

Constantine and Licinius were now the only competitors left in the running. Up to the present, their cooperation had been highly successful. It was now to be tested, and the identity of the inspiring and creative partner in the coalition ascertained.

A noticeable change came over Licinius. Not only did the increase of his power make him less dependent on Constantine, but the various interests, demands and necessities of his new dominions now began to influence him and to give him a new point of view.

It was a matter of course that the Church should enjoy her new freedom; it was to the advantage of Licinius that the name of the persecutor should be erased from all monumental inscriptions, and that he should be branded as a tyrant. Licinius had the sympathy of the Church when he proceeded to arrest and execute the chief agents of the persecution—Peucetius, Culcianus in Egypt, and Theotecnus in Antioch. It was a matter of course that he should execute the children of Maximin, who might transmit a claim to the empire. But there has always been something subtly treacherous in the air of nearer Asia—something that tempts men to go too far, do too much, and step over the margin of safety. This dangerous intoxicant began to affect Licinius. For him to execute also the son of Severus was hardly neces-

Actions of
Licinius

sary. To execute the son of his old friend Galerius was a mistake. It underlined a little too strongly some thoughts that interested Constantine.

Now, Galerius had married Valeria, the daughter of Diocletian. Their young son Candidianus had been still a child when Galerius died. Maximin Daia had proposed himself as the next husband of the widow. Her lack of enthusiasm for this prospect had caused Maximin to send her to the edge of the Syrian desert, there to meditate upon his advantages as a husband. Her mother, Diocletian's wife, accompanied her.

The expostulations and representations of Diocletian concerning his wife and daughter and grandchild were unavailing: and it is possible that the hold which Maximin possessed over these hostages had some effect in preventing Diocletian from giving in his adherence to the edict of Milan. . . . The death of Maximin Daia seemed to set them free. Valeria and her mother hastened to Nicomedia taking the boy with them. . . . This boy, the son of Galerius and grandson of Diocletian, was the Candidianus whom Licinius slew. Valeria and her mother attempted to reach Diocletian at Salona. Before they had got past Thessalonica they were detected and caught. Their bodies were cast into the sea.

This story is obviously one calculated to arrest the attention of the most casual hearer. It arrested the attention of a much larger number of people than was convenient for Licinius. He could hardly have announced more clearly that he intended to make a bid for **His imprudence** the throne of the whole empire, and to stop at nothing on the way. . . . He had also, by removing all these lives, left his own life the sole bar between Constantine and absolute supremacy. . . . And all this was highly dangerous in a world which contained Constantine—a man with the habit of striking first.

VII

To strike first, it is usually expedient to have a reason for striking. But so advantageous was the moment that Constantine was not long in dragging to light precisely the pretext required.

After his marriage to Anastasia,[1] the patrician Bassianus had been created Cæsar by Constantine, and had been given certain functions and status not now quite clear, but in any case not exactly according to the scheme of Diocletian. Constantine possibly was not yet quite settled in his mind concerning his future policy; and in any case, the dominion he held at present was hardly large enough to require the kind of lieutenant provided by Diocletian's plan. Bassianus seems to have been disappointed at this. His attitude may have been unreasonable; whether it was at all dangerous, the modern historian is in no position to judge. We only know that it was indiscreet; for Licinius knew enough of his feelings to offer polite condolences. Licinius was not interfering without cause. The appointment of Bassianus had been made with his approval, so that he had a certain say in the question. The statements made by the friends of Constantine amount to the assertion that Licinius was caught in a secret correspondence with Bassianus, in which he was urging the latter to take by force the rights he could not obtain by persuasion. Bas-

The
Cæsar
Bassianus

---

[1] See *ante*, p. 164.

sianus was arrested, tried, and executed. The smaller fry in the conspiracy bolted for the Illyrian border and took refuge with Licinius.

Licinius was merely supercilious when Constantine demanded the surrender of the fugitives. But Constantine was not interested in the fugitives. What he wanted was an excuse for knocking out Licinius; and he thought he had got it. His army (which, like most armies, did not guarantee its enthusiasm for wars of aggression) was satisfied that it had a just cause.

Early in October, 314, he crossed the eastern frontier, probably from Noricum, where the Striking Force had been waiting. He had only about half his full strength, and he marched fast. How sudden his start, and how swift his march, can be seen from the fact that he was at Cibalis within fifty miles of Sirmium before Licinius could throw himself across his path. Constantine took up a strong defensive position between hill and marsh, and dug in.

Licinius had his own Striking Force, which was at about full strength. All assaults of the Illyrians were repulsed by the Britons, Gauls and Germans of Constantine. Driven out into the open plain by a vigorous counter-attack, the Illyrians rallied. They were always hard stuff to deal with, and they suffered no dishonour at Cibalis. Only towards evening Constantine led in person a cavalry charge which turned them and threatened to cut them off. Licinius promptly and precipitately withdrew, in order to keep his line intact. During the night he had leisure to take stock. More than half his total force were casualties. He made up his mind to retreat on a point of concentration. His retirement

Battle of
Cibalis,
Oct. 8,
314

was conducted with secrecy and rapidity. Passing through Sirmium, and breaking down the bridge behind him, his columns took the grand trunk road by Naissus and Sardica to Thrace. After him the roads were crowded with British and Rhineland and Gallic troops, pack on back and sack over shoulder, coming down on his heels: and all the garrisons of Moesia and Macedonia were marching by converging routes to meet Licinius at the appointed spot. . . . It proved to be the plain of Mardia, where the new army could cover Hadrianople.

Only those who arrived before, or at the same time as Licinius, were of much use to him, for the pursuit of Constantine was upon him at once. The struggle at Mardia was as fierce and unflinching as the struggle at Cibalis. For over a century, Illyrian troops and Illyrian generals had ruled the empire. They did not mean to let their supremacy slip out of their hands now. But in the midst of the action Constantine managed again to turn their position. The Illyrians simply formed up back to back and went on fighting, until the battle petered out for lack of light to see by. When daylight came, they had retired towards the Macedonian mountains: which was a confession of defeat.

Battle of Mardia, Nov., 314

Licinius acknowledged it as completely as he thought necessary. He sent in envoys to admit that he had had the worst of it—though he was quite willing to continue, if Constantine preferred. His spokesman then made the remarkable announcement that he was prepared to discuss terms on behalf of the emperors, his masters. . . . This was the publication of the fact that, during the retreat from Sirmium, Licinius had created one of his principal commanders, Valens, a Cæsar.

If the crafty old fellow had wished to drag a red herring across the trail, he could not have done it more effectively. Constantine was furious. Did Licinius think, he demanded, that he had come all the way from York to swallow any Cæsar he chose to present to him? **Negotiations** He had not put down Bassianus to make room for an outsider like Valens. Before any terms could be discussed, Valens must go. . . . Having in this manner drawn off the worst of Constantine's temper, Licinius, with many apologies, instructed Valens to embrace euthanasia. Valens, with military correctness, did so. After this, Constantine and Licinius sat down to discuss practical business.

VIII

The treaty they framed has some interest. First, it divided the Illyrian realm of Galerius into two. Constantine took the whole of what we call the Balkan peninsula, with the exception of Thrace, which last was left to Licinius: each side, in short, kept what it had got at the close of the battle of Mardia. While this division was not fated to be absolutely permanent, it was a great step towards the permanent division between east and west which was to come a couple of generations later. At any rate—a matter of some historical importance—it abolished the old solid bloc of provinces which had hitherto been Illyricum. Never again, from that day to this, has Illyricum recovered its unity.

The treaty contained in the second place an agreement concerning the creation of Cæsars. Constantine was to **The Treaty** have the right of appointing two; Licinius, the right of appointing one. Such a proportion established beyond doubt the superior dignity of Constantine.

In spite of the violence of their contest, a noticeable amount of grim amiability distinguished the relations of Constantine and Licinius. They respected one another's abilities. A permanent peace between them was hardly possible, and was not seriously to be expected; but for nine years the treaty agreed upon after the battle of Mardia held good. When the contest was renewed it was by no idle squabble, but evolved straight from principles of the utmost importance.

IX

During the nine years' peace between Constantine and Licinius there were few great events. Both men spent the time in busy reorganization; and if the vast and far-reaching changes introduced by Constantine seem to our eyes to transcend the puny work of Licinius, it is only because we, at this distance of time, know the permanent effects they were destined to have. Contemporaries, who had no means of knowing, could not tell but that the work of Licinius might be equally important.

To those engaged in them, probably, the domestic events of these years—the births, marriages and deaths —bulked as large as the epoch-making political revolution which was proceeding before their eyes. The modern reader, who is doubtless prepared to be impressed by the fall of empires and the crash of worlds, may not be able to adjust himself all at once to the next scene in the story. We see the conqueror of Licinius bending over

Birth of Constantine II, 315-316

a cradle. . . . But after all, the crash of worlds is only a by-product of the domestic interests of men. It is round cradles, coffins and wedding breakfasts that the real sting and energy of human life centres. The child who lay in its cradle represented passions and ambitions whose repercussion has hardly yet died out; he was to be the indirect cause of crimes and tragedies which, though now cold and dead, once lived with lava-heat; he was the eldest child of Fausta and Constantine, and the grandson of two emperors—Constantius and Maximian Herculius.

Constantine had been married eight years: this was his eldest son, and no child had ever been born hitherto in the Roman dominion with an ancestry so august. Not only was he what in later ages was called "porphyrogenitus"—born in the purple, the child of a reigning emperor—but the uncles and aunts (there were six) who formed the necessary chorus of admiration, were every one of them porphyrogenitus too. With Constantine, that haunting ill-luck which dogged all the former emperors, and had condemned them to be barren, seemed to have changed. The baby grew up in a world which was a new kind of world—an imperial family, even an imperial tribe: a world in which every face was imperial.

The imperial family

In after years benevolent historians, with no objection to a little stretching and decoration of the facts, liked to discourse upon the wonderful symmetry with which the tenth year of Constantine's reign was graced by the promotion of his eldest son to the dignity of Cæsar. The symmetry was not quite so exact as they made out. The tenth year was well worn, and was verging on the eleventh, when Constantine elected to implement the treaty with Licinius, and to nominate the two Cæsars he was entitled to appoint. But their compliments mean something. Evidently the birth of his son was particularly pleasing to the emperor: and when we are searching for relevant facts amid all the obscurity and suppressions which afterwards hid the full truth, this pleasure is a significant index to his thoughts.

X

Pride of Constantine

In any portrait of Constantine there must be a certain absence of intimate detail; but this is not so much a defect in the portrait as an essential feature in it. If we could meet him face to face, we should in all probability be left with the same dissatisfied sense of a personal contact we could not quite establish, a revelation of character that was never quite candid, and a demonstration of motive that was never quite complete. Something profoundly reticent marked him—a reserve that was never broken. He would have eluded our personal scrutiny just as he eludes the examination of the historian. But for all this, we can identify in his actions a deep and complex motive which had much influence in moulding the future. He was moved and excited at the thought of that imperial ancestry of his baby son. It would be surprising if the episode of Bassianus had not put the finishing touch to his distrust of the system of co-optation which had been usual in the past, and was typical of Diocletian's system. It seemed to be impossible to find anyone whose sense of identity with the imperial interest was sufficient to make him proof

to temptation. Practically everyone, tested, had broken
down. Galerius had broken down; Maximin Daia had
broken down; he himself, Constantine, had broken down.
If experience taught anything, it taught the futility of
resting any expectation upon co-opted successors. The
only hope of maintaining an unbroken succession, free **The hereditary principle**
from civil war and party strife, was a hereditary suc-
cession. But a hereditary succession involved a number
of things. It meant getting away from human vanity,
passion, and ambition, to the impersonal qualification of
mere birth. Short of simply casting lots and trusting
to chance, hereditary succession was much the most impersonal method. Besides, it had an advantage. It enlisted on the side of order and permanency that curious
human instinct which men have towards their own family and kinsmen. If the method of tossing up for the
empire were adopted, it would indeed remove the succession away from the dangerous faults of human
choice; but then nobody would be expressly interested
in the result. . . . But one father, one mother, three
uncles, three aunts and an indeterminate number of
other relations were all expressly interested in the little
Constantine. . . . And if anyone objects to this argument, they must get over not only the logic which links
its terms, but the historical experience, extending over
many centuries, on which it rested.

Long before this—indeed, before the Italian campaign and the conquest of Italy—Constantine had fore-
seen some of these things. He had realized that if such **Pedigree of the imperial family**
an imperial family ever came into being, it could not
start suddenly and crudely. There would be difficulty
in persuading the world at large of the sacro-sanctity of

this imperial caste. In order to mark it off with some especial quality of its own, lacking which no claim to the throne could be upheld, it would be necessary to show that some such quality had always distinguished it. Before he left Arles, therefore, he had—whether truthfully or not—encouraged the theory that his father was in some way connected with the family of Claudius Gothicus. Old Constantius might have been considerably surprised to find that all along he had been an aristocrat without knowing it. . . . But the step was necessary if the right of succession were to be circumscribed.

In later years a quite simple and rational genealogy was worked out, linking Constantine with the first Illyrian emperor, who had begun the regeneration of the empire. It may have been true. There is nothing improbable or inconsistent about it. No one would ever have doubted it but for the uncertainty of its terms when it was first proclaimed. But whether it were true or not, it was politically expedient; and if it were a fiction, it was adopted for a rational purpose and for a beneficial end.

XI

For us, the case is all the better illuminated by the existence of Crispus. While the little Constantine, born in the purple, was only eighteen months old, Crispus was approaching his eighteenth year. It was for Crispus that the genealogy from Claudius Gothicus had first been devised. . . . Faint though the aura now may be that shone around Crispus, it is unmistakable in its suggestion of accomplishment and ability.

Crispus belonged to the older world of ideas in which

Crispus

men reached the imperial throne by merit—that is to say, fought their way to it, destroying in the process more than the utmost genius could ever replace. . . . Constantine's thoughts had moved since those days at Arles. His attention was not now fixed upon Crispus but upon the baby whose status gave him such curious and novel importance.

Constantine therefore implemented the treaty with Licinius by nominating both Crispus and little Constantine as Cæsars. Crispus was intended to take some of the substantial work of government off his father's shoulders, and on the first day of March, A.D. 317, he took over the old provinces of his grandfather Constantius—Britain and Gaul. The significance and purpose of Constantine junior still lay in the future.

Crispus becomes Cæsar, March 1, A.D. 317

Licinius at the same time followed the example of Constantine by creating the baby son of Constantia his own Cæsar under the treaty. The child was three years old.

Even if Licinius had known the trend of Constantine's thoughts, his interests would still have directed him to Crispus as an ally. No way existed by which the little Constantine could be made useful to the purposes or hopes of Licinius. But with Crispus a relation could be established: and Licinius had every personal reason for encouraging the young man and strengthening his position. He would in any case prefer the succession to proceed upon the old model—that is to say, he would prefer Crispus to succeed his father upon the old established terms.

Now, Licinius had used his position, several years earlier, in such a way as to gain the reversionary right to Constantine's dominions. Constantine's present action over the Cæsars had two aspects. First, it provided him with a mature successor whose prior claim would forestall that of Licinius. Secondly, it established a second successor with claims of a peculiar sort. Licinius "paired" the latter with his own little son; but towards Crispus he took a bolder and a wiser policy. He had no grown son; but he had a grown daughter; and he negotiated a marriage between them.[1] If, therefore, Crispus should ultimately succeed to Constantine's dominion, his children would unite the hereditary claim to both east and west, and Licinius, as much as Constantine, would be the ancestor of the coming dynasty.

Marriage of Crispus

This arrangement was obviously liable to create a number of determined enemies for Crispus. Licinius may have thought that it only repeated the earlier position of Constantine himself, who had not apparently suffered much from it. The point that Licinius possibly missed was that Constantine might presently realize with dislike that Licinius had once more managed to insert himself into the future of the empire! If Constantine transferred his sympathies to the opponents of Crispus, the position of the latter might become unfavourable. . . . Exactly how unfavourable no one, of course, could predict.

XII

Diocletian died the year before the appointment of Crispus as Cæsar. He was seventy years of age: and his departure marked the definite passing of an era. He

---

[1] It is impossible to prove this; but short of proof, every probability in the case points to this as the fact. See Gibbon, II, p. 209, f.n. 18.

had been among the greatest of those great men who drew the Roman empire from its slough and set it upon its feet again. Whatsoever we say or think of him and of his age, whether we admire or condemn, like or dislike, it is as impossible to ignore him or to get away from him as to ignore or neglect Augustus. Death of Diocletian, A.D. 316

Although he was one of the most successful men who ever lived, and was not unreasonably old when he died, the age was a time of such rapid change that he was destined to realize his own failure, and to see himself left behind by the new generation. He had never been a proud nor an overbearing man: but he lived to be wounded and humbled in his old age through the persons of his wife, daughter and grandson. He had only intended to restore respect for authority: and he lived to be a man whom the Christians pointed out to their children as subject to the wrath of God. He lived long enough to be astonished and bewildered at the world into which he had strayed.

There was deep appropriateness in the day of his death, on the eve of the appointment of the new Cæsars. They marked the utter passing away of the co-optative directorate, the Board of Emperors, which he had designed for the Roman world. It was the greatest, and it was the last, effort of its kind. Never again did any great statesman attempt a co-optative monarchy. The future was marked out for hereditary monarchy, as Constantine was beginning to see.

Had he, therefore, failed? Not quite. He was a man of the people, with a natural belief in the possibilities of the average man. He transmitted to the new monarchy the whole of that tradition of the career open to talent Verdict on his work which had marked the old. We may surmise that he was a faithful servant as long as he served. A great part of his success and his failure was rooted in his habit of counting on the obedience he had himself given. He had had a deep experience of a certain limited sort. He had known a little world in which all servants were faithful; and he made the natural—but erroneous—deduction that in the great world also all servants were faithful. He did not realize the fringe of secret disobedience, rancour, jealousy and fear which surrounds the master-man. He did not, when he began, know the ring that such men can draw round their masters. . . . But he learnt it. In the days of his retirement at Salona, he uttered strong and bitter words which have been recorded and handed down. "A monarch can see only with the eyes, and hear only with the ears, of his ministers; and they take a great deal of trouble to deceive him. So he advances bad men and neglects good ones—to the profit of those who are arranging the graft."

His life in retirement Some of this is visible in the dramatic exit he arranged. The sacred monarch put off the purple and the diadem and the human being emerged from the panoply and walked off into the wings to become ordinary again. It would have been hard to underline more neatly the principle of the difference between the office and the office-holder which is the essential element in the republican idea of magistracy. In the later kingship there was no such distinction. All the actions of Diocletian after his abdication were calculated to deepen the impression that the monarchy he founded was based upon a distinction between the office and the man. It was a very ordinary fellow who lived at Salona: not even a high-brow philosopher who would pause to make remarks upon metaphysics, but only an average man who grew cabbages. Those who bowed down to the new Augustus worshipped no man. They worshipped an idea—the idea of the unity of civilization.

XIII

The real magnitude of the figure of Diocletian comes home chiefly to those students who have to trace the history of late Roman or mediæval institutions. We are cut off by a gulf from all direct touch with earlier Rome. That gulf is the anarchy of the third century— the "First Death" from which Diocletian rescued the world. It lies, an impassable barrier, across the stream of history. The Rome with which we have direct touch, and from which we have direct tradition—the Rome which affected our beginnings, influenced our growth and formed our institutions—is the Rome of which Diocletian was the creator. Old Rome, the city of Fabius and Augustus, is a dream to us, known only by books. But the Rome of Diocletian is a reality.

Diocletian and Rome

Something vague and uncertain in the outline of the man warns us that he is real. He has never been sharpened and retouched into that definite outline which is the sure sign of human art. Cæsar has become an epic, a myth, a romance. Diocletian remains, like the men we know in real life, a somewhat puzzling figure, not perfectly consistent or fully realized. He was not very clever, nor perfectly good, nor altogether wise: he was a man of genius, a giant whose labours are immortal.

CHAPTER VIII

THE NEW EMPIRE

I

For nine years after the treaty between Constantine and Licinius, the Roman world had peace. It was a peace full of activity, in which the work of Diocletian was surveyed and revised. The revolution which had placed Constantine at the head of three-quarters of the Roman empire rendered such a review inevitable, and made it peculiarly important. Up to this point bishops had been men who kept tactfully to the back street and the kitchen entrance. They were now called upon to share in reshaping a world. Many must have thumbed over their Old Testaments with anxiety. Whatsoever the defects of that volume may be, considered as a guide to biology, its claims as a political treatise are not to be despised.[1]

Constantine was not, for the most part, a deliberate innovator. Much the greater part of the work he carried through was a process of simplifying and systematizing—"Rationalization" is the word we employ in the current use of the moment. He abolished redundancies, cut down excess, joined up loose ends, and gave

Reforms of Constantine

[1] A diligent student of that remarkable book is presented with an unequalled panorama of a civilization evolving from the tribal stage into that of the political empire; and it would not be difficult to make out a strong case for considering Isaiah much superior to either Plato or Aristotle as a political philosopher. Whether by accident or by inspiration, the Old Testament constituted by far the best collection of political data available in the age of Constantine and for some time after it.

their proper legal position to irregular usages which had grown customary. Some things, doubtless, he had to refound: some he needed to deal with as they came, and not in the order he would himself have chosen. He had to grapple with problems which Diocletian had failed to solve—the religious question, and the problem of the currency were two of the most important of these.

Meaning of the process

Scholars have not succeeded in distinguishing with perfect accuracy or completeness between the changes initiated by Diocletian, and those made by Constantine: and up to a certain point the two men were employing a very similar policy to deal with the same set of current problems. But at some point, not now to be indicated with exactitude, Constantine gave that policy a peculiar twist and a particular character. Some things both men had to take as they found them. The social evolution of centuries was not to be altered by a little legislation. There will presently be opportunity to observe precisely what those policies were, in which Diocletian failed and Constantine succeeded.

II

Constantine started, therefore, with an amount of accumulated material, which he gradually reduced to order. He accepted in their main outline the reforms of Diocletian; he accepted the underlying principles which gave them coherence—the new mobile Striking Force which he had already improved and perfected into a finer weapon than Diocletian ever wielded; and the apparatus of taxation designed to support it. He did not accept the quadruple division of the empire.

Wheresoever there was a great logical tendency in the evolution of the Roman dominion, he accepted it without question: but he accepted it all with a difference. Both the policies he accepted and those he changed were linked together by particular characteristics.

All the circumstances of his accession made him the point of unity for various parties and interests. In taking over the idea of levying taxes in kind, which Diocletian had systematized, he did not adopt it without qualifications and reservations. He followed Diocletian in abolishing the method of farming out the taxes. They were assessed and collected by the appropriate department of a regular Civil Service. But he did not endorse payment in kind as the only method, or the permanent method. He took the earliest opportunity of setting the currency upon a new and improved basis. He abolished altogether the last traces of the dream of military emperors, that fiduciary money, or "token" money, would pass current at its nominal value when the law commanded it to do so. He refounded the coinage on a gold basis. His new solidus, struck at seventy-two to the pound, remained for many centuries the standard and sterling coin. Those who cared to do so could always pay their taxes in money.

Although this could not, by itself, restore what had been destroyed, it relaxed the pressure of high prices and low production, and prepared the way in the east for the gradual restoration of commerce and a money economy. As we shall see, the west was destined to go another way.

His whole attitude towards the commercial classes was encouraging. The powers of a statesman have their limits, but what he could do, he did. He pursued the path marked out in his first favourable words to the Roman senate, by revoking the famous measure of Gallienus by which senators were excluded from military employment. He provided a special branch of the new imperial guard [1] as a kind of training corps for the sons of senators. Deep distinctions of social structure, which were only now becoming visible, caused this measure to have different results in the west and in the east of the empire. The senatorial class had moreover undergone a great change in status and type.

III

The unification of the Mediterranean states under the hegemony of Rome had originally been effected through a policy of favouring the propertied classes. In spite of the horror which such a policy nowadays excites in the breasts of even the most conservative historians, it was by no means ill-judged. It engaged in the interest of the central government at Rome precisely those social elements everywhere which were most stable and most permanent. Men may come and men may go—and Roman methods idealists, in particular, are apt to come and go at ir-

[1] The military changes made by Constantine may be briefly summarized. He reduced the old legionary frontier garrisons to the rank of second class troops. The best corps he drafted away into his Striking Force, which was now divided into two classes—the Comitatenses and the Palatini, the latter forming the picked corps. The frontier troops were commanded by Duces, the Comitatenses and Palatini by Comites. Constantine abolished the Prætorian Guards, and reorganized the new imperial guard which had been slowly growing up. The *Protectores* were of picked troops chosen for good service. The *Domestici* were the sons of senators, as mentioned above. Besides these, Constantine organized the Scholæ, five squadrons of German horse for special attendance upon his person —his "mousquetaires." It was a highly efficient military establishment, as we can see from its actions.

regular and inconvenient times—but property remains; and property holders stepped into a sympathetic interest with the government as if it had been a part of the estate. . . . We must remember, too, that to worry about the individual element and the cultivation of personality in an age which produced not only Alexander and Hannibal, but also Manius Curius and Agathocles the Potter, might have seemed quite unusually superfluous. Human personality? The age overflowed with it! The Roman turned his eye upon property because he wanted something solid and calculable; something that could be put into figures and was not a matter of opinion. . . . When we lay foundations we do not scatter roses. We put down concrete. The Roman, laying the foundations of a state, did not employ poetry. He employed property.

His choice of property proved his appreciation of the main duty of the statesman—which is to protect and further the material prosperity of mankind. It was particularly the urban form of property—the kind which centres round a market, and is related to the active exchange of commodities—which interested the Roman. His support of property worked out, therefore, as support of the local urban oligarchies throughout the Mediterranean.[1]

An urban civilization

This fact was, however, far from implying the obliteration of popular government. Even after the imperial government at Rome itself had ceased to depend

[1] Professor J. S. Reid puts this far more strongly when he begins his book by saying that the city is "the chief, or it would be nearer the truth to say the sole, ultimate constituent element in the structure of the ancient Roman empire." (Reid, *Municipalities of the Roman Empire*, p. 1.) He thinks democratic government more typical of the Greek east than of the Roman west. (*Ibid.*, p. 440.)

upon popular election, the government of the local
urban communities continued very much as it had
been.[1] It was never suppressed nor overthrown.

The decay of popular government was the result of
forces which were rather more economic than political.
The attention which the Roman government continually gave to the interests of property, though not always affectionate, and sometimes harsh, had the ultimate effect of concentrating political power into the
hands of the local oligarchies. Long periods of peace
and prosperity—especially when accompanied by a reign
of law, incorrupt justice and clean administration—are
apt to make man forget the asperities of party and principle. The election of magistrates grew rarer. More
and more the local senates became bodies fraternally co-
opting their members. By the reign of Constantine they
had become closed rings.

IV

The closing of the municipal oligarchies implied that
the ancient cities were dying. They were destined to   Decay of
                                                         the city
arise again transformed—but that is altogether another
story which does not concern us here. Their condition
in the age of Constantine betokens clearly that the city,
which had already lost its position as the basis of imperial
government, was losing it as the basis of local government. There was a very appropriate symbolism in the
language of the Apocalyptist when he prophesied the
downfall of Rome as the fall of the great Babylon. The
city on the Euphrates had been the most famous of the
earlier imperial city-states, and had become the type of

[1] On this point see Prof. Reid's decisive words, *op. cit.*, pp. 448-449.

them. Of such states, Rome was the last. Already her status as a city-state was fading into forgetfulness. Imperial Rome was not a city, but a monarchy whose capitals were at Nicomedia and Milan. Her aristocracy was no longer composed of Italian landholders who sat in the senate at Rome, but of men who owned vast estates in Africa, Spain, Illyria and Gaul. The units composing the empire were not now cities; they were great districts ruled by men who in all but name were kings. The ancient east had ended in a somewhat similar condition—and had stayed in it. Would Europe stay in it?—or would she use it as the basis for further giant strides forward?

V

The differences were connected with a fundamental change which had come over the inner structure of the central power. The Persian government, the final fruit of Asiatic evolution, had been a tribal body, the Persian monarchy a tribal monarchy. Even when Alexander succeeded to its power, he remained a Macedonian king reigning by Macedonian troops. But the government over which Constantine ruled was a political government. It was not tribal. Its members were of all races, and probably of all creeds, and of a pretty fair variety of opinions—all united by voluntary obedience to a common law and tradition. . . . According to their understanding of the situation, they were members of the same Roman *respublica* to which Camillus and Cincinnatus had belonged, but which had, under the first Augustus, cast off the limitations of a city, and become a Law whose local habitation was the world itself.

They were no longer a mass given shape by its limiting circumference: they had become morally vertebrate, and the name of the backbone which enabled them to walk erect as men was Law: the Roman Law, built up by Roman discipline and Greek astuteness. Everything was drifting away from the anchorage of the city.

Constantine could not know which elements, out of all the work he did, were destined to prove permanent. Much perished; but among the most permanent of his reforms were the changes he introduced into the central government.

These changes deserve a little attentive consideration as we pass them in review, for they are apt to vary their aspect according to the light by which we examine them. . . . The idea not merely of a Law, but of a principle, directing men to the right rather than merely restraining them from wrong, had become, from their own experience, familiar to Romans; and the introduction now of one or two conceptions derived from the Mosaic law strengthened rather than weakened it. While (according to the Christian view of the case) the Mosaic law was superseded, and therefore could exercise no direct influence upon Roman law, it nevertheless suggested vividly the thought that law could be—and under certain circumstances was—divine in origin. It suggested this without being strong enough to suggest the old tribal notion that it was therefore immutable. . . . But this was not all. If the Mosaic law were superseded, it was by Grace, the inspired guidance of God. Superior, therefore, even to a divine law, was a direct divine guidance. . . . One of the first notions that a bishop, consulting the scripture, would arrive at, was

New conception of law

the thesis that law was of divine origin, and that man was guided by a grace even more directly divine. . . . No one worried if a little Roman law and a little Hebrew tradition were mixed with a few imperfect recollections of Stoicism and a rather more complete acquaintance with the New Testament. Some mixtures are highly explosive; and this one was destined to be somewhat more powerful than dynamite.

VI

The whole atmosphere of Christianity favoured the sense of being detached from dependence on geography. When the Christian remarked that this world was but a temporary abiding place, he might or might not be thinking very much of his permanent heavenly one; but he was very certainly suggesting that a band of brothers might be equally at home anywhere in this world. A feeling of such a kind was the very foundation of the new monarchy. It approached with striking closeness to the tribal feeling that the tribe is the tribe, wheresoever it may be. And yet it had an altogether different intellectual ancestry.

Government detached from locality

We have been using such phrases as "the government over which Constantine ruled"; "band of brothers"; and "tribe." To what precise kind of reality do these phrases point? What was that government? What bonds united its members? We must consider this question before we proceed.

The whole story of the struggle between the army and the senate has shown us that while the army triumphed, its power and organization had in the public interest to be modified by its own leaders. Diocletian **Nucleus of** had fundamentally altered the nature of the military **government** guild on which was founded the imperial power. He had divided it, and opposed its sections, and tightened its discipline, until the real power of the army lay in a small group of leaders who now emerged into publicity as the "Consistorium." Under Diocletian the members of this body were not fixed. They were determined by his summons, and they were convoked at uncertain intervals. Constantine carried through the revolution of transforming this indefinite, fluctuating body into one that was fixed and definite. He created permanent members, and his consistorium met regularly. This consistorium, comprising the heads of the civil as well as of the military administration, was the secret of the new monarchy. It claimed to be something more than a Cabinet Council. On at least one occasion it is called by a remarkable name—*Comitatus*, a companionship: its members were usually known as *comites*, companions.[1]

Anyone who reads the history of the seven centuries after Constantine will find the word *Comitatus* and the words *comes*, comte, conte, count, and all their many derivatives and parallels, bulk large in the story.[2] This is the point at which they began to be of serious importance. Yet even here, Constantine was no surpris-

[1] The Consistorium, however, was not yet the complete comitatus as afterwards understood. It was only the senior, or ministerial half. This senior half, however, was the real origin and substance of the comitatus.

[2] A member of the Consistorium was "comes consistoriani," a count of the consistory. Members were occasionally co-opted for special work. The consistorium had a secretariat of its own, fairly numerous. There were other counts, not members of the consistorium. A modern British Privy Councillor is not necessarily summoned to meetings of the Council.

ing innovator. Diocletian, who created the consistorium, must not be forgotten. . . . Those comparatively slight changes which transformed it into a regular and permanent institution were nevertheless epoch-making. For the first time a machine of executive government came into existence, capable of controlling a large political state, and itself capable of being controlled by its chief.

The departments of government, the chiefs of which met upon the common ground of the consistorium, were systematically planned and organized. The ministers of Constantine would have astonished the early Cæsars. His President of the Council (the legal adviser who presently became Quæstor—or Chancellor, as men afterwards learned to call the office), his Secretary of the Public Treasury, and Secretary of the Private Treasury, his Commanders of the Domestics (the forerunners of our Ministers of War and Marine) his Chamberlain, his Secretary of State [1]—these show the complete form of the ministry which for sixteen hundred years was to mark not only European government, but all the governments derived therefrom. His sketch of the ground has lasted from then till now.

VII

One of the changes that has come over our point of view respecting Constantine and his age concerns our attitude towards late-Roman administrative methods.

---

[1] To translate "Magister officiorum" by "Master of Offices" is misleading, and is no translation at all. He was Chief of the Civil Staff, and he was in this respect more like the American secretary of state, or his English equivalent before the office was split up.

Gibbon could not help a kind of nervous giggle as he related the monstrous story (as it seemed to him) of multitudinous government departments, with hundreds of clerks in them. A modern man sees nothing peculiar about it. To us it is a natural thing. Any highly developed civilization will show the characteristic. Gibbon imagined that such a development must be due to some fantastic corruption in the state. But modern governments are as elaborately organized as that of Constantine, and in spite of the critical remarks of which all of us probably are sometimes guilty, we regard our age as at any rate no more corrupt than that of Gibbon.

We are therefore less disturbed than he was at the idea that the Secretary of State is recorded as having eight departments and a hundred and forty-eight secretaries under his direction. He was the head of the im- perial civil service, and all departments requiring trained assistants applied to him for their supply. Any section of the service not under the express control of some special minister was subject to him. Among them was the office of the director (a Count in rank) who planned and organized the emperor's movements. As the Chamberlain was occupied with the administration of the imperial household, the Secretary naturally took over questions of court ceremonial and imperial audiences; and by this means found himself in the position of Minister of Foreign Affairs, as far as any foreign affairs could exist for a world-state. With this was associated a corps of interpreters. The Secretary was also in charge of the famous *Cursus Publicus*, the official posting service, so might be regarded as Minister of Communications. He was the official head of the imperial secret police and of the Scholarians, who were special executive agents rather than merely a life-guard. We can easily understand that he required a moderately large staff for the supervision of all these departments.

The Secretary of the Public Treasury could, however, easily beat the Secretary of State with eleven departments and a much larger number of secretaries. He had entire charge of the assessment, revision and collection of taxes through the authorized channels. The importance and status of his office can be seen by the fact that out of twenty-nine principal assistants scattered through the provinces, eighteen were Counts. Since most of the mines of the empire had come into the hands of the government, the treasurer was also the Minister of Mines, and disposed of their produce. The Mint, naturally, came under his control. He was responsible for collecting the dues payable on trade entering or leaving the empire; which gave him a supervision over foreign trade in general. It is not at first sight so obvious why he should be in charge of the government woollen and linen factories; but as these were conducted at the government expense, and for government purposes, their product was no doubt felt to be part of the revenue. The manufacture of military stores, however, belonged to the department of the Secretary of State.

The Public Treasury

The Secretary of the Private Treasury was the official Administrator of the vast properties which had gradually been accumulated in the hands of the emperor. They were "crown-lands"; they were private property in the sense that the wearer of the imperial crown could produce legal proof of ownership, but they were certainly not considered as such, in the sense that individual

emperors could treat them as they liked. The imperial
estates had gone on increasing ever since the first days
of the empire. When we recollect the difficulties which
had attended the state-owned lands under the republic,
we can only admire the superior efficiency of the doctrine of private property.

The nature of these estates is worth attention. They
were a sort of "pool" into which went a very large as- **The**
sortment of various properties which from time to time **Private**
had been earmarked as "dangerous." A good deal of **Treasury**
the property of the men who fell in the senatorial struggle with Tiberius probably went into it. A famous passage of Pliny speaks of the six men who owned half
Africa. Nero expropriated them; and their estates went
into the pool. After his conquest of Asia, Constantine
dropped into the pool some of the estates of the wealthy
hereditary priests of the old cults. They were quite
large enough to make a splash. And all these properties,
stretching from Egypt to Britain, were under the administrative control of the Secretary of the Private
Treasury. No other single man in the empire controlled so much.

VIII

The Private Treasury had, as a consequence, very
great influence upon the land system of the empire.[1]
Its head was the largest landowner, whose policy could
determine that of many other smaller men; and he received from his predecessors a policy of remarkable con-
sistence and continuity. An estate which came into the **The**
"pool" usually remained there, and was subject, often **imperial**
                                                         estates

---

[1] For the whole subject see Mr. Heitland's *Agricola* (1921).

for centuries at a time, to one systematic policy. Generally speaking, the Private Treasury had always made a point of offering permanent tenures to good cultivators. It set itself the aim, as a business proposition, of securing the best tenants and keeping them. It was in a position to offer favourable terms. The administrative tradition of the imperial court was of that shrewd kind which understands and provides for the passion men have for justice and fair dealing. A square deal was the rule on the imperial estates, and the emperor was accessible to see that it was enforced. There was no difficulty in securing for his estates certain advantages which greatly benefited them. All the larger imperial estates became "peculiars"—that is, subject to special laws which made them little worlds in themselves. They were never vacant and never neglected. The Private Treasury practised just that rule of being a model employer which the British Government in more recent times has set before itself.

Other landowners had to compete with this system. They found it to their advantage to copy as far as possible the policy of the imperial "peculiar." Hence the policy of the imperial estates was decisive in either creating or demonstrating the trend of economic evolution, as far as agricultural production was concerned.

For a long time past—almost ever since the beginning of the empire—this trend had shown several features which deserve to be noted. The system of great estates, the *latifundia*, had not been very seriously modified by time. Land still tended to concentrate into a few hands. But a revolution had occurred in the methods of management. The slave-trade had diminished; the supply of slave labour had contracted to a normal average; the old capitalist exploitation of agriculture by large-scale cultivation with chain-gangs had become impossible; and the system which replaced it under the earlier emperors was a system of leases to cultivating tenants. Both parties seem to have felt the advantage of a leasehold system over one of small peasant-proprietorship. When some of the large confiscated estates were taken over by the Private Treasury, or its earlier equivalent, they brought with them a system of pairing both these systems. The old landlords had run a certain portion of their estates on the old method, by slave labour, and had let the rest on leases to free cultivators. In order to keep down their own expenses, they had stipulated that the extra labour needed for certain seasonal activities should be supplied by the lease-holders. Apparently this system worked well. It worked so well that the chief trouble seems to have been a tendency to try to wangle an unfair amount of contributory labour out of the lessees.

All these various tendencies were welded into one upon the imperial estates. We can see arising a series of vast rural districts governed by special laws peculiar to themselves, cultivated on a double system, partly by direct slave labour, and partly by free lease-holders. All the great landowners of the empire were approximating to this model.

IX

The significance of these facts will become clearer in a moment. We must recollect that they were affected by the vast perturbations of a century of unrest—the

Changes in land tenure

Evolution of a new system

war, the plague, the barbarian raids, the civil strife, the commercial ruin, the collapse of the currency—all the legacy of disasters to which Constantine was heir. These disasters struck with especial force at the municipal system and the municipal oligarchies which had once been the real aristocracy of the empire. In spite of Constantine's efforts to preserve the commercial and urban elements, the new rural system rapidly began to emerge as the prevailing system of the age. It brought its own alarming problems with it. All the reforms of Diocletian had not effectively stabilized the condition of the empire, and it was the lack of stability more than anything else which was the trouble. Nothing would stay put. With commerce well-nigh vanished and money driven out of civilization, with many estates wrecked by Gothic or Frankish plunderers, land had fallen in value, while labour had risen. Left to itself, the economic situation might have resulted in a series of "landslides": a prospect which evidently alarmed the government. Land demanded labour; and if the cheap land which was available tempted the free cultivator to transfer himself thither, the consequences might have been wholesale migrations, the fall of land values in other parts of the empire, and a general uncertainty which would throw still more of the economic system of the empire out of gear.

As far as we can make out, there actually was a movement on the part of labour, which continued for more than a generation, to take advantage of the economic situation. Men of all kinds left their positions: and it is almost certain that in many or most cases they broke contracts in order to do so. The government naturally

Effects
of the
anarchy

enough regarded this movement as a shirking of responsi-
bilities. That those concerned thought that they were
bettering themselves is of course beyond question: men
voluntarily leave their accustomed positions only when
they see a chance of doing better elsewhere.

The imperial estates were the interest most profoundly
affected by the movement, and the secretary of the
Private Treasury was the man who possessed the greatest
power of stemming it. His reports must have given
Constantine the clearest attainable view of what was
happening. . . . Had the problem been entirely new
and sudden, it would have been more difficult still. As
it was, the trouble had been growing over a long series
of years, and the efforts already made to grapple with
it had left their mark. Landlords in many instances held
contracts of old standing by which they were entitled
to restrain their leaseholders from abandoning their
leases. It is very probable that they did not always
hesitate to strain rights of prescription and rights of
custom towards the same end. The situation was a mass
of various rights derived from different sources and
often intended to apply to very different circumstances.
Modern analogies hint that probably there was reason
on both sides.

Movements of labour

X

Constantine had not invented these circumstances; he
did not impose them upon unwilling subjects; all he did
—and it needed doing—was to seek to stabilize the existing situation. It might possibly become better; at any
rate, once fixed, it could not become worse. To fix, to
systematize and to regularize a difficult situation is a

process that always has its drawbacks, and always involves some amount of hardship for those concerned besides some amount of discredit for the man who carries out the task. But it has the advantage that the healthy elements can at once begin their work of healing.

Probably no two actions that ever were performed by any man have been the subject of more bitter comment than Constantine's toleration of Christianity and his "closing of the castes." His reason for both was perfectly simple, and in both cases it was the same; they were the natural and obvious things to do. Short of destroying the world and creating it afresh (which is not an enterprise for a statesman) there was nothing else to be done. . . . So done it was; and to the best of our knowledge the comments of his critics have not disturbed his rest.

The "closing of the castes" consisted of a large number of measures spread over many years; and Constantine did not live to see the end of the process. But to him has always been ascribed the chief part in the conception and execution of the policy. He tied the cultivator to the soil. It became no longer legal for a cultivating tenant to throw up his holding and to take fresh land under another landlord. He was, however, legally protected against arbitrary increases of rent. The land could not be sold without him; and, of course, he could not be sold at all. To protect him against eviction was almost unnecessary,[1] as any decently competent culti-

---

[1] This was the legal beginning of the system of serfdom; and these Roman cultivators would in after days have been called "villeins." The system lasted until revival of commerce restored a money economy throughout Europe. During the twelfth and later centuries, when agriculture had recovered, and Europe was once more completely cultivated, there was no such competition for tenants,

vator would have been instantly besieged with landlords offering him a tenure. Even as it was, the larger and more powerful estates still stole away tenants from the smaller and weaker ones.[1] A slave who knew his job and cared to put his back into his work could be reasonably sure of a holding and eventual freedom. Only the less competent and less trustworthy need remain in a servile condition. The cultivator

By this means the existent condition of agriculture was pinned, and prevented from getting out of control. Succession to these fixed tenures became, as a matter of course, hereditary. The tenant was given a right that was to all intents a right of property. He got the rough and the smooth together: if he had not the right to do as he liked, he was not driven into the city to live on a Gracchan dole.

The reasonable expectation was that by degrees, and through the operation of natural causes, the deficiency of labour in certain provinces would be made good without disturbing those which were normal. On the whole, this expectation, in so far as it was not disappointed by entirely extraneous causes, was realized.

XI

The estates of the urban landlords, the decurions, the "curiales," enjoyed this system equally with those of Fate of the cities

and no assured room for them. All that the reader needs to note here is that the principle of tying soil and cultivator together is not one single system, but many: and the status, rights and social conditions of serfs varied widely in various ages and different places.

[1] According to tradition, there was a great deal of cattle-stealing and maverick-hunting on the old western cattle-ranches of America, exactly analogous to this tenant-stealing.

the rural landlords, the new senatorial barons. As the latter were much the larger owners, they commonly had all the pull that size gives. It was logical for Constantine to tie the landlords as well as the tenants. The doctrine of stabilization was finally extended to every class. In this case, equality of treatment was far from producing equality of result. The great rural landlords hardly noticed the difference. They were confirmed in powers and privileges which they already possessed. The soldiers, who held land in consideration of military service, became a military aristocracy; but this was no great change. But the curiales were pinned to a falling market and a decaying system. Constantine's efforts to restore commerce—determined as they were—did not suffice to bring the municipal system back to its old prosperity. The municipal aristocracies began that long death-struggle which is one of the most melancholy stories in ancient history. To sell out was now practically impossible. It was possible to sell; but who would buy properties burdened with hereditary liabilities which could not be avoided? The only way out was to hit a bargain with one of the barons, who, in return for an adequate consideration, would use all the influence with the officers of the revenue that was provided by his cellar, his larder, his strong-room, his private retinue of killers, and his personal friends at court. . . . Aurelius Mercuralis was, by the end of this process, a little less dapper than when it began. As fast as the great rural estates came on, the municipalities receded.

The process of stabilization reached down to the urban trades and crafts. By the agency of the collegia

—the "guilds"—men were fixed in their professions, and The Guilds
given an hereditary property in them.

It is not easy to see what could have been done, in the circumstances, other than this process of stabilization. Some modern old gentlemen are in the habit of believing that they could have run the Roman empire better than any of the bull-necked men who tried it. We shall see, later on, what ultimate meaning the process had. Its immediate meaning was that the new system was daily less and less compatible with the urban and commercial life which had been the secret of ancient civilization. Commerce and industry are activities conducted by enterprise, adventure, risk and individual initiative. The instant these are cut off, commerce begins to decay. As soon as they are extinct, commerce is dead. . . . And if not yet dead, it was certainly dying.

XII

When all classes of the community were thus becoming fixed in hereditary castes, the smallest and supreme class, which was employed in governing the empire, System of castes could hardly be left out. We have already seen whither Constantine's policy tended. He dropped Diocletian's system of co-optation, and rested his hopes upon a hereditary monarchy, fixed in a certain family that was almost a caste in itself.

The more we examine this system, the less we are able to point to any particular details in it that are original to Constantine. Most of it had been growing, developing through the centuries. Yet the more we look at it, the more we are impressed with the novelty and originality of the total. Some of the fundamental principles were new. It is a commonplace that Rome rose to power on the maxim, to rule men, divide them. Little as this may represent the full truth, there is a sense in which it is true. Early Roman statesmen had never liked the sight of men who were representatives. They possibly owed a certain weakness in this respect to their tradition as citizens of a city-state, and it prevented them from some political successes. But Constantine had no direct tradition behind him that was derived from the city-state. The real originality he showed was his readiness to confer with representatives. The most famous of all his policies—his attitude towards the Christian church—was only one example of a principle which he followed in all things. It was his deliberate policy, not to divide men, but to collect them, to confer with their representatives, and to make them collectively responsible. It is a testimony to the power of this principle that the two men who most carefully followed it produced an almost unequalled effect upon the institutions of mankind. Constantine was one: the other was the English king Edward the First.

Principles of Constantine's policy

In all the institutions which we have examined, as typical of the new empire, we have seen none intended for the purpose of collecting and expressing public opinion. Constantine, his biographer tells us, showed a friendly spirit to petitioners and deputations—the most usual method in those days of communicating public opinion to the government. The method was crude. It was the church which offered the best means of expressing public opinion. She acted as an informal parliamentary system. Her organization covered the whole empire, and was based upon the civil organization. The divisions and subdivisions of the ecclesiastical body almost exactly corresponded to those of the secular state. Her uniform system and hierarchy enabled her to guarantee a certain normality and representative character in her spokesmen. And although it is true that the sense in which we can say that bishops were elected would not altogether satisfy an advanced modern liberal, or an Athenian democrat, it is no less true that most men, in most ages of the world's history, would consider them to have been appointed on a respectably popular franchise. A full council of bishops was by a long way the most representative conference the empire could produce. This fact Constantine appreciated. At all events, the bishops themselves thought that he paid particular attention to their views.

Value of the Church

Not only did he listen; but from the first he intervened to preserve the order of the church. He retained the office of Pontifex Maximus among his imperial powers in order to possess a legal right to supervise religious questions.[1] The October after the Edict of Milan, he appointed the bishop of Rome,[2] with a committee of bishops, to enquire into the Donatist controversy in the African church. Ten months later, he convoked the Council of Arles to deal with the question, and after close enquiry and debate he issued in the year 316, a formal judgment in full consistorium. He did not prevent the Donatist split, but he gave the whole weight of his official support to the side which was undoubtedly in the right. These ecclesiastical conferences

---

1 Bury, *History of the Later Roman Empire*, I, p. 367.
2 The writ to Melesius is still extant in Eusebius, *H.E.*, X, 5.

were something entirely new. The expenses of the bishops were paid, and they were given official authority [1] to use the government travelling service.

The policy he followed in this respect was original, and its importance as a precedent was beyond reckoning. He set the pattern which later monarchs copied for centuries to come. Its peculiar nature is simply that instead of repressing great parties and great movements, he accepted their existence and controlled their activities: and this alone was a revolution. We shall see by his subsequent conduct that he was no ignorant partisan in religious matters. He could be cordial enough to the unorthodox, and his actions were in all cases based upon careful enquiry into the facts. If we could trace the details of his legislative action in other matters, we should probably find that it was based upon a similar process of official enquiry. Only the accident that the ecclesiastical record is partly preserved when the other has perished causes us to think that he treated the Church in such respects with special benevolence.

Originality of Constantine

XIII

Finally, one characteristic which marked the Church gave especial importance to his support of it. It was a strictly political organization, recruiting its numbers from every rank and class without distinction, and untouched by any gentile influence. As we have seen, not even Galerius could turn it into a hereditary caste. Days were to come, long afterwards, when some such fate did threaten the Church; but they were remote in

[1] The writ to the bishop of Syracuse is preserved by Eusebius, X, 5.

the age of Constantine. The greatest spiritual power in the empire, and the body which best represented its public opinion, thus directly traversed the whole tendency that was turning secular society into fixed hereditary grades. It upheld the banner of brotherhood and free speech. Indeed the leather-lunged and bellicose bishops who conducted the Donatist schism nailed it with defiance to the mast. The Church prevents the entire closing of the castes

We can hardly say of the contemporaries of Arius and Donatus, that they were servile and fawning persons. Even less can we easily depict them as degenerate and effeminate, either in body or mind. The revolution which was taking place in the constitution of the empire, whatsoever it may have signified, very surely did not signify that. Men themselves did not understand the economic evolution which had them in its grip. They had only the most confused notions of what it was that bore them upon an irresistible stream. The sins, the selfishness, the follies, the fears of twenty generations were producing their reward; and the men who struggled with the flood had neither the time nor the temper—nor the material either—to investigate too closely the causes which had evoked it.

CHAPTER IX

THE CONQUEST OF THE EAST AND THE
COUNCIL OF NICÆA

I

IT was over this crucial question of representation [1] that Constantine and Licinius had their second and final contest. Licinius had all the old imperial dislike of associations and of rich men.[2] In Illyricum he had not had very much contact with either. As soon as he became the ruler of Asia, he found himself deeply involved in the problems presented by both.

Licinius
in Asia

A much duller man than Licinius might have become worried as he perceived the power which was given to the Christian Church by the universality of her organization. All that occurred in the east was instantly reflected in every province throughout the empire. The Church was an unequalled whispering gallery: and we need not wonder if Licinius had an uneasy consciousness that at the other end of the gallery Constantine was intently listening.

He was soon involved in the difficulty that the very measures he took to stop this process only originated new grievances and intensified the trouble. He attempted to prevent the bishops from meeting in synod, where

[1] The question presents itself in modern times most vividly as the claim of trade associations to "recognition": i.e., a right to engage in negotiations with employers through official representatives, as a more or less corporate body. Constantine had been granting this kind of "recognition"—notably to the Church.

[2] Eusebius, Vita C., I, 48.

they could discuss their situation and arrange concerted action. Those that defied him he ejected, and confiscated their property. He enacted a number of somewhat odd laws. He forbade women to attend churches with men, and insisted upon priestesses for them. Finally he prohibited the use of churches altogether, and ordered all services to be held in the open air. These laws intrigued and scandalized the whole empire. If his object were to circumvent the natural activity of the feminine tongue, he signally failed to achieve it. It might indeed have been difficult to think of measures more beautifully calculated to set all the tongues at work. Licinius was quite serious. He removed all Christian officers from his army—a step which he would not have taken without what he thought good reason.[1] But he was wrong in principle: and when the principle is wrong, no adjustment of minor details will put matters right. *His struggle with the church*

Constantine never made any great step in dependence upon the support of the Church alone: and it is possible that Licinius might have continued his struggle with the Church almost indefinitely had he not alienated the landed interest. He introduced changes into the measurement and assessment of land for the purposes of the public treasury, so that the rate of taxation upon land was raised.[2] The coalition of interests so established made it possible at last for Constantine to take a step for which he had long been waiting.

[1] *Ibid.*, I, 44-47.
[2] *Ibid.*, I, 48; *H.E.*, X, 8.

II

Before he took it, he needed to secure the Danube frontier. On his way south from Britain, some years before, he had carefully inspected the Rhine frontier, and had attended to its safety. On his way eastward from Italy he paid similar attention to the line of the Danube. The possibility of an attack in the rear was not to be neglected. Licinius, after his lifetime of experience in the Danube valley, could not but possess a wide acquaintance with the tribal chiefs north of the river, who might not always turn a deaf ear to any suggestions or requests he made.

The appearance of Constantine upon the Danube marks a stage, not only in the history of the Roman empire, but in that of Europe at large. The strategic centre of the empire was shifting eastward, and he was following it. The chief points of danger were no longer on the Rhine or on the upper Danube, but on the middle and lower Danube. Marbod's kingdom had long ago vanished from the upper Elbe; Irmin's kingdom had never come to fruition. But on the Vistula the great Gothic realm was steadily growing. It had extended eastward; it had crept up the head-waters of the Vistula until it reached the Carpathian divide, and it had spread down to the Danube valley. The Goths were always in more or less force, and were continually aggressive along the Danube. The existence of this Gothic menace was the outstanding strategic fact of the third and fourth centuries of the Christian era. It had determined the political strife in favour of the Illyrian emperors, Claudius Gothicus and his successors. Political power

The
Danube
frontier

had drifted into the hands of the men who could deal with the Goth. The epic tale was not forgotten, how the Goths had reached the Tauric Chersonese and then, in their ships, had come through the Straits into the Ægean, outflanking the defences of the Danube. They might do it again.

A great deal of interesting history has been lost for ever along this Danubian frontier. We know · just enough about it to realize the nature and extent of the loss. That great raid of the Goths, and their defeat and destruction at the hands of Claudius Gothicus, was followed by fifty years not perhaps of peace, but of comparative quietude with occasional bickerings. Then the vacant places filled again with youths who knew not Claudius, and the pressure on the frontier began afresh. What men will do under the stimulus of hope and necessity is a continual wonder to their quiet descendants and contemporaries. The new generation of the Goths pushed their way south with the determination of the Conquistadors whose ancestors they are reputed to have been.

Constantine's Danube campaign was no trifling skirmish. He attacked the Goths on a front of some three hundred miles. Great battles at Campona, the Margus and Bononia mark the spots where the line was forced; but the Margus, apparently, was the place where the real break-through occurred. Constantine repaired the old bridge at Viminiacum. His advance took him deep into the Dacian land, which now for these many years past had been abandoned by the Roman government. After hard fighting, he gained his principal objects. The unconditional surrender of the Goths was rewarded by terms which have imperfectly come down to us.

It was afterwards a matter of satisfaction to Constantine to think that he had succeeded so rapidly where Trajan had found all his work cut out. His nephew Julian thought this second conquest of Dacia a remarkably brief one, which sprang up and soon withered; but Julian was more concerned to be witty at his uncle's expense than to discover his motives. Constantine had no immediate use for Dacia, and certainly did not intend to waste several years in conquering it. The surrender of the Goths was probably secured by an undertaking on his part, as a set off, not permanently to occupy the country. The terms represented a compromise, and a drawn game.

III

Constantine was now free to turn south, as he wished. The impressions produced upon his mind by the Gothic war no doubt added weight to all the other motives which impelled him. It had been a struggle of unusual magnitude. Although he had got what he wanted, he had obtained it under difficulties. The trouble was that there seemed to be no prospect of any end to this Gothic threat, which did not retreat nor diminish but seemed, if anything, to increase. Unless the whole of this Gothic frontier could be grappled with and held, the old danger was not removed, but only suspended. This was as much as to say that Illyricum would never be safe until its possessor held Asia also: for Asia outflanked and "contained" the Gothic lands. The events of the next year gained fresh point, it may be, from these considerations.

Influence
of the
Gothic
struggle

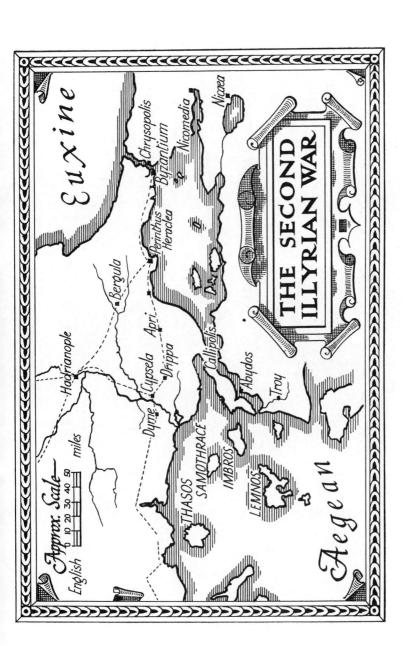

If the magnitude of the struggle left this impression upon the Roman side, it is no difficult guess that the Goths were little less impressed. The new empire was something unlike the empire of Claudius Gothicus. It was a power at once beautiful and strong which, like an angel with a flaming sword, easily destroyed the utmost efforts of men who nevertheless possessed an inward conviction of invincibility. They could not at first understand what had placed this barrier in their way. A few years yet were to pass before the secret dawned upon their minds.

A hint of the importance attached to this year's campaign lingers in some of its indirect results. Two new festivals were instituted—the Sarmatian Games in November, and the Gothic Games in February, to celebrate its successful end.[1]

IV

With his rear secured, and his troops fit and practised with a season's hard work, Constantine was ready for the contest with Licinius. In the course of his Gothic campaign he had trespassed upon territory technically belonging to the eastern Augustus, so that they had a sufficient pretext to publish to the world. Constantine notified Licinius of his claim to be the only rightful Augustus, and ordered a concentration at Thessalonica. Crispus was recalled from Gaul. A hundred and twenty thousand men were assembled at Thessalonica early in the year, comprising the whole three mobile classes of the reorganized army, the palatini, the com-

[1] Gibbon, I, 435, with Bury's note. They illustrate the fact that Constantine was on perfectly good terms with his pagan subjects; for these Games were pagan festivals.

itatenses and the pseudo-comitatenses; the last named of whom had been released from garrison duty. A scratch fleet had been raised among the Greek sea-board cities, to co-operate. . . . It was ordered to assemble at Piræus. It numbered two hundred vessels, none of them large.[1]

Licinius was perhaps now too old a man for heroic measures; and in any event he was a great deal too shrewd to take the offensive with his own imperfectly trained troops against the veterans of Constantine. His fortified lines in front of Hadrianople were defended by a hundred and fifty thousand men, as well as fifteen thousand of the Asiatic cavalry who were slowly becoming the most fashionable arm of the day. Three hundred and fifty ships from Egypt, Phœnicia and Asia Minor held the Straits. It was not unreasonable to regard this as a defence that would take some penetrating. On the defensive, the inferior training of the Easterners would be less noticeable.

Advance of Constantine

The advance of Constantine was along the coast road which, crossing the river Hebrus at Dyme, runs by Cypsela and Apri to Heraclea. There it met the main road from Hadrianople. The whole position was a vast triangle, of which the entire base, from Hadrianople all the way down the Hebrus to the sea, was defended; from this base the roads converged to Heraclea, where rested the apex. The Gothic campaign of the year before had perhaps been a rehearsal of the converging attack which Constantine directed upon the position of Licinius. While Hadrianople was kept engrossed by the advance

---

[1] Gibbon (I, 437, f.n.) well points out that this decay of naval resources was due to the decline of commerce. Athens alone could once have put four hundred three-bankers on the water: but those were the days of commercial enterprise and discovery.

along the main road, the principal break-through was successfully made near Dyme. The first stage of the battle concentrated round the bridge which Constantine ordered to be thrown over the river. While the struggle was proceeding, a body of five thousand archers crossed the river elsewhere, and took the defenders in flank. This drew the advance of Licinius himself, who left his fortified lines to take part in a struggle upon open ground. Constantine then delivered one of the cavalry charges which were his usual method of giving the final blow. The story is that he swam the river with only twelve horsemen—doubtless his personal guard of Scholarians; but far more than twelve must have followed. In the disaster which overtook Licinius thirty-four thousand men are said to have fallen.

Battle of Hadrianople, July 3, 323

The camp of Licinius was stormed the same evening. The survivors of his army, after spending a night scattered in confusion through the hills, readily surrendered to the fresh advance which pursued them the next day.

v

Licinius had probably not an unlimited amount of time in which to reach Byzantium and close the gates to pursuit. His position, though bad, was not desperate. He still held a firm foothold upon the European side of the Straits. His fleet held the Straits themselves; and all the wide recruiting ground of Asia Minor lay open to him. The Anatolian peasant of those days was certainly not inferior to his descendant of today. A fresh army could be raised, capable of barring Constantine's way and of forcing a diplomatic compromise.

No man ever illustrated more neatly than Licinius the disadvantages of a mere defensive. So powerful a defensive was it, that the only weakness in it was that it was a defensive at all. Byzantium was well fortified and well supplied. The only practicable way of reprovisioning the western army was by sea; and the eastern fleet held the Straits. Byzantium might have added to her laurels by destroying the man who was destined to recreate her as Constantinople, had he not got his blow in first. He recognized the peril of attempting to sit down outside the city. But the fleet of Licinius, fully possessed of the defensive notion, was simply idling in the Straits. In an urgent conference at head-quarters, the masters of Constantine's fleet were directed to force the Straits at all costs, and young Crispus was despatched to undertake the general command. The chance of success probably seemed to those concerned a slight one. But human energy works wonders, and Crispus inspired the fleet to excel itself. The first day's battle ended in mutual exhaustion and withdrawal. But at mid-day on the second, a southerly wind arose, which gave Crispus an advantage which he pressed steadily home. A hundred and thirty of the great ships of Licinius were destroyed, the Straits were opened, and Byzantium was isolated.

The situation was now reversed. The western camp was open to revictualling and supply by sea, while Byzantium was cut off. Constantine had always been a driver, and at this point, with life and death in the balance, he drove for all he was worth. Mounds were raised against the walls of Byzantium, and on these were erected towers from which the banquettes were commanded by mechanical artillery, while the foot of the walls was attacked with the battering ram. Before a month was over, these labours brought their results. It became clear that Byzantium was doomed. There was still an opportunity for making a bolt by sea, and Licinius took it. He arrived at Chalcedon in safety, and took command of the new army which—strengthened with a division of Gothic auxiliaries—was coming from Bithynia to raise the siege of Byzantium.

Constantine was hot upon his heels. The Striking Force was hastily ferried across the Straits. At first Constantine parleyed, either because the military task before him was not an easy one, or out of pity for the amateur army which came so confidently to its destruction. Perhaps both reasons had their weight. Licinius, however, was determined to try his fortune. The new eastern army fought with all the indomitable courage which might have been expected from it; but it was ill-trained, out-fought and out-generalled. It had been warned beforehand to look out for the labarum banner, and to avoid it as much as possible. . . . The Striking Force took the cliffs at Chrysopolis by storm, and twenty-five thousand of Licinius' men were left upon the field.

Battle of Chryso-polis, Sept. 18, A.D. 323

Licinius hurried to Nicomedia. The game was up— or very nearly so. His last line of defence was his wife. Constantia went to see her half-brother. Possibly the situation was a somewhat difficult one. Constantine did not wish to refuse his sister her request for the life of her husband; though whether he thought the better of Licinius is questionable, and whether he seriously contemplated the permanency of the arrangement, still more questionable. It was not as if Licinius were a Sunday-school teacher. . . . However, that could wait. For the time being, Licinius, having duly performed the act of submission, was received with the kiss of peace, dined at the imperial table, and was appointed a pension and residence at Thessalonica. . . . The large majority of men who have been prisoners of state would have thought Licinius singularly fortunate in his fate.

What happened afterwards may as well be told here and finished with. He was executed a few months later. As Eusebius tells us that he was executed according to the laws of war,[1] we may safely take it that he was felt to be too dangerous a prisoner to retain. . . . It was said, later on, that he was in correspondence with the Goths.[2] If this be an invention, the inventor had an uncanny genius for hitting upon precisely the accusation that would be likeliest to be true and hardest to prove.

VI

Many reasons combined to make famous and noteworthy the crowning mercy which Constantine found at happily named Chrysopolis. It undid the work which, thirty-seven years earlier, Diocletian had done in appointing Maximian his colleague. It restored unity once more to the empire. The battle of Chrysopolis opened the prisons throughout the east, and set free all who were suffering for their Christian faith. Constantine's first proclamations may have been those which officially announced his own accession; but the second

Effects of Constantine's victory

[1] Eusebius, *Vita C.*, II, 18. Cf. also *H.E.*, X. 9.
[2] Gibbon, I, 440. Socrates, I, 4.

were those which recalled the Christian exiles,[1] freed those who had been condemned to slavery, restored their confiscated property, and replaced the dismissed Christian officers in their old rank in the army.[2] It was provided that the property of the martyrs should go to their next of kin, or, failing heirs, to the Church in whose cause they died. All confiscated property found in possession of the treasury of Licinius was promptly returned to the owners.[3] Any that was in the hands of private persons was ordered to be reported to the government; but it was directed that the interim owners need not render any account of profits received. . . . Eusebius tells us that the emperor showed good will and good feeling towards the pagans as well as towards the Christians, and possibly this may have been one of the ways in which he did so. **End of the persecution**

Not only were the Christians relieved from the penal laws, but the civil law itself was altered to enable them conscientiously to take part in the government of the empire. Constantine appointed many of the new faith to official positions, and in doing so cancelled those requirements which were inconsistent with the profession of their religion. The official sacrifices were abolished, in order that Christian magistrates might not be in an invidious position.[4]

[1] The minister who drafted the revocation of Licinius's persecuting measures did his work so hastily, that all the laws of Licinius were revoked, and this had subsequently to be put right.

[2] Eusebius, *Vita C.*, II, 20. A considerable number of people in good position had been reduced to slavery and were working in offices or mills. The dismissed military officers were given the choice of return to the service, or of taking the pensions to which they would be entitled.

[3] *Ibid.*, II, 21. Chapters 30 to 41 purport to be a copy of the original document issued by Constantine. It will no doubt be surprising to many readers to reflect that martyrs actually possessed property.

[4] *Ibid.*, II, 43-44.

In this way terminated the last traces of the attempt to suppress Christianity, which Galerius had begun twenty years before.

These were not the only results of the battle of Chrysopolis. It marked that shifting eastward of the empire's centre of gravity which ended in the division into East and West Roman. Had it produced no other result, it would yet have been one of the decisive battles of history, for the entire evolution of Europe, from then until now, was determined by this division, which fortified the east against the invasions from Asia, and protected the slow independent growth of a new policy in western Europe. . . . But possibly even the eastward shift would not have split the empire save for one more factor: and that was the destruction of Crispus. Had Crispus followed his father as emperor, he might have preserved for ever the unity of the Roman dominion. Destiny had determined otherwise.

VII

Crispus

If nothing else had done so, the forcing of the Straits might have opened the eyes of men to the brilliance and worth of Crispus. That famous episode was the crown of a career by no means undistinguished. It drew the eyes of the world to the eldest son of Constantine: a man like his father in all things—a successful governor of Gaul and a successful soldier. Eusebius, penning the last lines of his *Ecclesiastical History* [1] before he turned to other subjects, noticed with enthusiasm the promise of the young Cæsar, and allowed himself glowing words

[1] Eusebius, *H.E.*, X, 9.

of admiration. Crispus was the first-fruits of a new system of human cultivation—a Christian education. Lactantius had been his tutor: and Lactantius, in addition to the qualities he could boast as a scholar, had an experience of the world which possibly may have given his teaching a point and pith not always characteristic of the training of princes. He had himself been a witness of the great persecution and its beginning at Nicomedia: he was the man who penned those chapters *Of the Deaths of the Persecutors* which remain one of our chief sources of information for the events upon which they touch, as well as a very lively bit of Christian propaganda. . . . A young man who combined the brains he derived from a father like Constantine with the training he could obtain from a teacher like Lactantius might go far and fare splendidly—and there were many who confidently anticipated that young Crispus would do so. . . . And he might have done so had his qualities attracted the interest only of friends. But among those who noted his success were enemies with an interest in seeing that such a brilliant promise was never brought to its fruition.

Education of Crispus

The dangerous undercurrents at work can be traced within a month of the battle of Chrysopolis. In October, the appointment of Crispus in Gaul was terminated, and he left his provincial government in order to return to court. In November, the little Constantius, the eight-year-old son of Fausta, was given the commission of utilizing his extensive experience and proved ability in the guidance of Gaul. It is impossible to doubt that a party at court had become suddenly conscious of the desirability of having Crispus under closer surveillance.

Crispus withdrawn from Gaul, Oct. 10, 323

Constantine was not absolutely satisfied with the machinery of government he had set up in Gaul and elsewhere. This sense of dissatisfaction was probably used by the enemies of Crispus for purposes of their own. Complaints had evidently reached the emperor that those who represented him did not always do so in the way he would have wished. We know that the charge was true, although it is little likely that Crispus was much to blame. During this autumn Constantine issued a notice inviting complaints from all who felt that they had ground for grievance, and promising personal investigation by the emperor, so that no guilty party should escape through the importance of his position. . . . We have no record that much came of this; but the fact that Constantine thought it necessary shows that he had doubts concerning some things and some persons.

VIII

The conquest of the east, and Constantine's accession to the government of the whole empire, were no merely formal events. They produced results of the utmost moment. Those great pagan vested interests, which battened on the corruption of the people, had played no small part in inspiring the persecution; they now reaped the consequences which they had no doubt expected and feared. The cult of Serapis was suppressed. The scandals connected with Heliopolis and Mount Libanius were terminated. It was high time. These were great and dangerous powers which for far too long had been allowed to exist and to exercise influence. Whatsoever the faults of Christianity may be, similar accusations have not been part of the historic case against it.

It was round about this time that Christianity spread a successful propaganda through Persia to India itself, to Abyssinia, and into the Caucasus. The events connected with the persecution drove abroad many vigorous men who took their faith with them.[1] But at the very moment of its highest energy and its widest dispersion, it showed some ominous signs of trouble within its own ranks.

Constantine grasped very clearly one aspect of the Church—its educative, controlling and representative power. This, rather than its theological orthodoxy, was the principal feature which commended it to the interest of a statesman. But its usefulness in this respect depended very much upon its unity, and upon its ability to maintain one great uniform organization extending over the whole empire. There had never before been any such educative power capable of directing public attention simultaneously and everywhere to one end. Constantine did not mean to lose its offices without a struggle. Even before the contest with Licinius he had seen the impending threat. His action over the African schism furnished a guide and a precedent. He determined to deal on the same lines with the information which now came to him.

Trouble in the Church

This information, which he appreciated at its full value only after a personal visit to the east, was the news of the great Arian controversy.

[1] Socrates, I, 19-21.

IX

Hosius, bishop of Cordova, who acted as an informal ecclesiastical secretary to Constantine, took an early opportunity of visiting Alexandria, the seat of the trouble, and of bringing back a report. Hosius was not commissioned to interfere in any way with the controversy itself, but only to urge upon the parties the desirability of preserving the unity of the Church. He returned to inform the emperor that the position was far more serious than they had supposed. The Church was threatened with a quarrel that would rend it from top to bottom.

Arius

The dispute which had broken out between the bishop of Alexandria and the priest of the great church down by the docks was the beginning of a division only a little less serious than that which a long time afterwards broke out between a German bishop and a monk of Wittenberg. Arius, the priest in question, was neither the originator nor the chief exponent of the views he professed. He merely reflected wide-spread current opinions; perhaps he brought them to a convenient focus; certainly he would never have been dangerous unless the bishops themselves had been deeply imbued with the beliefs he taught. He taught that Christ, the Logos, the second person of the Trinity, the divine Son, had been created by the Father out of nothing; and although this act of creation had taken place before the beginning of time, there had been a state when the Son did not exist, and the Father reigned alone. Not only was the Son created, but like all created things he was subject to change. . . . For these beliefs,[1] the bishop of Alexandria and a synod of African bishops expelled Arius from his cure and from the Christian Church.

x

The expulsion of Arius was the signal for real trouble. Arius went to Cæsarea in Palestine, and laid his case before a sympathizing world. Many of the Asiatic bishops could hardly believe their ears. That any man should have the audacity to expel a Christian priest for these reasonable, logical and unobjectionable beliefs outraged their sense of decency. They wept (figuratively speaking) upon the neck of Arius, and proceeded to write to Alexandria. The bishop of Alexandria, when his wicked conduct was pointed out to him, circularized his colleagues at considerable length,[2] saying, in effect, that he could not conceive how any respectable Christian bishop could even listen to such revolting blasphemies as these abhorrent doctrines, which had evidently been inspired by Satan. To this standpoint he firmly adhered in the teeth of protests. It was at this stage of the controversy that Hosius arrived to implore all the parties to be kind to one another, and not to endanger Christian brotherhood. Both sides drew his attention to the inexcusable wickedness of the other; and he hastily returned to inform Constantine of the situation.

The controversy

[1] On the teaching of Arius see Stevenson, *Studies in Eusebius* (1927), pp. 75-76.

[2] Socrates, *H.E.*, I, 6. This letter is printed as part of the works of Athanasius (*Nicene and Post Nicene Fathers*, Vol. IV, p. 69) and is thought to have been drafted by him.

Constantine had a faith in conferences and discussions which alone should be enough to clear his memory of any charge of autocracy. He determined now to call a general meeting of bishops at which the controversy could be debated and settled. Ancyra was the place appointed.

Before it met, a comparatively minor event had added fuel to the flame of controversy.

The persecution was probably responsible for certain marks of nerve-strain which revealed themselves among the bishops. Men who, with varying success, had defied the torture-chambers of Maximin and the executioners of Galerius were not likely to turn tail at the mere verbal strictures of rivals whose theological views they despised. A group of bishops met at Antioch to consecrate a successor to Bishop Philogonius. They filled in the time by discussing and formulating a creed expressing the views held by the supporters of the bishop of Alexandria. Three of their number, who declined to sign, were promptly excommunicated, with right of appeal to the forthcoming council at Ancyra. Of the three, one was Eusebius, bishop of Cæsarea, the future biographer and friend of Constantine.

As a manœuvre, this was good. The catholic party would now go to Ancyra as the party in possession; and possession is traditionally nine points of the law. Constantine saw that it would be necessary to exert his authority if he were to preserve the unity of the Church and the concord of its representatives. He therefore transferred the meeting place from Ancyra to Nicæa, a town conveniently near Nicomedia, where it would be more under his watch and control.

Synod of Antioch (margin note)

XI

The bishops went to Nicæa. A deep and subtle mind had calculated some of the effects which would be produced at the council: not all of them had reference to the controversy about Arius. . . . It was all very novel. Instead of the bishops setting out with caution, and in some cases on foot, with much counting of pence and discussion of itinerary, the imperial Government paid all expenses, furnished free tickets for the public post transport, and even sent carriages for bishop and servants. . . . The reverend men no doubt had leisure for reflection on their journey—and not always reflection about Arius. At Nicæa, some three hundred bishops found themselves assembled: and it is very probable that to many of them their own numbers were startling. No minions of the law came to drag them away to gaol. In fact (bewildering thought!) they were guests of the emperor.

No church council ever held in later times was quite like the Council of Nicæa. It included a missionary bishop from among the Goths, and Spiridion, the sheep-raising bishop of Trimethous in Cyprus—a very holy man and a first-rate sheep-farmer. There was Hosius, the emperor's adviser, more or less fresh from Spanish gaols: and Eusthathius of Antioch, from an eastern one. Most of the assembly had been in prison, or at the mines, or on the run. Paul, the bishop of Neo-Cæsarea, had lost the use of his hands under the torture. Two Egyptian bishops had each lost an eye at the hands of Maximin's men: of them, one—Paphnutius—had also been hamstrung, and was a cripple. They had had faith, and had believed in the coming of Christ and the victory of the good: it is hardly surprising if most of them supposed that such ideas necessarily implied the approaching end of the world. There certainly seemed no other way of realizing them. . . . And yet here they were, Paphnutius and Paul and all the rest—safe, important, and protected. Lazarus can hardly have been more surprised when he found that he had risen from the dead. . . . It was the doing of their unknown friend, Constantine. . . . Where was he? . . . He was coming later on. . . . But after all, human nature is very elastic. A large number of bishops, inspired by a sense of duty, settled down to write to him, warning him of the character and opinions of certain colleagues whom they knew and he did not.

On the twentieth of May the Council opened for its preliminary discussions. No emperor was there to overawe it: and its sessions were open, not only to laymen, Opening sessions but even to non-Christian philosophers who had been called in to contribute their special knowledge. It spent several weeks in talking. When the members had said all they had to say, and the edge was off their first ardour, Constantine began to appear in the offing. At Nicomedia, on July the third, he had kept the anniversary of the battle of Hadrianople; thence he came on to Nicæa. On the day following, the bishops were to see him. A large hall had been prepared, with seats all round its sides. In the midst was a chair, and a table bearing an open copy of the gospels. There they waited for their unknown friend.

XII

Something of the thrill still survives, of the amazing moment when they saw him—the tall, aquiline, majestic man in his purple silk robe and pearled diadem. No soldiers accompanied him. In compliment to his audience he was accompanied only by civilians and Christian laymen. . . . That they themselves were convulsed with the sensation of the moment is clear, for their emotion a little embarrassed him. He coloured, halted, and remained standing until he was requested to be seated. Then he took the chair.

His reply to the address of welcome was brief. He had, he said, wished nothing more than to find himself amongst them, and he owed thanks to the Saviour of the world that his wish was accomplished. He referred to the importance of agreement, and told them that he, their fellow-servant, was pained to see dissension in the Church of God—an evil worse than war. He entreated them to forget all personal feeling—and here a secretary produced a large bundle of letters from bishops, which he dropped into a glowing brazier, where it was burnt unread.

The Council then got to work in earnest under the presidency of the bishop of Antioch, while the emperor looked on, and occasionally intervened. When Arius came before the Council, it was evident that Constantine did not like him; a distaste which is not hard to understand if the traditions are true concerning Arius's supercilious airs and jaunty self-confidence. The crisis came when Eusebius of Cæsarea, one of the victims of the Synod of Antioch, rose to justify himself.

Arrival of Constantine

Eusebius put before the council a creed, or confession of faith, which had been used in Cæsarea. Constantine intervened to remark that this creed of Eusebius was perfectly orthodox. Eusebius was therefore restored to the fold. The next step was to take this creed of Eusebius and universalize it. There was no chance of a local creed being accepted by everyone; a creed which could be generally subscribed would need to be evolved by the efforts of the whole council. As neither party was very willing to accept any proposals put forward by the other, final recourse was had to Constantine. The emperor was primed by Hosius with the form of words which would probably satisfy the majority of the bishops, and he proceeded to move its adoption. As soon as the creed was put forward from this neutral source, most of the bishops accepted its phrasing.

The only difficulty which then remained was to get as many of the waverers as possible roped in to the true fold. While a certain number of irreconcilables were sure to stand out and to decline accommodation, the object of Constantine was to gain the agreement of as large a majority as possible, so that the unity of the Church should be preserved. Eusebius of Cæsarea was typical of a certain sort of bishop. He was hopelessly muddle-headed and incapable of grasping exact philosophical definitions; but he appreciated the emperor's desire for unity, and at some strain to his own conscience he decided to sign the new creed.[1] On July 19, the

The creed formulated

---

[1] Constantine had invited Acesius, the Novatian bishop, to the council. On talking to him afterwards, he was surprised to find Acesius so orthodox, and asked how, in such a case, he came to be in schism. Acesius started to explain the controversial points; but Constantine merely said: "You must get a ladder, Acesius, and climb into heaven all by yourself." This famous anecdote Socrates (*H.E.*, I, 10, 13) had from Auxanon, a priest who accompanied Acesius to the council.

creed was read out by Bishop Hermogenes, and was
signed by the acceptors. The result was a triumph for
Constantine and for his policy of conference and agreement. The new creed, together with all the other pro-   Results
ceedings of the council, was approved by a substantial   of the
                                                         Council
majority of the bishops; and in due time it was accepted
throughout the Church.

XIII

The success so obtained by Constantine at Nicæa was
much more than a theological victory. That victory,
important as it was, the Church owed to the bishops;
and it is probable that Constantine was only to a very
secondary degree interested in the theological aspect of
the case. His chief interest lay in preserving the unity
and uniformity of the Church; and this he had tri-
umphantly accomplished. The Arian controversy was
perhaps the most difficult and delicate of all the problems which were to trouble Christianity. To steer her
safely through it without disaster was a much greater
triumph than any of the ecclesiastical statesmen of the
sixteenth century ever succeeded in achieving; and that
it was done at all was due to the council of Nicæa, and
to Constantine whose work it was. . . . Much was to
happen, and much trouble was to be suffered, before the
Arian question was concluded—but the main difficulty
was overcome at Nicæa.

In all probability it never could have been overcome
had the matter rested with the bishops alone. An outside force was needed—an outside force not too much
interested in the theological merits of the case—to apply
a gentle and indiscriminate compulsion. . . . Historians

have talked about the disadvantages imposed on the Church by its alliance with the State. These disadvantages—though serious—do not trouble those who reflect that but for Constantine there might now be no Church at all.

It may, of course, be asked, What did the unity of the Church matter, anyhow? But in this, Constantine saw further than his critics and questioners. The unity of the Church was the spiritual integrity of civilization. We ourselves, nowadays, are beginning to feel the pressure of the forces to which Constantine was instantly responsive—we feel the harm done by the disunion of those who deliver to us the moral standard, and the necessity that it should be declared with one voice. Our material civilization, our daily life, can never be satisfactory—it can never even be safe—until we have secured at the back of it a unity of will and ideal. . . . That for which we are working, the crown and consummation of our efforts, is by the programme a thing which will be achieved only through our united labour; and for this reason the quality of unity is not to be despised.

XIV

After the council was over, Constantine's Vicennalia—the twentieth anniversary of his reign—was celebrated: not by any means by his abdication of power, but by a magnificent banquet at Nicomedia, to which he invited the bishops. . . . And though some of them had found engagements interfere with their attendance at the council, none of them found any engagement which prevented them from attending the banquet: for the council embodied only the difficulties and trials of the Church—but the banquet embodied her wonderful safety and incredible triumph.

Perhaps the bishops wished to fix the miraculous facts in their memory. One, at least, chronicled his sensations at passing between the armed guardsmen at the palace gate. No one apprehended him as a criminal. The emperor's table was crowded with bishops. One hopes that he took wine with Paphnutius.[1] . . . If the martyrs were allowed to know anything of the proceedings of a world which had unpleasant memories for most of them, they had at any rate the satisfaction of knowing that they had not died in vain. Though differences may have disturbed Nicæa, the proceedings at Nicomedia were apparently quite harmonious. All present took away with them handsome gifts graded according to their rank and dignity. It was a famous day.[2]

XV

Constantine spent the summer in Asia. He made a tour of the Holy Places of Palestine, and had the Holy Sepulchre (which had been wilfully defaced) restored. He had certain thoughts in mind which we shall meet with again shortly. Nicomedia was no new ground to him. He had lived there for many of the most impres-

---

[1] Paphnutius was a man of character—an ascetic, who, at Nicæa, defended the existence of married clergy, while himself maintaining a life-long vow of chastity. His view was that Christian marriage was no infraction of chastity, and a married man who was ordained should not be required to part from his wife. This view prevailed at the time. Constantine appreciated Paphnutius and invariably saluted him when they met by kissing his eyeless cheek: an action significant and symbolic. Socrates, *H.E.*, I, 11.

[2] Eusebius, *Vita C.*, III, 14, 15.

sionable years of his youth, when Diocletian was lord of the Roman world. There he had seen the Church of Nicomedia levelled with the earth, the First Edict posted up, and the man George and the Christian chamberlains meet their hideous ends. . . . Perhaps he stood there, sometimes, in the evening, and in imagination enacted over again that dusk when he walked down the steps of the palace, took the reins, and mounted for the long arduous ride to Boulogne. . . . Boulogne! . . . And here he was, back again, after many adventures. . . . Most men in his place would have felt a certain dislike of Nicomedia. Memories can sometimes be disturbing.

He leaves for Rome

Towards the end of October he made ready to leave for Italy. Probably he did not want to go; but having celebrated at Nicomedia the beginning of his twentieth year of reign, decency seemed to demand that he should celebrate at Rome the completion of it. He travelled by easy stages through Naissus to Sirmium, the city of Galerius, and thence by Aquileia to Milan, the city of Maximian Herculius. From Milan he travelled to Rome, where he arrived early in July.

He did not know what was waiting for him there.

CHAPTER X

ROME AND CONSTANTINOPLE

I

EARLY in July, Constantine rode into Rome. He had not come back altogether to the Rome he had left. No man ever does. A few years' rest from the gaieties of Maxentius had done wonders in restoring the self-confidence of Romans. They were not liking Constantine very much. They carried on with him the feud they had begun with Diocletian. He need not expect to be admired in Rome if he displayed too clearly his preference for Milan and Nicomedia as capitals. He need not expect to be admired in Rome if he neglected the old Roman gods and the old Roman rites—the old, old venerable things that had seen the fall of the Tarquins and the coming of the Gauls, the retreat of Hannibal, the triumph of Augustus and the presence of Marcus Aurelius. . . . Rome, plunged into a dream of antiquity, did not like those men who lived too actively in the current day.

Above all, it did not like the manners of this new generation. When it saw Constantine and his men, with their silken tunics and curled hair, their Asiatic chargers and the pearl-embroidered fillet that crowned his head, it laughed. The Romans had always despised millinery; and here were the men-milliners in force.

Constan-
tine arrives
at Rome,
July,
A.D. 326

243

II

Change
in public
opinion

The trouble began almost immediately upon his arrival. He came anxious to please, and eager, on principle, to be on good terms with the senate. If he offended Roman taste it was because he had not heard of its rules and prohibitions. The day after his arrival he wrote to the senate asking for a list of those of its members who had suffered from the government of Maxentius and Licinius, and promising his interest on their behalf. This does not appear to have been received quite as warmly as might justly have been expected. The underlying lack of sympathy gradually became clear. The fifteenth of July was the famous procession of the knights "from Castor in the Forum to Mars without the wall," which is familiar to every English reader through Macaulay's Lay of the Battle of Lake Regillus. Constantine declined to take personal part in a celebration which included sacrifices to an idol. This refusal may have involved some slight change of ground on his part, and a shifting nearer the official Christian position. It deeply offended the knights. But worse was to come.

On the day of the procession the emperor and his comites were interested spectators. The Romans had laughed at their silks and satins. It was now their turn to remind the Romans that the men in silks and satins were old professional soldiers who were not proof against the temptation to smile at the proceedings of the amateur soldiers of Rome. . . . The news spread instantly. The amateurs were furious—none the less so because they had themselves given the first offence.

So acute was the feeling aroused by this incident that it gave rise to the almost complete social isolation of the imperial court in Rome. Constantine himself could not pass through the streets without popular demonstrations of hostility. It was of course quite obvious that no such demonstrations could take place without the connivance of the authorities. A meeting of the imperial council was called to consider what action should be taken. Some members were in favour of strong measures, and the use of military force: but others gave very different advice, and thought it better that the emperor should take no notice of hostile demonstrations. . . . Constantine finally accepted this latter point of view. It was observed that he left the meeting with a calm countenance.

A story which in after days was current about Constantine may possibly have arisen at this time. Some member of the court came in with the news that there had been stone-throwing, and that Constantine's statue had been hit on the head. . . . After a moment's pause, Constantine passed his hand over his head and remarked: "I can't say I feel it!"[1]

III

But old Rome had not yet done her worst. Constantine had neglected her, stolen her empire, disbelieved in her gods, and laughed at her processions—and he had had the hardihood to put his foot within the magical circle of her bounds; he was not going to escape so easily. He was not destined to tear himself away without leaving his most precious possession behind.

[1] De Broglie, *L'eglise et l'empire Romain*, II, 90-95.

The whole imperial family, with the exception of his mother, Helena, had accompanied him into Italy, and in the comparative leisure and isolation of their life in Rome, some of its dividing lines deepened and took on a fresh ominousness. With little to do but think over its own domestic squabbles, the imperial family employed the time at Rome in blowing up for a first class storm.

Perhaps the root of the whole matter lay in Constantine himself. All the indications point to one peculiar quality in his mind which was the immediate reason of all that happened. Clever as he was in some special ways, rapid in decision and sure in his instinct for the right course, he nevertheless seems to have possessed some of the ingrained unworldliness which often distinguishes men of special gifts. Only a particular limited part of his mind was lit up by that brilliant light which made him great. He does not seem ever to have been a man of deep and subtle knowledge of human nature—least of all his own human nature. That power of handling the calculus of human motive which marks men like Richelieu and Talleyrand was foreign to Constantine. He remained all his life a little unsophisticated, and, outside his own special work, somewhat "innocent." [1]

Limitations of Constantine

A great many facts of various kinds find their due and comprehensible place when we see them related to this characteristic of Constantine. He was liable to accept men's own account of themselves. The ancient historians have noted one or two men who struck their

[1] Lactantius represents Constantine as unsuspicious in his dealings with Maximian (*De M.P.*, xxix). In xviii, the dialogue between Diocletian and Galerius, the former speaks of Constantine as a mild and amenable person—and Galerius does not deny it. Compare also Eusebius, *Vita C.*, IV, 54.

contemporaries as remarkably successful in the art of hoodwinking Constantine. One was Ausonius, whom the emperor employed to collect information concerning Christianity and Christians: the other was Ablabius, his Prætorian prefect. Both seem to have been able and efficient ministers: but (so men rightly or wrongly believed) they used their positions freely to feather their own nests. Constantine was anxious that his friends should feel as he did on political and religious subjects. A large number of people, who did not particularly care what they believed, were perfectly ready to oblige him. The conviction of the world at large was that Constantine showed a simplicity bordering on the credulous in the way in which he took their professions at their face value. . . . He probably owed much of his success and his power to a capacity for working with all kinds of men—and therefore for bearing with their peculiarities. He was liable to bear just a little too far.

Analysis of his character

The danger of this lay in that he was a very long way from being a fool. Every now and then he would awake to the consciousness that he was being deceived; and then there was trouble. We have already seen that just before he left Asia he had begun to entertain some suspicion that not all the complaints that were addressed to him reached him. While he resembled his father in possessing a tolerant, easy-going temper, which liked to be at peace with all men, there was somewhere in him a nerve which, when touched, roused him to far greater violence of reaction than Constantius had ever displayed. It is a familiar fact of human experience that the more implicitly a man trusts, the more he resents betrayal. Those who give little, often expect little; but those who have given more than anyone wanted sometimes ask for more than anyone will give.

IV

More than anyone will give: for it is the safest plan (if safety be any object) to expect nothing from man—neither faith nor truth nor gratitude nor charity: for these things are like fortune and happiness—pleasant surprises, on which we must not calculate. . . . Men afterwards shrank from explaining what happened at Rome this year. They surrounded the events with a wall of darkness and silence which it is now hardly possible to penetrate: we can do no more than catch shadowy glimpses in the gloom. Eusebius, the biographer of Constantine, is silent; Lactantius, the tutor of Crispus, has no tale to tell; Zozimus, who lived long afterwards, was a prejudiced and hostile witness, and in any case did not know much. From other sources come faint scraps and hints, from which we can put together, after long controversy, a silhouette with few details. But one or two things we do, as a result, seem to know. It was around the person of Crispus that the explosion occurred; and Fausta's was the hand that fired the train.

What
happened
at Rome

Crispus had been at the height of his fame and success that year. Every day he had grown to be a more dangerous rival to Fausta's children, had forced them more surely into the shade, and had made it more certain that they would never reign. The whole drift of Constantine's policy tended to favour the prospect of a single successor, a single emperor to step into his shoes. Unless

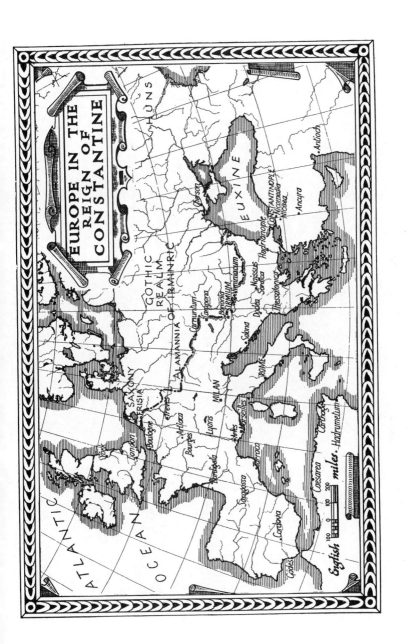

EUROPE IN THE
REIGN OF
CONSTANTINE

this could be changed, it might be too late ever to change
it. During those idle days at Rome, Fausta changed it.

V

But first of all, of Fausta herself.

The character of Fausta is not directly known to us;
but it can be reconstructed from the known characters **Fausta**
of her father and her son. Old Maximian Herculius had
been an egoist of really remarkable depth of dye. There
must have been something engaging about the simplicity
with which he held the doctrine of his own importance.
He never doubted that the noblest achievement of the
universe was the person of Maximian Herculius, and
that no benefit could be bestowed upon the world greater
than the privilege of being directed in the right path
by his wisdom. He could not sit down quietly in a
world which lacked proper appreciation of his virtues:
he could not stamp with enough ferocity on the persons
who opposed his beneficial supremacy. He felt that he
was justified in almost any measures which would give
the world the advantages that followed from obedience
to him.

This anxiety to stamp on opposition is visible enough
in the character which Ammianus Marcellinus gives of
Constantius, the grandson of Maximian and son of
Fausta. Constantius lived in a world of pitfall and of
gin, and he spent most of his time in searching out
enemies and in discovering conspiracies. He lived in a
sort of William le Queux world, in which he was the
hero of a hundred sensational novels. Constantius was,
moreover, a strong silent man. When he rode in his

Explana-
tion of
Fausta

Triumphal procession he looked neither to the right hand nor the left. No sign broke the fixed and awful calm of his imperial dignity.[1] . . . . A man needs to be a good deal of a poseur to carry things to that length; but even allowing for pose, the cold hard-heartedness of the man is clear. And such egoism, such ferocity, such passion for intrigue, such cold vanity as we see in Fausta's father and son, would explain Fausta also.

VI

What did Fausta do?

Strictly speaking, at this stage of the affair, it is not clear that she had done anything. The question of her share in events must wait. The thing which first came to pass this summer at Rome was the arrest of Crispus, his examination before the emperor, and his removal to Pola in Istria.[2]

Exactly what then happened to Crispus is not clearly known; but apparently he was held at Pola for some short time. His removal put a distance between father and son that was fatal to any explanation between them; and it laid Constantine open to influences against which no counter-influence was at the time available. Pressure was brought to bear. To produce the consequences it did, the pressure must have been extraordinarily strong and convincing.

---

[1] Amm. Marc., XVI, 10.

[2] All the evidence germane to this affair is assembled by Dr. Wordsworth in the *Dictionary of Christian Biography*, article "Constantine." De Broglie, *L'eglise et l'empire romain* is very good. The description in the text is obtained by taking all the passages cited by Dr. Wordsworth, and is the logical result of accepting them as nearly as possible without alteration or amendment.

Constantine signed his son's death-warrant: and Crispus was secretly executed at Pola.

This action is one of the most sensational and con- Arrest and execution troversial acts in human history. What can it have of Crispus meant? On what evidence was it based? As we have seen, Constantine was far indeed from having the reputation of a Brutus. If anything, his repute was for softness and generosity. How does it come about that he stands with Junius Brutus, one at each end of Roman history, as a man who executed his own son?

Slender and fragmentary as the evidence may be, it nevertheless produces a coherent story. We must remember that Constantine's visit to Rome was connected with his Vicennalia—the celebration of the twentieth year of his reign. Now Diocletian, when, a generation earlier, he designed his system, had intended to review his position in his twentieth year; and he had intended all his successors, in their turn, to review their position every ten years of rule, giving place if necessary to appointed heirs. Galerius would probably have obeyed this regulation had he not died before the time came. But Constantine's accession to the empire had been effected under wholly different circumstances, never contemplated by Diocletian; it had taken place by stages, and it had introduced a new atmosphere, of pure monarchy, totally unlike Diocletian's curious Board of Empire. . . . Constantine had brought it in almost unconsciously; and being much less of a doctrinaire than Diocletian he had not put forward any definite theory or any hard and fast programme, so that it remained not quite certain how much of Diocletian's system he had retained, and how much he had abolished. This incerti-

tude provided an advantageous field for the intriguer.
. . . Let us remember further the very peculiar circumstances in which Diocletian resigned. He had doubted and hesitated; and Galerius had taken a vigorous course and had forced his hand.

The charge against him

All these considerations indicate that the charge against Crispus can only have been that he intended to take upon himself the part of Galerius, and force his father's abdication.

The astonishment and scepticism of Constantine are not very difficult to picture. In his doubts he evidently had the support of some of his chief advisers.[1] On the other hand, it is clear that the charge must have been made and the witnesses produced by some of the less important members of the court. Constantine's half-brothers, the sons of Constantius and Theodora, do not seem to have been involved. Finding themselves in the dangerous position of having their testimony rejected, with all the consequent prospect of reprisals from the party of Crispus, the accusers appealed to the real author and instigator of the charge. That instigator was Fausta.

VII

Fausta intervenes

The advent of the empress entirely altered the position of affairs. Not only was she a witness who could not be easily rejected or smiled away, but she was one who could give her evidence under circumstances particularly difficult to deal with. She did not need to come into court. It is probable that she still met with aston-

---

[1] The famous distich of Ablabius, mentioned on p. 366 below, certainly indicates that Crispus had friends ready to show rash partisanship on his behalf. As Prætorian prefect, Ablabius was a very important person indeed.

ished incredulity. . . . At this crisis (for it was now either Crispus or herself) Fausta played the winning card. She charged Crispus with having offered to make her his empress.

If, to the modern reader, such a charge seems wild and improbable, it had a very different sound to Constantine. Its nature deserves careful observation. A good many centuries of Christianity have caused most of us to forget some of the customs of earlier non-Christian civilizations. But to Constantine the brother-and-sister marriages of the Egyptian dynasties, and similar oriental customs, were reasonably familiar; and he is hardly likely to have been ignorant of the means by which gentile descent was artificially secured among the tribesmen of northern Europe. He certainly knew things far more recondite than that, which he could have heard of a hundred times, over any camp fire on Rhine or Danube. The custom of a king securing his title by marrying the wife of his predecessor was known long after Constantine's day. English history, five hundred years later than Constantine, provides one well-attested instance of a king seeking to secure his title by marrying his father's wife: King Æthilbald of the West Saxons, King Alfred's uncle. . . . Constantine—and Crispus too—were old Rhine frontiersmen, well acquainted with the life and thought of north-western Europe. There was nothing impossible in Crispus having thought of the plan. There was nothing improbable in Fausta disbelieving in it and denouncing it. She had saved her husband in that way once: she might do so again.

Nature
of her
charges

Later Roman authors had heard a story that Fausta herself had made the proposal to Crispus, and, in order to save herself when he declined it, had laid the charge at his door. Not being men of the Rhine or eastern frontier, they were unable to make head or tail of this story, and supposed it to be a version of the tale of Phædra and Hippolytus.[1] But her charge was deadlier than that. No such accusation would have been believed. The doctrine of securing a title by marriage with a predecessor's wife was a different matter. Linked with the other story of Crispus' plans for the Vicennalia, it made a straight tale—and a particularly odious one.

It was on this tale that Crispus was sent to Pola. Had Constantine had time for thought, his belief in the story would instantly have begun to fade. But Fausta knew her husband. He was swift. She tempted him to be a little too swift: and he fell.

One of the peculiar characteristics of calumny is that **Crispus' death necessary to Fausta** it cannot be withdrawn. Once this charge had been made, and Crispus was at Pola, it became urgent that he should never return. It was absolutely necessary that he should die. An empress can do a good many things that no ordinary woman can do. Howsoever it may have been done, done it was. Crispus died at Pola.

Some thought that it was Ablabius himself, the Præ-

---

[1] The Duc de Broglie is probably right in dismissing the assertions of Zozimus; but the fact remains that Zozimus made them—and the best way of interpreting them is to suppose that he simply filed incomprehensible facts under the most applicable heading he could find. The story that Fausta herself made the proposal might conceivably be part of the unsuccessful case put up by the friends of Crispus when hurriedly called upon to defend him. The *tu quoque* argument is often quite good business. If unsuccessful, however, it would make matters worse for Crispus—all of which fits the course of events.

torian prefect, who wrote, and stuck up on the palace
notice-board, the little distich:—

> "Back to the Golden Age again?
> We've got as far as Nero's reign!"

VIII

The state of pause that followed was, we may believe, no especially happy one. It lasted just long enough
to chill the anger and faith of Constantine: and it was
broken by the arrival—too late to save Crispus—of the
avenging fury: not (as later historians supposed) his
grandmother, St. Helena, but a far more effective agent
for the purpose, his wife, Helena, the daughter of Licinius. . . . Old Licinius, in his youth, had been no slouch;
nor was his daughter. A young woman out to avenge
an admired and beloved husband is not likely to hesitate
at trifles. Helena arrived in a mood to tear out the eyes
of anyone who disagreed with her. She burst upon Constantine with some of the effects of a fireball or an earthquake. Having first been driven one way before the
storm, he was now driven another. Helena possessed
one advantage—she had the truth on her side. Fausta's
tale would only hold good until it was questioned.

Arrival
of Helena

It was questioned now by a young wife whose natural
feelings were given point and edge by the special insult
of the pretence that Crispus had ever proposed to himself any forgetfulness of her. If Fausta had had any
chance of escape, she must have lost it through the form
she had given to her charges. . . . Constantine, to his
horror and consternation, gradually became conscious

how completely he had been duped. The death of Crispus had been not only the unjustifiable and unnecessary murder of an innocent man, but one of those irremediable actions from which there is no way out: which cannot be palliated or made right by any repentance or remorse. . . . The criminal could not now be deprived of the reward of her crime—for nothing now could prevent the reign of Fausta's children. They were innocent in word and deed: they could not be punished for their mother's act, nor deprived because of the failure of Crispus.

The very success of her crime may have been the destruction of Fausta. Since there was no way of lightening or palliating the deed, she had to pay for it. . . . It is very unlikely that Constantine could have endured to see her again or be reminded of her existence. No man, in such circumstances, could have endured it. If Constantine permitted her death, he only solved the difficulty of an impossible situation, and saved Fausta the misery of a life-long imprisonment in which her memory would have been a torment to him, to herself, and to all about them. She had entered into a conspiracy to procure the death of an innocent man: the penalty for which, even in modern days, is the penalty for murder. And there were no extenuating circumstances.

Fausta's death-warrant

All those who were involved in the conspiracy suffered the penalty of the law. It was traced step by step back to its source, and the prime mover identified. The historians agree that Fausta was suffocated in the steam of a hot bath. . . . That was the end of the daughter of Maximian Herculius. Though she died, the evil that she did lived after her—how long it lived, and the full depth of its degree, no man can say.

IX

Constantine left Rome soon after.

Few men would have entertained any passion for that ancient city after such events as those of the past summer. It had wreaked its revenge on the apostle of change. His plans for the future were destroyed. No single monarch could now step into his shoes when the time came. The future must be left to its own devices.

But as the tradition testifies, the moral effect of that summer in Rome left its mark. The legend—symbol of his state of mind rather than historical fact—is that he so deeply repented of the death of Crispus that he consulted the priests of the old religion. They told him that the guilt was too deep to be washed out by any expiation. He turned to the Christian Church, which offered him forgiveness. So he became a Christian.

Results of Crispus' death

Little as this may accord with the facts of his life, it no doubt accurately represents a process at work in his mind. He had had some experience of Christianity as a factor in the political life of the empire. He now had experience of it in relation to his own personal life— and we need not be surprised if the shock was great. The old religion was poor stuff—a pill to cure earthquakes—when confronted with such a spiritual crisis as that of Constantine after the summer in Rome. It had nothing to say and nothing to offer save a few decorative rites of purification and a little cheery sentiment as distasteful as it was shallow. It is very probable that

Constantine did not want any cheery sentiment. He may have realized now for the first time the realities which lay behind the power of the bishops.

The
moral
problem

The problem of Fausta contained greater difficulties than that of Crispus. The latter he might meet again in another world, and he might make his explanations and reach a satisfactory peace. But did he want to meet Fausta again? The inconsistencies of a man's own feelings in such a matter can tie a knot of paradox in his mind. When we have known them for a long time with intimacy, even our enemies become part of our lives. The servant of the Lord, with his wife and his children, his manservant and his maidservant, his friends and his enemies, his ox and his ass, his dog, and the stranger within his gates, all together go up for judgment. What is to become of the things and the people we cannot do with and cannot do without?

Even from the narrower point of view, Constantine had not altogether reflected credit upon the religion he supported. Ablabius had scored with that vengeful word "Nero." Was the court of the first Christian emperor to be distinguished with scandals from which even Diocletian's was free? Constantine seems to have appreciated this aspect of the case. From the very first, with a panic-stricken secrecy, all the circumstances connected with the deaths of Crispus and Fausta were studiously concealed. The writers nearest the imperial person scarcely even mention them. His enemies knew

The facts
concealed

them only imperfectly.

He was wrong. To hide such things is the surest way to an invidious and unfair publicity. Since Constantine's day, few historians of his age have been able to refrain from speculation, not always friendly. Had Constantine taken the world into his confidence, it might have sympathized. But to give it hints, and half-facts, and suggestions, and provoking silences, is above all to stir the worst part of the human mind into enquiring activity: and the punishment he has suffered is that although he was tricked into executing in good faith a son he loved, and only executed a woman who had justly incurred the penalty of death—still, from that time to this, he has been given the repute of a murderer and a tyrant.

X

Constantine turned back to the east. He had business there in which he could forget the horrors of that Roman summer. He had determined to protect the eastern frontiers by establishing a new centre of empire, a new Rome, in some position where it could command the whole of the eastern provinces. Alexandria was too far south. Antioch was not in the right position. Both had far too much separate provincial life of their own for the purpose. . . . Nicomedia had not satisfied Constantine. He had thought long and deeply on the subject, and evidently had discussed it at length with others. A site near Troy had been suggested; and there was real vision in the idea. Old legend predicted the return of the Romans to the city from which they sprang. . . . There were serious objections. Troy was not altogether a cheap site to fortify, and it had no very convenient harbour. Thessalonica and Sardica had been considered. Constantine's choice had finally fallen upon the old Greek city of Byzantium. It has never been disputed

Constantine returns to the east

that this was the best choice from all points of view that could possibly have been made.

Byzantium stood at the centre where the great land route between Europe and Asia crossed the great sea route between the Euxine and the Mediterranean. It controlled both these important routes, and barred the way of any invader seeking to pass from one area to another. It was within comfortable reach of both the Danube and the Euphrates frontiers. It was easily to be fortified. It was warmer than Sardica and less relaxing than Alexandria. Finally, it had a magnificent harbour. Communication between the capital and all parts of the empire was a far easier matter with Byzantium **Byzantium** than it ever had been with Rome.

The future of Byzantium and the particular function in history it was destined to fulfil were strongly affected by the conditions under which Constantine refounded it and established it as his capital. As a political capital, a centre of direction and administration, it had its importance; but such a centre would naturally grow up in any place in which the emperor fixed his usual residence, and in the circumstances of the Roman empire at that time, the exact position of this centre did not very much matter. The factor which gave Byzantium its importance sprang from its position as the military base for the Striking Force. In years to come, the whole history of Europe was to be altered by this factor. Everything that was in the military sense accessible from Constantinople was held and retained by the Roman empire. Everything that military force alone could do, Byzantium enabled the emperors to achieve. When the city at last fell, it fell in reality to a prolonged blockade.

Probably no single act ever done by a soldier was quite so far-reaching as Constantine's when he approved the decision to build at Byzantium.

The foundation of the wall which was to mark the bounds of the new city was laid on the fourth of November, in the year 326—a date memorable in the history of mankind.

XI

Something unintentionally symbolic marked it . . . The emperor was turning his back upon Rome. What he carried with him was the heritage of civilized mankind, as it had been modified and improved by Rome, rather than the particular local spirit of Rome itself. A little difficulty arose in distinguishing between the thing and the word. For long, the name of the new city was uncertain. It never lost its old name of Byzantium. The intention was, to call it New Rome. This, however, proved a complete failure. Before Constantine's death, the name *Constantinople* had been evolved by public opinion, and it stuck. The new capital

There was meaning in these trifles. The process of disentangling the Roman empire from the local associations of Rome, begun by Diocletian, was carried a step further by Constantine. Even the principate founded by Augustus had been a recognition of the fact that the Roman empire was more than a product of Rome. The empire always had been largely Greek. It is only an illusion of perspective which makes us think of it as wholly Roman. We are so engrossed with the magnitude of the great Roman figure of Cæsar which leads the way, that we do not notice the crowd of push- The Greek east ful and keen-witted Greeks who surge forward in his track. Some may have been freedmen or slaves—distinctions of great importance in their day, but to us meaningless. Weighed in the balance of human power, these men were as important as Cæsar. The Italian peasant might despise them, in the spirit in which the old-fashioned rustic Englishman despised the urban Frenchman; but the Greeks pulled their weight and were half the team. . . . We must not forget that even the leading Romans were Greek by education. The empire was a Greek empire as much as an Italian one, long before Constantine arose to give its Græcism a local habitation at old Byzantium. . . . If anything, he segregated the Greek element, withdrew it from the west, and concentrated it in the eastern provinces, leaving those of the west once more purely western, de-Hellenized—even, to a certain extent, barbarized: for Hellenism was eight-tenths of human civilization.

How much of this process was consciously intended it is beyond our power to tell. Constantine very certainly did not found Constantinople without knowing very well what he was doing; but the amenability, the strong tendency to go where he was pushed, to follow the current, and to obey the call, which we have seen function as weakness in relation to the episode of Crispus' death, could function as great strength in matters of statesmanship. It gave him a kind of preternatural intuition into the immediate circumstances. He was not imposing his iron will upon a shrinking world, but was anxiously feeling his way, with sensitive touch, interpreting the needs of the moment, quick in response to its demands . . . not always particularly clever when he

Significant
of the
change

had to trust to his own unaided intelligence, but only a little less than unfailing when it was a question of sensitively registering the subtle language that is spoken by events and things. . . . He was no Greek himself. He used Latin as his familiar language. In it he composed his speeches, which, at necessity, were translated and delivered in Greek by interpreters. It is very clear, therefore, that he was not a deliberate apostle of things Hellenic. He was only following the trend of the day.

XII

We need not look far to discover the cause of this growing influence of the Greek east. The eastern peasant and merchant had been far less deeply injured by the economic collapse than those of the west. They were rapidly recovering their prosperity, while the western farmer was still in difficulties, and the western trade was well-nigh beyond help. The age was thus a Greek age. Even if Constantine accentuated the trend by his policy, the trend was there to begin with. It was one of his characteristics that he always went with trends rather than against them.

XIII

Constantinople was nearly four years in building. Old Byzantium stood upon a long tongue of land, surrounded on three sides by water. By building a new land-wall further inland, Constantine enclosed a much larger area of the tongue for his new city. The beauty of the site is famous. It is a dry bracing land of sun-

Site of Constantinople

shine and violent colour, where high winds battle with the sun and a fierce current sets through the Straits. It lies comparatively low, running up southwest by the watery expanse of Marmora to the cliffs of Gallipoli, and the huge mountains of Greece, Asia Minor, and the Ægean islands: while north-west, beyond the plains of Hadrianople, rises the vast Balkan plateau, cut through by the roads to the Danube. North-east, the Straits form a sea gateway into the Euxine, where the Danube delta, the great plains and rivers of Russia, and the wild northerly edge of Asia Minor along to the Caucasus, are accessible, and without too much trouble men could even then reach the Caspian. It has something of the climate of Marseilles or Venice, but to this day is a wilder and less conquered spot. One thing it never has been—it has never been the home of a dull and effete convention.

Constantinople long kept the peculiar touch it gained from the hand of Constantine himself. He and his architects worked out the ground plan that gave the city its unique character, and most of the features which have become famous. Santa Sophia, the Palace, the Hippodrome, the Golden Gate—such names are a music ushering in a new and astounding age. . . . They were not yet what they were to become. No such domes rose over the first Santa Sophia as hung dream-like over the latter; no such mosaics lined it. But the general plan, and probably some of the architectural quality, remained unaltered. . . . We are obviously parting, gently but irrevocably, with the world of Antoninus Pius and Marcus Aurelius, of Cicero and Cæsar. Old things are passing away and all things become new.

The
new era

XIV

Constantinople was the first purely Christian city ever built.[1] No pagan temple was open for public worship within its bounds: though there is no reason to suppose that the private exercise of any religion was interfered with. The old temples of Byzantium were preserved as public monuments.

We may deduce that Constantine himself hardly shared the ordinary Christian view that the pagan gods were devils. At any rate, he collected a number of important memorials of the old religion, especially those of artistic or historical interest, and preserved them in Constantinople, where they formed a striking link with the famous past of Hellas. His architects did not hesitate to utilize an old Greek Apollo as a statue of Constantine himself, carefully removing the head and replacing it with a portrait of Constantine wearing a seven-rayed nimbus. The remains of this statue and its pedestal still survive, battered and blackened, to this day, as "the Burnt Pillar." It is a curious testimony—like the Labarum itself—to the bridge over to the Christian faith that was formed by the sun-cults of later Rome. Tradition alleged that in the base of the pillar Constantine had deposited the Shield of Pallas, the thrice-famed "palladium" of Rome. If so, it must be there still.

Several other relics of the sun-cults were among the renowned decorations of Constantinople. The Pythian Apollo was brought from Delphi, together with the

The old cults

---

[1] Euseb., *Vita C.*, III, 47, is quite definite. Bury, *History of the Later Roman Empire*, I, p. 74.

tripod, the twisted Apolline serpents, which the Greeks consecrated at Delphi after Plataea. The Sminthean Apollo also, one of the most ancient of all the Greek sun-gods, and possibly pre-Hellenic, was brought to Constantinople. . . . Exactly what motive urged the emperor to collect these relics of the old religion has never transpired; later ages accepted them much in the spirit in which an Englishman accepts the Elgin Marbles. Bishop Eusebius was certainly mistaken in fancying that they were set up as marks for opprobrium. They received none until, eleven centuries later, the conquering Sultan Mohammed, with exquisite symbolism, showed his distaste for the votive offering that once had been made by the exalted victors of Plataea.

XV

Constantine wished his personal friends and supporters to fix their homes in the new city. After ages believed that a considerable migration took place from Rome itself. The emperor granted sites for town houses, and legend has it that to some of his friends he paid the compliment of presenting them with exact reproductions of their houses in Rome. Not all his friends, however, came from Rome, and Milan probably was the severest sufferer, at any rate for the time being, when the officials and servants of the court transferred their permanent quarters to the east.

Some of these migrants may have found, after a little experiment, that residence at Constantinople had advantages to which Rome or Milan could lay no claim. It is certain that the new capital, once built and popu-

Settlement of Constantinople

lated, flourished. It offered openings for the investment
of capital and for commercial enterprise upon which the
new citizens were not slow to seize: and while Rome
continued in the imposing grandeur of a dying city,
Constantinople was growing into the active and progres-
sive commercial capital of the empire.

The present age, which has seen the building of new
Delhi and of Canberra, can conceive from these modern
examples some of the work and the cost that were involved in the founding of Constantinople. But they
illustrate only the building of the administrative capital.
Neither of the modern examples is ever likely to develop
into so wonderful a military base, or so prosperous a
commercial port, as the city which Constantine
founded.

Commer-
cial
advantages

XVI

So the amazing deed was done, and the man who had
ridden away from Nicomedia at nightfall long ago had
now returned to the place whence he had departed,
bringing with him not only the triumphant army of the
west but even the laurels, the prestige, the age-long
harvest of Rome itself, to build a new Rome on the
Bosphorus. He had transferred the centre of the empire
to the east, which Antony had failed to do. He had
founded a new capital; he had set the empire travelling
on a new orbit of triumph and success; he had secured
the future safety of Europe. . . . And as we shall presently see, he was now about to set going the process
which in a few generations was to create in western
Europe the national states whose slow growth Constantinople was to guard and to nourish.

XVII

Dedication
of Con-
stantinople,
11 May,
A.D. 330

On the eleventh of May, 330, Constantinople was dedicated. As the Christian Church had at that date no experience in founding cities, the consecration was probably carried out with some, if not all, of the time-honoured rites which in their day had served for Cumæ, and Massilia, and Syracuse, and even for Rome itself. It is improbable that everything was finished; but the city was sufficiently advanced to allow the new empire to move into new Rome.

CHAPTER XI

THE PROBLEMS OF THE NORTH, AND THE PROBLEMS OF THE SOUTH

I

NONE too soon was Constantinople started upon its career. Its first task, the beginning of the wrestle with the Goths, was at hand. Constantine's invasion of Dacia had had the results which usually followed such campaigns. The prestige of the old Gothic leaders was weakened; in the course of a few years new men stepped into their shoes with a more aggressive and uncompromising policy, and the Gothic advance recommenced.

Gothic menace, A.D. 331

The Sarmatian tribes settled along the Theiss and Danube were the first to feel the pressure. Now, however, they had grown wiser. They made only slight attempts to match themselves with the Goths, but as soon as they had sufficient evidence of aggression to prove their case, they laid it before the Roman government together with a request for help.

Constantine recognized both the danger involved in the Gothic advance and the advantage given him by the appeal of the Sarmatians. He immediately notified the parties that he was prepared to intervene. The reply of the Goths was to anticipate and prevent action on his part by themselves promptly crossing the Danube and beginning the war in Roman territory.

This Gothic invasion was by far the most serious that the empire had known since the days of Claudius Gothicus. Great as it was in military magnitude, it owed its importance even more to certain elements which lay behind the military. All the following winter the Goths remained in Illyria, living upon the country and destroying its taxable value. The winter was taken up in active preparations of the imperial government; and the means which it employed, the following year, to break up and expel the Gothic army, will give us a clear hint of the knowledge it possessed concerning the events which were changing the face of central and eastern Europe.

II

The great raid of the Goths, back in the reign of Gallienus, had been rendered possible by their use of the Black Sea ports, particularly the port known as Cherson, near the mouth of the Dnieper. This was one of the very ancient Greek settlements which, like Massilia and Cumæ, had been made in the earliest age of Greek commercial expansion. It had lain there, on the edge of the wild steppes, almost unchanged by the events of the Mediterranean world: a medium by which Greek products, and possibly a number of Greek ideas, were exchanged for the raw materials of the Scythian plains. It retained its old Greek magistrates and its old self-government.

It is possible that Cherson had established direct relations with the imperial government during the building of Constantinople, for its neighbourhood contains quarries of variegated marble. The old town had not by any means been a mere cipher in the history of its own part of the world. Like Venice and Genoa, it had fought for its own interests and defended its markets with all the skill and vigour that men are apt to show when fighting for a good reason and for substantial stakes. The imperial government now approached the city with the proposal that it should co-operate with the Roman armies by attacking the Goths on their eastern limits during the forthcoming year. The government undertook meanwhile to push its own campaign upon the Danube, and very possibly it may have offered a substantial sum to help in the equipment of its ally.

Cherson accepted this proposal. Its army, although strangely antiquated, was quite adequate. The war-cars which it put into the field must have been nearly as startling to an officer of Constantine's age as they would be to one of today. They were, however, suited to the steppes, where indeed they had probably first been invented: and the archers, who drove into battle with their mobile shooting-platforms stacked high with ammunition, had no difficulty in dealing with the Gothic armies they met.

Had the Goths been organized as a loose alliance of tribes, or even as a number of independent kingdoms, the attack made by Cherson upon their eastern limits would have had no result whatsoever upon the situation in the Danube valley. But the calculations of the imperial government seem to have been correctly made. The campaign in Illyria drove the Gothic King Araric out of the lowlands into the hills. There, as the season wore, the Goths, without food or supplies, died in great numbers from cold and exposure. No help or diversion came to their aid. Their surrender had to be abject. The son of King Araric was retained as a hostage. Con-

Goths expelled from Illyria

stantine treated the Gothic chiefs well, and dismissed them with rich presents. It may not have been a wise plan; but what wiser plan was there, in dealing with such men?

III

Constantine and the imperial government seem to have felt that their utmost gratitude was due to the friendly offices of Cherson. Municipal honours were showered upon the city. Her commerce was freed from all customs duties in Euxine ports. Subsidies were promised. The government was clearly under the impression that the action of Cherson had in some way signally helped the empire against the Goths. If it was right—and presumably it knew its own business—then the Gothic power with which Cherson fought in Southern Russia was the self-same power with which the empire was fighting on the Danube, and a military reverse which the Goths suffered upon one front would affect their power upon the other.

The kingdom of Irminric

The strong presumption is, therefore, that already, in the year 332, the kingdom of Irminric was in existence. So much interest has Irminric to a student of Constantine, that we may profitably survey the identity of that famous Gothic king, and his place in the history of Europe.

When we examine the traditions of the northern peoples of later, post-Roman Europe, we realize that they run back to a certain period, and no further. If this period is laboriously calculated with the aid of the old genealogies, as far as these will help us, it turns out to be round about the year A.D. 300; that is to say, round about the reign of Constantine. At this period, therefore, some remarkable revolution took place in northern Europe, and the institutions and traditions which we find prevailing in later times had their origin.

The Goths themselves, later on, came so into the circle of Roman history that the substance of their traditions has been preserved in very old forms. Bishop Cassiodorus, the minister of the Gothic king Theodoric, learnt from the king, and embodied in a book, the genealogy of Theodoric. Counting back along the list, we find that he had an ancestor, Irminric, who must have been born approximately in the year A.D. 304, and who would thus be perhaps twenty-eight in the year in which the city of Cherson made its campaign against the Goths.

Evidence of Theodoric

Irminric, whose existence is thus attested, was an extraordinarily famous figure in northern tradition. Theodoric knew stories of him which have now perished. He stamped his name deeply and ineffaceably upon the memory of succeeding ages. He was the Old Man, the patriarch, from whom all things came, and whose prestige overshadowed everything. Although Theodoric knew the names of men alleged to be Irminric's ancestors, he evidently knew nothing of them except their names, which culminate in the first name, Gapt. This name, Gapt, has a strong resemblance to the name Gaut, which was the name of a god to later ages. Theodoric's ancestors, according to his own version, came from Scandinavia.

From this account, which comes from a man as reliable and as worthy of credence as King Alfred himself, we see that Irminric was the first king of the Goths distinctly known to the Goths themselves, and that he was in some sense absolutely the first Gothic king; that he had a divine ancestry, descending from a god, and that his ancestors were thought to come from Scandinavia.

Evidence of Ammianus Marcellinus

But our knowledge of Irminric does not depend upon Theodoric or upon Cassiodorus. An earlier writer, Ammianus Marcellinus, who lived and wrote within a couple of generations of Constantine, knew the story of Irminric. The famous old Gothic king, according to Ammianus, died in the year A.D. 375. He had founded an immense Gothic realm in the valley of the Vistula, including many peoples of whose existence we have no other record. For long he was the greatest power north of the Danube. After living to be very old, he killed himself to avoid seeing his kingdom fall into the hands of the Huns.[1]

We know, therefore, these further facts concerning Irminric, that he reigned for many years, and died in the year 375; that he was very old when he died, and that in his heyday he conquered and ruled the whole of the great land which extends from the Black Sea to Pomerania, together with a good deal of the land north of the Danube. Precisely where his frontiers lay is not now ascertainable; but it is fairly sure that at any rate they bordered on the Black Sea, the Danube and the Baltic.[2] He was the first Gothic king to hold this do-

Extent of the Gothic empire

---

[1] Amm. Marc., XXXI, 3, (2). From the way in which the record is phrased it seems just possible that Irminric was a priest of Othin, who was a god of the other world—and that he "cut the runes upon his breast and bled away to Othin" as a voluntary self-dedication. All this would be quite in keeping with very ancient and dignified traditions.

[2] There is a well-known introductory passage to Snorri's *Heimskringla* in which the migration of Othin from the Black Sea to the North is described. This passage probably describes a historical fact of some kind; but what fact? Prof. Chadwick (*Cult of Othin*, pp. 56-7) puts the introduction of Othin into Sweden

minion in his own hand. If, in the year 332, an attack on the Goths by Cherson could affect the situation on the Danube, it is fairly sure that at the age of twenty-eight Irminric was already over-king of the Goths. If he died in A.D. 375, as Ammianus tells us, he would then be seventy-one years old—by no means an incredible or excessive age. There is nothing unlikely in the story.

What was the cause, then, of the fame and greatness of Irminric? And what was his relation to Constantine?

IV

The answer is, that Irminric was the first political king of northern Europe; the first man who ruled by political, and not by gentile means. He was the man who began the overthrow of the tribal system which hitherto had been the prevailing system in northern Europe. What the Cheruscan Irmin and the Suavian Marbod had attempted, the Gothic Irminric did. And he succeeded because he copied, not the Augustan principate on which Irmin and Marbod had modelled their attempts, but the monarchy of Constantine.

Nature of Irminric's power

In this sense, he was the first king of the Goths. Indeed, he was the first European king—the first who was not an elected tribal war chief, such as the old Saxons

between the limits A.D. 50 and A.D. 500. In Angeln we may safely cut this date down to A.D. 350, the proximate date of the English King Wihtlæg. Irminric's suicide suggests that he was a priest of Othin—i.e., *was* "Othin." Snorri's passage may therefore be a description of the spread of Irminric's realm to the Baltic: successors of his may have brought the cult into Sweden. Whether this be so or not, Snorri in any case recognizes some drift north-west from the Euxine, connected with Othin-worship, which we know to have been connected in turn with the new kingship. There are traces of political change in Sweden round about this date.

continued to possess until the days of Charlemagne, but was the chief of a political organization, a "comitatus," [1] or military guild, through which he fought and conquered and administered the territory under his government. He was not an elected magistrate, watched and controlled by tribal elders, to whom in peacetime he surrendered back his authority. He was a sovereign ruler, as Constantine was sovereign. On this point the traditions concerning Irminric are very decided. Nothing impressed the north more than this sovereign power, this imperial authority of Irminric—his apparently irresponsible power of saying "Do this!" and of seeing that he was obeyed. . . . Irminric was not quite so irresponsible as men fancied. He had to carry the public opinion of his *comites* with him in all that he did. But to be free from the tribal elders, and to ride rough-shod over the tribal medicine-lodge seemed to the ancient north as good as absolute power. No man before him had ever possessed it. Irminric was a man of his age. The swords which slew the Cheruscan Irmin, and drove Marbod into exile, were impotent against Irminric. He battered down the fierce with a ferocity greater than their own. He knew how to handle his subjects. Long

His
prestige

[1] The idea that the "comitatus" was a primitive Teutonic institution rests upon the testimony of Tacitus in his *Germania*. But Tacitus, who gives us the earliest connected account of Teutonic institutions, wrote under the emperor Trajan, about A.D. 98 or 99. When he wrote, the Germans had been in close—sometimes uncomfortably close—contact with the imperial system for something like 110 years, a period not much shorter than that which divides a man of the present day from Napoleon. The comitatus which he describes as a German institution was simply the copy of the Roman imperial military guild which had been begun by Irmin and Marbod, but had fallen into partial decay after their deaths, though it never entirely died out. Cæsar had not heard of any comitatus. His description in *B.G.*, VI, 21, refers to a tribal war band, similar to those which exist in all tribal communities. See the present author's *Tiberius Cæsar*, pp. 187-191.

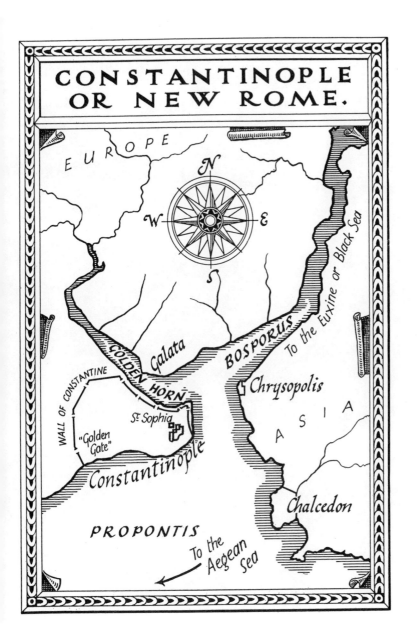

CONSTANTINOPLE OR NEW ROME.

after his death, they spoke of him with bated breath and whispering humbleness. He was the first, the fountainhead, the patriarch—the prototype of all later European royalty.

V

By no possibility could a monarchy formed by delegated authority have risen upon the basis of the tribal system: nor did any man anywhere ever achieve it. The existence of Irminric's monarchy became possible when the Illyrian emperors, from Aurelian to Constantine, began to see the need of finding a basis for sovereignty apart from the mere choice of an army. The north was not sunk in sleep while Constantine was working out the steps towards a primary monarchy, hereditary and sacred, so set apart as a caste that no military cabal could tamper with the succession. Keen and interested men were watching. . . . The stroke of genius which created the kingdom of Irminric was his perception that he himself possessed ready-made all the elements of monarchy which Constantine and his predecessors had assembled.

Relation of Irminric to Constantine

How did this come about?

The ordinary modern man lives so remote from tribalism that he is liable to have only very vague notions of it as a working mechanism. Most men picture the ancient peoples of the north as nations in the modern sense, composed of individuals of varying status. But far from this being the case, they were composed of kindreds, clans, and families of varying status. The variation was sometimes remarkable. When we hear of the Sarmatian slaves revolting, we presently find that instead of these slaves being individuals scattered through the Sarmatian nation, they were a tribe, with a name and tribal organization—the "Limigantes." The tribal system is in fact a caste system, in which the castes are created by blood-relationship and hereditary descent. These tribal castes frequently had laws and tabus peculiar to themselves. Some ruling Saxon castes never married into other unauthorized castes. Certain castes we know to have been sacred. They descended from gods; their heads were priests. . . . Of these, one was the caste to which Irminric belonged. He traced his ancestry remotely to a person named Gapt, who may have been a god; but immediately to a person named Amal, who was without doubt a sacred person, and divine. The Amalung were a sacred tribal caste, and Irminric was a member of it—possibly its head. It was not the only one. The present king of Spain is descended from the Baltung, of whom Alaric was the most famous member.

Gothic sacred castes

On these qualifications, which man had not given him, and man could not take away, Irminric founded the northern political kingship. The head of the sacred Amalung, fenced with their immemorial privileges, formed round himself, soon after the year 322, a political organism founded upon the model of Constantine's "comitatus"—his consistorium, and his comites.

It was probably not a slavish copy. Irminric adapted the Roman pattern to the circumstances and needs of the north European peoples, and he adapted it so skilfully that it took root and grew as if it were a spontaneous product. The north European kingship constantly tended to vest itself in the whole of the members of the caste, and to become a committee or board of kings like Diocletian's, rather than a true monarchy. A hard struggle was needed before the Roman rules of primogeniture and monarchy finally prevailed. . . . But it retained throughout, and it retains to this day, the two peculiar notes of Constantine's monarchy—the hereditary caste working through a political organization.

VI

In spite of the defeat of the Gothic invaders under King Araric, Constantine made no attempt to carry reprisals north of the Danube. No doubt he had his reasons. He rested content with the expulsion of the Goths. Neither was any serious campaign ever again conducted north of the Danube by Roman armies. The campaign of Constantine in the year A.D. 322 was the last of its kind.

No reprisals against the Goths

The imperial government did not even attempt to defend its allies. When, two years after the defeat of Araric, King Geberic arrived to conduct punitive measures against the Sarmatians, no move to assist them was made. In a pitched battle, the Sarmatians were defeated and their king slain.[1] Driven to their last extremity, the Sarmatians resorted to the expedient of arming a subject tribe, the "Limigantes," which worked for them as cattlemen and shepherds. So reinforced, they fought a successful battle with the Goths. The Limigantes, however, once armed and independent, were not likely to surrender very readily the liberty they

---

[1] The Sarmatian kings were members of a Vandal tribal caste. Apparently they were tribal kings—i.e., they had no comitatus independent of tribal institutions.

had acquired. They claimed an equality with the Sarmatians which threatened to pass into mastery. The old Sarmatian power dissolved in the face of these disasters. Some tribes went over to the Goths; others joined the Quadi beyond the Carpathians. The larger part applied to Constantine for an allotment of land within the empire.

The Sarmatians broken up

In the condition of labour shortage which prevailed throughout the middle and western provinces, this application was immediately welcomed. Land was found for many thousand Sarmatian families in Pannonia, Thrace and Italy. The upshot of four years of war was, therefore, that a Gothic invasion had been repelled; but that the Goths had successfully broken the Sarmatians, and driven the larger part of them over the Danube into Roman territory. . . . In the course of this narrative we have seen sufficient of the military capacities of Constantine to realize that such a result was scarcely due to any inefficiency in his military methods. The simple truth was that the Goths were for the first time demonstrating what would happen when the tribal divisions of the northern peoples were superseded by political unity and central direction. . . . Three centuries earlier, the emperor Tiberius had expressed his views concerning the possible dangers to Rome of Marbod's Suavian realm. . . . These dangers were now at last realized in the kingdom of Irminric.

VII

Had Constantine been a younger man, it is possible that he might have taken a sharper and more personal interest in the new Gothic kingdom. It is possible that a touch of lethargy and indifference was eclipsing his sun. All his great deeds were done before the death of Crispus and Fausta. From that time onwards he was an old man, still able to take active interest in his new city and its first wars—but no longer the man he once had been. Lethargy of Constantine

He never visited their mother's delinquencies upon Fausta's children. As far as we can see, the episode of Fausta was utterly blotted out. Nothing was ever said or written on the subject during the life of Constantine and his sons; hardly anything was as much as thought. He continued their education on the lines he had originally projected. None of them was brilliant; and although all of them were competent men, not one had any touch of endearing quality or inspiring character.

Nevertheless, it was now afternoon. Something of his inspiration had worn off. He was perhaps conscious of it. Most of his work had been done, and he was merely marking time until the day came when he should make room for his successors. The results of the Council of Nicæa had not been all that he might have wished. The propaganda of the Arian party steadily continued. One great victory fell to them when they secured the deposition of Eustathius, the catholic bishop of Antioch, on charges which included scandalous conduct. The catholics contended that the real cause of Eustathius' deposition was that he had not been sufficiently polite to the emperor's mother. . . . Constantine had to investigate these charges and counter-charges. He did so without enthusiasm and without his former intui- The Arian question

tion. He heard the appeal of Eustathius in person, but did not take any steps to restore him to Antioch.

The next quarry of the Arians, and the next person to cross Constantine's path, was someone much more important than Eustathius—namely, Athanasius, the new bishop of Alexandria. The story begins with the emperor's half-sister, Constantia, the widow of Licinius, who had a favourite priest, a friend and supporter of Arius. During her last illness, Constantine frequently came to see her, and met this priest. She had never during her lifetime dared to attempt to sway her brother's views; but on her deathbed, having nothing more to fear, she ventured to commend the Arian priest. Constantine listened to his representations. With surprise, the emperor heard that Arius was a hardly treated man, who was unjustly excluded from a Church to whose doctrine he fully subscribed. Constantine was induced to send Arius an order to appear before him. When he came, he wrote out, at Constantine's order, the creed to which he subscribed.

Athanasius Constantine was no philosopher. The creed which Arius wrote out seemed, to the emperor, correct enough; and he accordingly recommended Arius to show it to bishop Athanasius at Alexandria. Athanasius at once saw that howsoever correct, as far as it went, it omitted the essential points on which Arius had been called in question, and he refused to re-admit him. The war was then on foot. By the advice of his friends, Arius appealed to Constantine, who sent Athanasius a request that he should receive Arius. This Athanasius positively declined to do.

The subsequent proceedings were of the highest and

most peculiar interest. As examples of a certain sort of controversial method they take high rank. What the Arians wanted was not to disprove the doctrinal position of Athanasius, but to get him out of Alexandria. In fact, the doctrinal question dwindled to comparatively small proportions, while the personal struggle expanded until it was all embracing. For this result, Constantine's policy of pacification and reconciliation was directly responsible. It was not worth the while of the Arians to prove Athanasius doctrinally unsound; for Constantine would merely try to find a ground of compromise, and would compel the disputants to compose their differences. The Arians did not want the existing position perpetuated. They wished to upset the settlement of Nicæa; and the quickest way by which to do so was to concentrate upon the overthrow of the Nicene leaders, and the destruction of their power. . . . The charges against Athanasius were thus not doctrinal but criminal. . . . He was accused of breaches not of the ecclesiastical but of the secular law.

The Arian method

VIII

Constantine was not prepared for this line of attack, and he was puzzled. He summoned Athanasius to Nicomedia, examined the evidence, and dismissed the charges as imaginary. The matter, however, was not at an end. A fresh set of charges was raised—by subornation of perjury, the Nicene supporters declared. One of the strangest was the production of a human hand, which the Arians asserted to be the hand of a priest named Arsenius. This hand Athanasius was charged with having cut off, and with using as a "Hand of Glory" for magical purposes.

The awkward side of an accusation of this kind is the difficulty of rebutting it. Athanasius could do very little except resort to the bloodless and unconvincing expedient of merely denying the charges. No one, of course, would be in the slightest degree influenced by so anæmic a defence. When Constantine ordered a synod to meet at Cæsarea, in the same year in which the Sarmatian settlements were made, Athanasius was far too wise to put in an appearance. He left the synod to kick its heels while he was devoting his energies to more profitable work.

Difficulties of Athanasius

Freed from the Gothic war, Constantine was able to attend more closely to the Athanasian question. Next year, accordingly, he came to grips. A synod was summoned to meet at Tyre. Thinking that they had now safely got Athanasius on toast, the Arian party persuaded Constantine to insist upon the bishop's presence. Athanasius, warned that if he declined to appear before the synod he would be fetched by military force, reluctantly journeyed to Tyre. In spite of all his efforts, he had not been able to lay hands on the priest Arsenius. The latter had, by frequent changes of hiding place, successfully dodged all the bishop's observers. Athanasius went to Tyre without the only witness who could effectually clear him.

At Tyre, however, a glorious surprise awaited him. Arsenius, unable to keep down his curiosity, and not being supplied in his hiding place with newspapers, could not resist the temptation of going to Tyre himself. Archelaus, a senator, and a supporter of Athanasius, was informed by his servants that while turning in to some drinking bar in the town, they had heard a report that Arsenius was in Tyre, and hiding in a certain house. This was news indeed! The gratified senator jumped at the chance, and instantly proceeded, with a few of his private punchers, to the place indicated. Haled from his hiding place, Arsenius protested to incredulous ears that he was not the man. He was produced before Paulinus, the bishop of Tyre, who identified him from old knowledge as certainly the missing Arsenius. Word was sent to Athanasius that all was well. *Capture of Arsenius*

The next step was to arrange that the Arians should fall into the pit they had dug. On being summoned before the synod, Athanasius defended himself with studied discretion. In response to his enquiry whether the members of the synod really knew anything about the alleged person Arsenius, a number of bishops signified that they were acquainted with the man, and were capable of identifying him. The next step was sensational. To the horror of the Arian party, Athanasius produced Arsenius before them, his hands hidden under his cloak. The now alert synod identified Arsenius beyond question. Attention was concentrated upon his hands. Had he lost a hand? Athanasius turned up one sleeve, and revealed an undoubted hand. This one was evidently certain. After a calculated pause, to let the situation have its due dramatic effect, Athanasius turned up the other sleeve. There Arsenius was revealed, with two unmistakable and verifiable hands! . . . The synod did not need the ironical enquiry of Athanasius, whether the Arians would kindly produce the third arm of Arsenius.

The chief witness for the prosecution hastily left the council chamber and disappeared into the crowd.

It would have been fortunate for Athanasius if all the charges against him could have been dealt with in this way. As this first one had broken down, the synod resolved to appoint a committee to investigate the others. This committee, however, the Arians succeeded in packing: and Athanasius, after protesting against the proceedings, left for Constantinople to appeal to the emperor in person. In his absence he was condemned unheard, and deposed from his bishopric. Among the bishops who signed the deposition was one whom Athanasius had been condemned by the synod for having murdered.

Athanasius appeals to Constantinople

IX

At the request of Constantine (who had not yet received any report of the proceedings of the synod) the bishops then adjourned to Jerusalem, where they were welcomed and entertained by his deputy Marianus. The gathering was a considerable one: a Persian bishop was the lion of the occasion. The object was the consecration of the great Church of the Martyrs which Constantine had built on the sacred site, and had decorated with unusual richness. It was the opening ceremony of Constantine's Tricennalia, the thirtieth year of his reign. No emperor since the great Augustus had reigned thirty years, and this was a historic occasion.

The synod at Jerusalem, A.D. 336

At Jerusalem, Arius was received back into the fold, together with his friends who had been involved with him. The assembled bishops certified that Arius repented of his heresy, and had acknowledged the truth.

. . . It was a very great and imposing festival. Those who took part in it realized that Constantine wished his thirtieth year to be marked by peace and concord; and they did their best. Eusebius of Cæsarea delivered a series of wonderful orations which were much admired. All was as merry as a wedding-bell. Athanasius was forgotten: until the time came when the post was due from Constantinople, whither the deposed bishop had retreated.

X

The modern reader will not, perhaps, be surprised to hear that at this point the cheerful party received a somewhat unkind letter from the emperor, who referred to its proceedings at Tyre in a way which must have hurt the feelings of the more sensitive bishops. He expressed the hope that all this squabbling—he employed a harsh word to describe it—might soon cease. . . . They thought, no doubt, that he was somewhat receding from the beautiful spirit he had once shown. . . . He went on to explain why he wrote.

Letter of Constantine

While driving in his carriage through the streets of Constantinople, he had been suddenly confronted and stopped by a group of foot-passengers who professed to be the bishop of Alexandria and his chaplains. He was not personally acquainted with the right reverend man, and would have had difficulty in identifying him had it not been for some of his suite, who both answered for the bishop and explained the circumstances. Constantine flatly refused to hear anything or discuss anything, and (as he told the synod) came very near to ordering Athanasius to be ejected from the imperial presence.

The man wanted nothing less than the removal of the synod to Constantinople, where the emperor could supervise its proceedings; and as far as he, Constantine, could make out, the request was a highly reasonable one, considering how the synod had gone on. He therefore called the synod to Constantinople.

He wound up his letter by remarking that he had by his own efforts converted to religion some of the heathen barbarians, who were now as a consequence living godly, righteous, and sober lives, and agreeing in the truth of God's holy word, while the bishops who professed to be the principal substance of the Church and the guardians of its spiritual life, could do nothing better with their time than squabble and fight, and promote the destruction of mankind. He would like them to remember that the first duty of everyone was to maintain the faith as contained in the scriptures, and to get rid of the people who crept into the Church under false pretenses, and did not believe her doctrine.

The synod disperses

It is hardly to be wondered at that, after the receipt of this devastating letter, only six bishops ventured to present themselves at Constantinople—and they were mostly men whose sees lay in the neighbourhood. The majority of the bishops dispersed from Jerusalem with promptitude and rapidity, and did not stop until they were home again.

Among those who went to Constantinople was, however, Bishop Eusebius of Cæsarea, carrying with him his successful sermon already delivered at Jerusalem.

XI

Constantine was in no temper for any further long and intricate discussions. As a soldier, he had less natural taste for words than the bishops had. The six bishops—most of them Arians and all of them acquainted with Constantine's character—appreciated this beforehand. When they arrived, they had forgotten all the charges on which Athanasius had been condemned at Tyre, and had thought of a bright new accusation—namely, that Athanasius had threatened to prevent the despatch of corn from Alexandria to Constantinople. . . . The emperor regarded them with a calm despair.

Problem of
Athanasius

There was just one last possibility. It was just possible that some of the trouble was due to Athanasius himself. When he had left Tyre, all the rest of the bishops had been a united family party. Conceivably, if he could be kept in retirement for a space, the harmony might continue, as Constantine wished it to do. Every man of the world knows that there are cases when trouble arises, not from difference of views or beliefs, but simply from difference of temper. It was remotely possible that the present instance was such a case. . . . Constantine cut short all discussion. He did not want any arguments. He banished Athanasius into Gaul until further notice. . . . The bishop settled at Treves—which, it is to be hoped, still celebrates the memory of its august visitor.

The deposition of Athanasius was suspended. No successor was appointed to the bishopric. Quite evidently Constantine contemplated his return, in quieter times, when they could all settle down peaceably again and forget their quarrels.

He was not altogether misled in this policy: and it certainly neutralized with extraordinary neatness the aims of the Arian party. Their efforts to get Athanasius out of Alexandria were likely to have very little result if his place were not to be filled, and if he himself were liable at any moment to return. All their work of intrigue had gone practically for nothing.

The Arians disappointed

But Constantine was quite intelligent enough to perceive that the policy of the Arians was not to discuss doctrine, but to discredit persons. He had set his face firmly for peace and concord. These things might be obtained by discussion; but they never could be obtained by a system of victimization. The last important ecclesiastical measure of his reign showed how little he had achieved in the way of reconciling the differences that distracted the Church. . . . Unity, agreement, common effort, common aims—these he had believed in, and sought to attain. . . . And where were they?

XII

Where, indeed? . . . Alexandria was never a very meek or peaceable place. When Arius returned to it, the city proceeded with enthusiasm to hurl itself into the fray. The emperor summoned him back to Constantinople.

Constantine and Arius

It was pointed out, in the emperor's presence, that the form of belief which Arius had signed and Athanasius had refused to regard as adequate, was gravely deficient. Did Arius accept the Canons of Nicæa? Arius declared that he did, and affixed his signature to the declaration. He was then called upon to swear to his belief, and he unhesitatingly did so. . . . The Nicæan party could not bring themselves to believe him. They felt sure that he did it with mental reservations and juggleries. The popular belief was that he carried his real and heretical creed written on a sheet of paper under his arm-pit, and swore then that he believed "what he had written," meaning this secret sheet. . . . Men are in a serious state when they can no longer believe one another's pledged words. Constantine took the bold course and the manly one. Right or wrong, he accepted the subscription and oath of Arius. He directed the bishop of Constantinople to receive Arius into communion.

The bishop—a convinced Nicæan—was in no happy state of mind. He did not know what to think, nor where the truth lay. Locking himself into the church, he spent the hours in earnest prayer; the zealous faithful (who no doubt took a sympathetic interest through the keyhole in his troubles) reported that he knelt on his bare knees, fasting and praying to be guided rightly in what he should do. To these prayers, the subsequent event was ascribed.

Arius came in grand procession to be received into communion. The minions of his protector, the bishop of Nicomedia, marched on every side of him, to guard him from possible assault. When they came to the Forum of Constantine, Arius did not feel very well. A pause was made. In a few minutes he collapsed and died.

Death of Arius

Such was the death of Arius: [1] the end, not of the great drama, but of the first act. . . . It was an event which shocked, horrified and convulsed not only Constantinople but the world. The supporters of Nicæa pointed to it as a beneficial miracle. Constantine himself is reported to have looked upon the event as a significant proof of the Nicæan doctrine. For long afterwards the tradition was preserved of the exact spot in Constantinople where Arius died.

XIII

This is anticipating. Let us return to the exile of Athanasius. Arius was still in Alexandria when Constantine, free for the time from the worries of ecclesiastical storms, began the celebration of his Tricennalia.

It was July, the thirtieth July since that day in the city of York when the army accepted the son of Constantius as emperor. The feast was being kept in Constantinople, that new and wonderful city on the Bosphorus which the man from York had founded. A very different world now lay beneath the sun from the one which Constantine had set out to conquer. He was **The Tricennalia of Constantine, July, A.D. 336** sixty-two that year. He had seen the Cleveland Hills, the Yorkshire Moors, the Hill of Calvary and the Arabian desert; he had known Diocletian and Maximian,

[1] It has been suggested (e.g., by Gibbon, II, p. 357, note 83) that Arius was poisoned. There is no evidence that such was the case; and the way in which he died is probably paralleled. From the account of Socrates, *H.E.,* I, 38, it is obvious that Arius was being very carefully guarded, and if he had been poisoned it seems almost certain that the fact could have been demonstrated. One need not be hostile to the Arians to suggest that they would not have missed the opportunity of damaging their opponents by proving a fact so fatal. It is of course conceivable that he might have been poisoned by an agent of the court; but such suggestions are the purest speculation. All we know is that Arius died in the way described by Socrates, I, 38.

Galerius and Constantius; he had lived into the days of Athanasius and Arius. A great life and a wonderful one. The Lord had added power to him. He had never lost a battle on land or sea. He had been the death of three emperors, and life to thousands of common men. He had founded an immortal city, and was leaving an immortal name. . . . That year he celebrated with great magnificence the marriage of his second son, Constantius. He showed no sign of memory or of regret; but he was not a fool, and he cannot have been ignorant that to leave an empire to three sons conjointly is a counsel of despair. He must have known that his reign was after all unfinished, imperfect and unsatisfactory, because it would not be followed by any adequate successor. All he could rely upon was what he himself had done. His ultimate fame would rest upon that.

Eusebius of Cæsarea had brought with him to Constantinople the sermons he had preached at Jerusalem, where they had been highly admired. He was now requested to repeat, for Constantine's pleasure, the address on the emperor's thirtieth year.

The six bishops, the sole remaining members of the great gathering which met at Jerusalem, therefore assembled with due ceremony. Constantine and his household and friends who were celebrating the Tricennalia were present. And there Eusebius pronounced the judgment of the age he lived in on the life, the work, and the significance of Constantine the Great. . . . It may or may not be our judgment: but it was what men at the time believed and applauded. . . .

Eusebius and his sermon

Let us listen to Eusebius.

THE IMPERIAL CASTE, A.D. 337

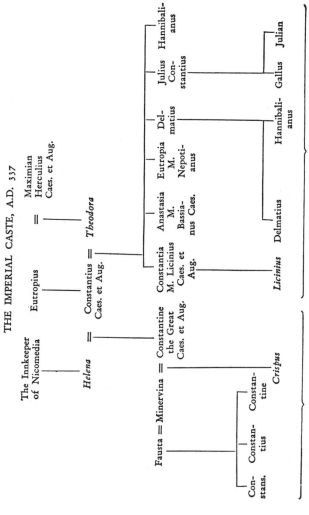

The descendants of Helena

The descendants of Theodora

CHAPTER XII

THE TESTAMENT OF CONSTANTINE

I

HAD Eusebius lived in modern times, he would have been a journalist. His famous Oration would have been issued as a special Tricennial Number of his newspaper; it would have been sold out soon after publication, and collectors would have competed for copies. He lived long before the invention of printing, but his speech occupies just such a place in the scheme of things as any similar attempt today to estimate, with sympathy and appreciation, the life's-work of a great contemporary. . . . His audience did not go to hear the opinion of modern times upon Constantine. They went to hear one of themselves sum up a career and a man with whom they all agreed; they were there to hear the explanation which, when their time came, they could themselves offer in their own justification to God.

Rank of Eusebius' sermon

What Eusebius had to declare and to illustrate is thus not the invention of a modern writer striving to deduce from fragmentary information some coherent truth. . . . For once in a way the age comes forward and speaks for itself: speaks in full, unmistakably, with no uncertain note. More than one man in that audience must have hoped that the words of Eusebius would reach future generations, and convince them of the deserving and the repute of those to whom they were addressed. . . . This speech therefore is made to us as much as to

An age speaks for itself

those who heard it. It is the message of another age to us—not to instruct us about our own age, but about theirs.

The doctrines, the hopes, the enthusiasms of Eusebius, moreover, are here countersigned by Constantine, at whose command the speech was given. If we wish to know what Constantine himself hoped was true, and believed was true, about himself—here it is, approved by his own presence and his own authority. . . . Those who are willing to listen to the words of Eusebius are not merely listening to an elderly bishop—they are hearing the words of an age, the gospel of a revolution, the message of an empire, speaking direct across the centuries to this.

II

It is the custom to look upon the oratory of the late Roman period as empty and pretentious, a string of words with little substance behind it. Against Eusebius, at least, no such charge can be brought. His sermon is close packed with ideas, led with art and system to one dramatic conclusion. . . . The sermon does not, indeed, altogether correspond at all points with the notions of the early twentieth century. Eusebius and his audience had no notion of being hurried hastily through a string of broken-backed sentences, so that at the earliest moment they could hurry out to their cars and their golf clubs. Far from it. The bishop and his audience are there to enjoy themselves—and enjoy themselves they do. Out of the bishop's discourse swiftly arises a vast and iridescent sphere, a rainbow bubble of words, which expands and enlarges and becomes more glorious,

Opening

while within it grows picture after picture, visual image, thought-image, one after another—all of them evoking in his hearers a certain orderly march of thought. . . . This is the real art of rhetoric, or Public Speech—shown by a man who truly loved the divine gift, and appreciated by hearers who shared his taste for this splendid tracery and gorgeous transparency of the windows of the mind. In the beginning was the Word—the activity of the Intelligence. They all had one ground at any rate in common—they all loved the art of rational intercommunication which for us is the first and chief expression of that Word.

Eusebius begins by remarking that they are assembled to celebrate the praises of a mighty emperor; and after his first few audacious phrases have made his hearers gasp, suddenly it turns out that he is referring to the Heavenly Emperor, the Father and Creator of all, "whom cœlestiall Armies doe encompasse, whom powers and Angels doe environ. . . . And here the Sun, the Moon, and other cœlestiall Luminaries are rowled and carried about, which shining in the entrance of his Palace, doe honour the Creator of the Universe, and by his command doe enlighten the dark places of the earth with daily light." [1] He then depicts the way in which the universe honours its ruler and emperor, namely, by the marvellous pageant of its obedience to his law, in which obedience resides their own glory. With a succession of phrases he depicts this glory. Modelled upon this, and taking it as a pattern, is an earthly empire, a Roman empire; and by the authority and institution of the Word, an emperor is appointed to rule it—Constan-

Obedience to Law

[1] So Wye Saltonstall translates (temp. Oliver Cromwell).

tine. As the Lord of Heaven guides men to their immortal welfare, so the lord of earth guides men to their secular prosperity. Constantine, leading to God this empire, as a bloodless sacrifice, was honoured with power, and fortune and prosperity, and with sons who, one by one, were coming forward to take up their place as his successors in the monarchy. So Eusebius said.

III

The magical word—monarchy—being spoken, Eusebius proceeds to decorate this theme. His argument deserves our particular attention; for the speaker is the adviser, friend, and vigorous supporter of the man who revolutionized the Roman monarchy, and turned the principate of Augustus into a new institution full of portent for the future. What Bishop Asser was to Alfred the Great, what Suger was to King Louis and Eginhard to the emperor Charles, so Eusebius was to Constantine. Short of the views of Constantine himself, we can get no nearer an official pronouncement than these words of Eusebius.

His opening is unexpected. Law, he says, is the king of all, and the supremacy of law proves monarchy to be the best kind of government. In an aristocracy there is insufficient authority; in democracy, no authority at all by which to implement law and so give men power to control the social environment in which they live. Now, the unity of God is essential to our conception of God. A plurality of Gods is a contradiction in terms. Hence there is one universal Heavenly King and Emperor, and one authority, which appertains to him—not

Necessity of unity

a dead law of the letter, written in books or engraved and set up on tablets, but a living law, a perpetual active exercise of living judgment. This authority, or Word of God, is the rational spirit by which we gain "the notions of reason and wisdom; the seeds of prudence and justice, the principles of arts, the knowledge of vertue, and the acceptable and pleasant name of wisdom: the reverend love of philosophy, the vision of God himself and piety and godliness of life, also all knowledge of goodness and honesty, and the establishment of humane kingdoms and empires." It is this which made man alone of all creatures fit to command and to obey. Our hope of a heavenly kingdom to come causes us to construct on this earth an earthly kingdom to begin with. Constantine's title to rule is rooted in his obedience to the divine authority. A man who does not obey the law of God in all its particulars has no title to government. That man alone is an earthly monarch whose soul is a mirror in which God can see his own face. Only that man is an emperor who realizes that what we all are, we are by the grace of God alone. Nothing has any virtue in itself; for as far as things-in-themselves are concerned, an emperor is only a magnified swine-herd or cattle-driver. The latter professions have, indeed, the advantage of being softer jobs. . . . Fame and wealth are illusions. Ultimately there is nothing in them. The pursuit of pleasure is the pursuit of death. Constantine was wiser. He sought the Kingdom of God, and carried his subjects with him. And the Lord, as usual, delivered the goods. We celebrate the thirtieth year of our emperor's reign; and no doubt the saints in heaven as well

Title to authority

as all good men on earth are rejoicing with us. . . .
So Eusebius.

IV

Then Eusebius draws a breath, and proceeds. The
Kingdom of God is eternal. He does not express it so
baldly as this; he blows his iridescent bubble of words,
and it expands, to the wonder of all beholders; and
within it we see the gorgeous and richly coloured picture
of the everlasting creation of God, infinite and boundless, with its tiny unseizable pomegranate-seed of a *Now*

**The
infinite
cosmos**

slithering about over its immensity. We could do nothing with it but for the divine idea of number and di-
mension, by which we divide it into finities which our
minds can deal with. Eusebius points out the lyric nature of numbers, that exquisite poetry of God, how by
its means the infinite is made into the clothed and smiling
world we know, with its turn of the seasons and its procession of the years, its white day, and black night "clad
with a starre-embroidered mantle. He stretched forth
the heavens like a curtain over the earth, and as a picture
drew on it the Sun, the Moon and the Stars." And in
the midst of the world is Man, the favourite of God, en-
dowed with mastery over all natural things. And the
governor of all this is the Word, the divine reason.[1]

Eye hath not seen, nor ear heard, neither can imagination conceive, the splendour of the rewards which are
the enjoyment of the good. This good is obedience to
the Word: of which a great and shining example is Con-

---

[1] Here comes a passage with which the modern reader need not be troubled,
in which Eusebius demonstrates the wondrous perfections of the number thirty,
the years of Constantine's reign. This little bit of rhetorical virtuosity probably delighted his audience. So much do fashions change!

stantine, to whom power was given to lead the whole world to obedience, and to root out error and falsehood. To him also was revealed the banner of the Cross, by which the Word overcame death and triumphed over his foes—and under this banner he too triumphed not only over earthly foes but over the devil himself. Man is double—a body and a soul. Fleshly weakness wars against his body; spiritual evil against his soul. This spiritual evil is represented by polytheism, or a belief in plurality of powers and causes. The understanding of man was gradually disrupted and destroyed by the increase of pluralism. At last with a suicidal mania men turned upon those who still preserved the correct and salving belief in unity, and sought to stamp out them and their ideas. But here God himself intervened. Those who were slain he took to himself in heaven. Against his foes he sent his armed champion Constantine.

The enemies of man

It was the pleasure of their emperor to be a servant of God. Evil men had sought to stamp out good ones. Constantine, in the spirit of his Master, had not sought to stamp out evil men, but rather to lead them to the truth. Two kinds of barbarism he had fought against— not only the old familiar kind, the wildness and crudeness of primitive people, but the devilish barbarism, the power of darkness working in the mind. He had thought it his duty to suppress idolatry: and he had taken every care that all dangerous worships should be suppressed.

V

What were these dangerous worships? Eusebius of Cæsarea lived a great deal nearer to them than the modern sentimental neo-Pagan, and his descriptions are not all of them suitable reading for a Sunday School class. He specifies the temple of Venus on Mount Lebanon as a hotbed of wickedness. This was suppressed by Constantine, and a loathesome source of moral infection removed. Not only so, but the suppression of these cults made for general peace and social order. What good had they ever been? Men from of old had filled their cities with splendid temples and had worshipped with zeal: and what had they obtained? Nothing but wars and dissensions. What was the good of a Delphic Oracle that could not foretell the date on which it was going to be suppressed for ever? Which of them foresaw the triumph of Christ and Constantine? And where (thunders Eusebius) are the men who defended them? Perished! "Where are now those Gyants that warred against God?" Over them towers the triumphant Cross, that sign in which Constantine truly had conquered.

If Constantine had cast down, he had also built. Eusebius enumerates the magnificent churches of Constantinople, those at Nicomedia, the metropolitan church at Antioch, and the Church of the Passion at Jerusalem, as well as three which marked the birthplace, the deathplace and the Assumption of Christ. These he built to the honour of that faith which had made him so mighty and bestowed upon him such strength. . . . And with a magnificent pageant of words, amid which Cœlestiall Quires sing and companies of Blessed Angels

Where are those gyants?

do laud, Eusebius brings the first part of his sermon to
its conclusion.

VI

Only the first part. He has still something to say.
He begins afresh with God the divine emperor. And
now his remarks are directed, not to his audience, but
over sixteen centuries to *us*. He has anticipated us
and our criticisms, and he replies to us in advance.

Some of us (he correctly observes) will think it un- *This
means
you* fitting that the head of a world-state should concern
himself with these memorials to which he has been referring. And others of us will say, would it not have
been better for him to preserve the old institutions of
his country, and to retain the worships which his age
shared with the whole world in common? For one argument applies alike to all. What proves the divinity of
Christ, proves the divinity of other gods; and what disproves theirs, disproves also his. . . . Well (says Eusebius, politely) no doubt our most august emperor derived his views and opinions from the direct inspiration
of God, and was guided by Divine Grace in all that he
did. It should be the bishop's humbler task to demonstrate their nature, and to interpret them to the
ignorant.

Some people are like men who, shown over a beautiful new building, admire the roof, the walls, and the
workmanship, but never think of admiring the archi-
tect. And the true founder of a state is not the man
who raised the buildings, but the man who created the
organization. It is the mentality that made the thing

which is important. What, then, of the mind behind the universe?

Eusebius discusses this—not in a perfectly modern manner, but then it is he who is doing the talking, and he was not a perfectly modern man. It is this mind, the **The divine reason** Logos, Word, or Divine Reason, which is the connecting link uniting God and Man; and if we doubt its existence —why, there is as much evidence for that as there is for the existence of a soul or personality in man: no more and no less. And it is in this Word that all things are related: which is the same thing as to say that by it they are created: it is the sole author of all things. Hence a belief in the plurality of causes is one of the earliest forms of ignorance and error. . . . He analyzes the process by which the pagan "gods" came into existence: some were the food and drink of man (such as Ceres and Bacchus) some were the faculties of the intelligence (such as the Muses) some were personified passions; some were deified men; the whole method was one of attributing causality or creative power to an intermediate process. Eusebius, having finished one catalogue, begins another. He, living so near pagan days, strings together a list of the known customs of human sacrifice. Not only bloodshed but vice and cannibalism were employed as forms of worship. Plurality of causes had its natural consequence in plurality of opinions, and human disunity. Because of the desperate state of humanity, the Word became a man in the person of Jesus Christ, in order to work direct upon men. He gave them methods and instructions by which to attain the right life: and in order to convince them of His power and reality, He performed the supreme miracle of rising from the dead. The knowledge that death was overcome enabled the Christian martyrs to face their fate and to move public opinion into sympathy. Finally, His death was an atoning sacrifice which overthrew the power of the devil, and broke the spell of his dominion. **Reason is Order**

This institution of a faith centred in the one genuine cause or creative power gave humanity for the first time a solid ground common to all. Rivalry, hatred, and internecine strife began to die out; and this growing unity among men was reflected in the establishment of the Roman empire.

Eusebius ends with an appeal to us to judge Christianity by its effects. We cannot visibly or tangibly, by means of the senses, perceive the intellectual part of man, nor can we perceive the theoretical principles of science. The power and the divinity of God are equally incapable of being presented to us in a glass case. In all these instances we judge of the reality of the power by the effects it produces.

The peroration of Eusebius sinks swiftly to its close. He draws a vivid picture of the practical effects of Christianity upon human character; its triumph over savage enemies; the victory, above all, of the personality of Jesus Christ, dissolving hatred, reconciling opposition, convincing belief; and he solemnly calls Constantine to bear witness, from the events of his life, as they are known to him alone, to the power and readiness of God to help those who seek His Kingdom.

VII

Such are the prophetic words which men can speak, hardly knowing what they say. . . . The curtain falls. The golden dream of ideas and principles dissolves, and we see once more a little grey-haired bishop pottering off the platform, carrying his notes in his hand. A few polite persons advance with bows to conduct him, not to the young man who rode from Nicomedia to Boulogne, but to a grey-haired emperor who rises to his feet to [1] salute the man of thought and spiritual discernment. . . . If the speech of Eusebius has come down to us, it is because the men who heard him bought copies, and some of these copies survived.

Constantine invited the six bishops to dine with him, and the six ate the banquet which, had not their consciences made cowards of them all, might have been shared by all the bishops who gathered at Tyre and Jerusalem. It was a truly imperial feast. . . . Eusebius does not tell us more; but perhaps his phrases are enough to convey to us the picture of six bishops, happily lost among gold plate and jewelled cups, while magnificent presences bear hither the flagon, and an imperial hand graciously directs the pouring of the chosen vintage. . . . It was, we may suppose, late that night when the six sought their several couches; and we do not know their dreams.

---

[1] In the case of another sermon of Eusebius, however, Constantine insisted on standing with everyone else as the custom was. At last the bishop showed signs of hurrying his sermon on this account; whereupon Constantine stopped him and told him to take his time. Being again requested to seat himself, he grew a little annoyed, and flatly refused. The military man certainly peeps out in his sharp rejoinder that he did not approve of slackness or negligence. (Euseb., *Vita C.*, IV, 33.)

It hardly matters. Athanasius, far away in Treves, They live spare who certainly had not supped off gold plate, was the man destined to mould the future. They live spare who walk with God.

VIII

Constantine only lived ten months after his Tricennalia. His work was done. As the days passed, he realized it more and more. Nothing really remained but to consider how he would leave this life. Eusebius tells us that the emperor had perfect health until his last days. He died because his aims and objectives had drifted out before him.

Two or three episodes occupied these last months. He received an Indian embassy, bearing with it remarkable gifts of gems and pearl, and animals such as were unknown in the west. It is probable that this embassy was by no means merely ornamental, but represented a renewal of those trade relations which for many years past had been tenuous or non-existent. He finished the building of the Church of the Apostles, where his own tomb was placed. In the spring, there was talk of a Persian war; but about Easter-tide a Persian embassy arrived, which soon put matters in a more satisfactory perspective. The reception of this Persian mission was the last important public business transacted by Constantine. Last days of Constantine

As he felt sickness coming upon him, he took a course of hot baths, first in Constantinople, afterwards in Helenopolis. At the latter place, named after his mother, he prayed in the Church of the Martyrs, and seems to have made up his mind that his death was at hand. He resolved to receive baptism.

It is not easy to ascertain the reasons why he had spent a large part of his life as a Christian, and yet had so long put off the necessary sacrament of entrance into the Church. He probably had many reasons. He was not willing to seem too obviously to take a side. His chief efforts had all his life been bent upon the task of conciliation and peace-making. In accordance with this plan, he had avoided any action that seemed like too plainly classifying himself. To his pagan subjects he had conducted himself as an enlightened pagan—very much, in fact, as his father had done. Taken all together, his legislation in favour of the Church had hardly at all exceeded the bounds of strict justice. Even a pagan might have thought it expedient to make most of the concessions to Christianity which Constantine made. . . . This aspect of Constantine's policy has hardly received the credit it deserves.

Question of baptism

Such a position on the fence was technically allowable so long as Constantine refrained from receiving baptism. His reasons were sufficiently good. Once he received baptism, his actions would necessarily be much more limited. Hence he had postponed it from time to time. . . . His own statement was that he had an ambition of being baptized in the Jordan.

But now that he felt his end approaching, and any concealment or hesitation became pointless, he showed his true belief. Had he been at heart a pagan, or indifferent, he might with perfect ease have died unchristened. The Church, from a secular point of view, could neither have harmed him nor helped him. He took the decided line just when it had the least worldly value: and this consideration is a reasonably conclusive indication of where his heart lay.

IX

He made his confession in that Church of the Martyrs at Helenopolis; and after he had been pronounced worthy to be received, he went to Nicomedia, where he requested to be baptized, undertaking to live henceforward until his death under a regular discipline. . . . So, as Eusebius observes, Constantine was the first Roman emperor to be received into the Christian Church. Constantine himself was impressed by this fact and all that it meant.

Returning home in his white baptismal robe, he lay down upon a bed which he was not again to leave. He never again wore his imperial purple. His officers were admitted to the room, a few at a time, to pay farewell to the great emperor. In reply to their condolences, he said that he had now for the first time begun to live, and to experience happiness, and he was eager to be gone. He made his will, which he gave into the keeping of his chaplain. He died on Whit Sunday, in the year A.D. 337, about noon—unusual even in the day and the hour of his death.

His death. Whit Sunday, A.D. 337

X

So suddenly and so decidedly did Constantine leave this world, that none of his sons were with him. An express post was sent to Constantius, the nearest; and in the meantime the body was laid upon a cere-cloth of gold, and covered with a purple pall. Candles were placed round about; and there lay Constantine, crowned and robed in his full imperial insignia, while his guardsmen stood to arms about him.[1]

His lying in state The revolution which Constantine had brought about can partly be seen in the mere narration of his lying in state. The fierce soldiery who had slain Aurelian and Probus were now under a far different discipline. While Constantine lay glittering on his golden bed, day after day the guard was changed, and all the business of the household went forward, with full etiquette, exactly as if he were alive. The senators, magistrates and citizens, who were allowed to pass through the chamber, were expected to conduct themselves in all respects as though the emperor were living. . . .

Nothing could more completely have justified the policy of Diocletian. The latter had ascended the throne amid circumstances which will be within the reader's recollection. His policy, which some men called servile and degrading, had had at least one effect—it secured that the machine should go on working though the engineer was no longer there to guide it. . . . Eusebius himself describes what he thought was the moral. Good kings never die. This was an idea which both the poets and the lawyers were destined to borrow.

His burial As soon as Constantius arrived, the body was carried to Constantinople. A mighty procession set forth, the troops going first, the civilians following behind. On each side of the catafalque paced the guardsmen, the Domestici, with splendid accoutrements and glittering

[1] Eusebius speaks as if this mode of lying in state, now a regular form of procedure, were then new, and especially invented for the Christian emperor.

spears. The body of Constantine was solemnly buried
in the tomb he had erected for himself in the Church of
the Apostles. Amid those quiet pillars for more than
eleven centuries he lay, until the Turks pulled down
and levelled the church to build the Mosque of Sultan
Mohammed the Second.

XI

Young Constantius, Fausta's son, found himself, without experience, without the intuition of genius, in charge
of the machine. And now a wonder came to pass!
The machine had a life of its own, and it proceeded to
go on acting independently of Constantius, and even to
a certain extent in defiance of his wishes.

Constantine had died upon the 22nd of May. For
more than three months—until the 9th of September—
the man silent in the Church of the Apostles continued
to be imperator and Augustus, and to rule the Roman
dominion, while outside a struggle was waged for the
elucidation of the new system of monarchy which he
had given to the empire.

The situation which confronted men upon the death
of Constantine was unique, and no precedent existed by
which to resolve it. The imperial family had so grown
in numbers, and had been so placed in positions of authority, and surrounded with a definite etiquette, that
it had become a "caste" fenced off from the classes in
contact with it. It was practically the first time a civilized European state had been confronted with such a
case. The trouble was to reconcile the existence of this
caste with the conception of monarchy. It is of course
quite obvious that if the imperial family went on mul-

*Problem
of the
imperial
family*

tiplying indefinitely, it would end by constituting an aristocratic order of a kind not distinctly contemplated by anyone. In this case, what would become of monarchy—that idea of a single indivisible governing person, who was not a committee, nor a congress, nor a delegation, but an individual?

Constantine had shirked this problem—perhaps not altogether deliberately. Had Crispus lived, no trouble would have arisen. His seniority and prestige, and perhaps his ability, would have founded the first precedent for a system of primogeniture. . . . But after the death of Crispus, Constantine seemed to lose heart. At the emperor's own death, none of the circumstances had been provided for. The ministers and the military counts who met one another daily in the way of business, and who had ample opportunity of discussing matters, formed certain provisional conclusions of their own. They decided to back the descendants of Helena against the descendants of Theodora.

What we do not know is whether any definite party was already backing the descendants of Theodora, and how far that branch of the imperial family had put forward any claims, or expressed any intentions. In any case, the supporters of the descendants of Helena determined to secure the exclusive rights of their own nominees.

XII

Immediately upon Constantine's death, travelling commissioners had left Nicomedia for the frontiers and the military stations. A general canvass of the army secured a satisfactory result. The troops undertook to support the sons of Constantine to the exclusion of all other candidates. Constantius, on his arrival, found that the elder branch of the imperial family was sufficiently perturbed by the course of events to make acceptable a solemn oath of good faith which he proceeded to take. But he was not his own master. His partisans took no cognizance of any undertakings he had given. According to one story, a forged will of Constantine, which accused his half brothers of poisoning him, was the weapon used. Some expedient must have been employed, and no means are known to us by which the unfortunate men could have been justly and rightly condemned. The three half-brothers, and two nephews of Constantine were tried before a packed court and executed, together with the patrician Optatus and the prefect Ablabius, who might with much more reason have fired off his famous squib now. . . . Of all the male descendants of Theodora, only two were left, Gallus and Julian.

Descendants of Theodora swept away

The first result was the division of the empire. It is possible to discern a glimmering of the reasons which led to the *coup d'état* at Constantinople, when we regard the other division that might have chanced. Had no *coup d'état* been made, the empire would have been divided among five Cæsars, with the consequence either of dissolution, or of another long and destructive civil war while one of the competitors was establishing a superiority over the rest. The three sons of Fausta represented the lowest limit to which it was immediately practicable to reduce the succession. Constantine took Britain, Gaul, Spain and part of Africa; Constantius took the east, beyond the Bosphorus; Constans took the central provinces of Italy and Illyria. All bore the title of Augustus. This was a far easier and much more promising arrangement than its possible alternative; but that it would be final was not very likely. It was only the provision of a breathing space for more careful consideration.

XIII

The sons of Constantine

The arrangement in fact, lasted only three years. At the end of that time Constantine and Constans reached a final disagreement concerning the shares to which they were entitled. The death of Constantine in battle left Constans master of the whole of the west.

Constans lasted ten more years. At the end of that time the Count of the Domestici, Magnentius, felt himself strong enough to do what no man since Diocletian had done. He snatched a crown. Constans, riding for his life, was caught and murdered near Helena, the ancient Illiberis in Spain, whose name his father had changed in order to honour the mother of Constantine the Great.

Destiny had now drawn the lot; and it had fallen upon Constantius.

He was no genius; but he was probably by far the ablest of the sons of Fausta. Something of his father's skill and the energy of his grandfather, old Maximian Herculius, clung to him. He met the emissaries of Magnentius at Heraclea in Thrace.

XIV

The conference was a memorable one. To it came the self-assured western counts, backed with the old sanctions that for centuries had been regarded by public opinion as sufficient title to sovereignty: the support of the army, and the might that makes right. They offered their alliance and friendship to Constantius on equal terms; they undertook to acknowledge his seniority; they pointed out the power which Magnentius held, and the certitude that war would once more prove the superiority of the European west to the Asiatic east. . . . And all they said was true.

Confer-
ence at
Heraclea

Constantius asked for time to consider the proposals made. . . . We have read the speech of Eusebius. We know what strange, novel doctrines of imperial sovereignty the old bishop had preached. These new doctrines were the creed for which the consistorium of Constantius advised its master to hold out. . . . Next day the epoch-making words were spoken. With full consciousness of his military inferiority, Constantius rejected the friendship of adventurers and usurpers, and defied a title which was founded upon force.

Mediocre though Constantius might be, he had among his supporters acute diplomats and expert planners who could out-think and out-manoeuvre the men of the west. His first victory was bloodless. Vetranio, the military governor of the Illyrian provinces, seceded from Magnentius and came over to the legitimate emperor. . . . Magnentius, with a host of Gauls, Germans and Spaniards, marched into Illyria. After a long period of playing for position, Constantius detached one of the important Frankish leaders. This success turned the scale.

Many centuries had passed since the armies of Cæsar and Pompeius faced one another on the battlefield of Pharsalus. The battle of Mursa was nearly as important and as decisive a victory. Constantius, after inspecting his men and speaking encouraging words to them, had the good sense to go to the rear and stop there, while the machine did the fighting. By nightfall, the mailed Asiatic horsemen had enveloped the western right and broken it, driving the unarmoured German foot before them. Magnentius, when all was lost, rode for his life and escaped. . . . To conquer the west was the work of two years. Magnentius killed himself. The revolt was suppressed. . . . In the person of Paul Catena, the imperial commissioner despatched to stamp out the last embers in Britain, the backwash of Constantine's conquests touched the place whence they had first started. At no time in history would an Asiatic commissioner in Britain be popular, and Paul was no exception to the rule.

Battle of Mursa, Sept. 28, 351

XV

Such are the consequences involved in an imperfect system of succession. The Roman empire was once more united under a single sovereignty; Constantine's work was restored; but the process was a costly one. . . . One or two little facts emerged. Given the new system, it could not be worked by one man without assistance. Constantine had worked it with the help of three sons and two nephews as "Cæsars," or as the later north would have called them, sub-reguli. Both

The logic of strife

branches of the imperial caste had now been very nearly extinguished. Of the three sons of Fausta, Constantius alone remained. Of the descendants of Theodora, Gallus and Julian survived. . . . The logic of strife was at fault.

Reconciliation between the two branches was reluctant, but it was necessary. Gallus was released from his polite confinement, and after a meeting with Constantius, at which they exchanged oaths of good faith, he undertook the task of governing the eastern provinces. But Gallus proved to be impossible. His mind had been distorted by the events of his childhood, and his idea of government was to defend himself from conspiracy. When his suspicions spread to his own entourage, they hastened to save themselves by conspiracy in earnest. Constantius, with the consent of his consistorium, removed Gallus from the stage.

Julian was left. Called to Milan, he found himself in a new and terrifying world of which he had never dreamed during his years of retirement and study. After he had been watched, scrutinized and criticized by keen and (as it seemed to him) hostile eyes, he was passed as good enough, and was allowed a personal interview with the emperor. . . . He was told to return to Athens; but a few months later he was recalled in earnest, was married to the emperor's sister and was given the title of Cæsar and a command in Gaul—the same command that Maximian Herculius had once given to Constantius.

Julian Cæsar, Nov. 6, 355

Not the least of the influences which compelled this measure was the pressure on the northern frontiers. These were years of unrest, during which Irminric was actively building up his Gothic kingdom, and all the tribes of northern and eastern Europe were seething. Raids of the Quadi and the Sarmatians called for the presence of Constantius himself upon the Danube. The Franks and Alamanni were active on the Rhine frontier. . . . Julian's entire ignorance was his salvation. Had he tried to work the machine, he would have wrecked it. With despair in his heart, he was content merely to press the button and follow whithersoever he was led; and the machine, which needed no assistance, led him to fame and triumph. In three years he had acquired the renown of a second Julius, and having begun by being a joke to the court at Milan, he ended by being the hammer of the Franks to the army.

Constantius was less fortunate. His campaign against the Persians was a failure. Anxious to restore his prestige, and to temper that of Julian, his ministers hit upon the device of ordering four of Julian's triumphant legions to leave immediately for the Persian border. The auxiliaries had in many cases enlisted for service in Gaul only. To send them to Persia was a breach of the agreement. The legionaries were not attracted by the idea of a Persian campaign. Since Julian was too humble and helpless a person to pass them the word, they passed it themselves. After imbibing as much Dutch courage as was necessary, an uproarious deputation of huskies aroused Julian one midnight, and clapped the crown upon his head. He was Julian Augustus, and they were not going to Persia. The panic-stricken Julian, after imploring them for three hours to spare him, allowed the machine once more to have its way. Perhaps he began to realize that it would see him through.

Revolt of Julian

XVI

It saw him through better than he could have dared to hope. His march across the headwaters of the Danube, and his sudden descent into Illyricum, are famous. The whole of the west accepted the triumphant soldier who seemed to be a second Constantine. When Constantius died at Mopsucrene near Tarsus, no further serious effort was made to dispute the claim of Julian. The last descendant of Theodora was the last member of the imperial caste.

Julian reigned three years. He died on June 26, 363, in the Mesopotamian desert, at the age of thirty-two, of wounds received in battle against the Persians. The machine had carried him thither; and it failed him only because it failed itself. So passed off the stage the last descendant of that Constantius who died at York, and the last man of the imperial caste which that Constantius had founded. With him ends one part of the story of Constantine the Great. The dynasty of Constantine perished. What became of the ideas and the principles which he had sought to embody, we must presently see.

Death of Julian

XVII

As for Julian—a great deal of pompous nonsense has been talked about him and the so-called pagan reaction he headed. He was an able man and in his natural instincts a good ruler—as by his ancestry he should have been; and he was unmistakably an unusual personality. But he had been a little warped from the normal by his early experiences, and had been given prejudices

Unimportance of being Julian

which, left to himself, he would never have acquired. His pagan reaction was a somewhat artificial revival of Stoicism which no longer represented any contemporary reality. The middle-class persons who cared were too few to count. The proletariat marched solid behind the banners of their bishops. As soon as they knew which way the procession was going, the aristocracy assumed their natural places in the front rank. And so the pagan reaction petered out into nothing. Nobody cared, except a few old gentlemen, who long after Julian's day were still performing with pleasure the rituals of Augustan culture and Antonine philosophy. . . . There are still Englishmen today who linger with fond tenderness over the age of Queen Anne. . . . The Lord, probably, takes Julian much less seriously than we do. It seems unlikely that Julian ever would have uttered the words: "Thou hast conquered, Galilæan!" It was far too true a remark for Julian ever to have thought of: and far too obvious for him ever to have said.

CHAPTER XIII

THE SECOND DEATH

I

THOUGH the dynasty of Constantine perished, the machine he created was taken over by other men; and the principles he had embodied in it endured, because they were the genuine product of the day, and fulfilled needs and ideals of which the age was conscious. The death of Julian was an extraordinary crisis in the history of mankind. It foreshadowed the series of changes by which the empire was to be divided; and while one-half preserved the tradition and the name of Rome, the other expanded into a totally new organization which we know of as modern European civilization. Had the house of Constantine endured, western Europe might have grown as the Byzantine empire grew, and have perished in the same way.

A would-be philosopher had nearly lost the Roman Striking Force in the deserts of Mesopotamia. An unintellectual man of the world extricated it. Jovian, who was hastily elected to succeed Julian, had been, like Diocletian, commander of the imperial guard; a cheery, pleasant, prosaic fellow, a professed Christian who perhaps had not studied the ten commandments so closely as he ought. He knew how to control the machine. He got it out of Mesopotamia at the cost of some prestige; but that could not be helped. The main thing was to get it out. . . . A year later he died, and Valentinian

Significance of Julian's death

Division of the empire

I., an Illyrian officer, who succeeded him, took the great step, which proved to be final, of dividing the empire into eastern and western spheres. Though, for a few years later on in the century, Theodosius the Great re-united it under one rule, the division instituted by Valentinian I. proved to be a permanent one. . . . After all the various experiments which we have noticed in the course of this book, the final arrangement was that there should be two Augusti, and that they should be hereditary monarchs.

And now a fresh and tremendous act in the drama begins. It was about the year 375 that the Huns began their career in eastern Europe. They destroyed the empire of Irminric, and the fierce old Gothic king died by his own hand rather than face defeat. The retreat of the Gothic refugees before the Huns finally stranded them upon the Danube—where, like the Sarmatians before them, they applied for land within the empire. The imperial government could not make up its mind. Goths were a very different proposition from Sarmatians. They had their sacred kings among them, and were a definite organized political power, as the Sarmatians were not. They were allowed to cross the Danube into safety, and were given subsistence while the government considered the problem. A little official dishonesty, a little Gothic pride and impatience, a little unfortunate accident—and the explosion came that blew a hole in twelve centuries of time. The Goths revolted, and began to take what they wanted. Valens the emperor hastened thither with the Striking Force. He was caught unprepared, with insufficient reconnaissance and defective dispositions. The Goths wiped out the Strik-

End
of the
Striking
Force

ing Force and Valens too. During the pursuit after the battle some Goths set fire to a house where Roman fugitives had taken refuge. Valens was there, and perished in the flames.

II

This was the end of the Roman army which had descended with unbroken tradition from Camillus. Theodosius the Great, who refounded the military organization, never troubled to re-institute the old legionary training. He accepted ready-trained recruits from the north. It was, indeed, practically impossible to find men susceptible of the old training. Legionary discipline had been the moral product of citizen-training. With the decline of commerce and town life, the supply of suitable recruits was cut off. Rural peasants, without any stiffening of townsmen, were incapable of taking the peculiar polish required by the old legionary methods. From the day of the battle of Hadrianople the imperial armies were largely filled with Germans.

Gradual decline

The events of the centuries which followed consisted of the adaptation of the principles and methods of Constantine to the whole of Europe. Among all the various channels by which this result was accomplished the chief was this Germanization of the army, which became the training-school through which all the European peoples directly or indirectly were educated and formed. Leo I. stopped the process of Germanization in the east, and isolated Asia from the changes which slowly transformed Europe into a new type of civilization.

We must not imagine that in Roman times the European lands north of the Danube were just, for the first

time, filling up their vast emptiness with population.[1]
. . . Northern Europe had been a thickly populated
country for many centuries before Rome was heard of.[2]
She had poured out stream after stream of emigrants,
whom we can only suppose to have been excess population: Aryans, Phrygians, Archæans, Dorians, Celts, Germans. She had not been an empty space awaiting colon-
ization, but a land always full to her capacity, and gradually, by one means or another, extending that capacity

**The
north**

to carry a larger population. Both agriculture and
commerce (perhaps with temporary disasters and set-
backs) had expanded in the area they covered and the
productivity they showed. Roman salesmen had been
far more successful than Roman soldiers in reaching
central Europe, and the markets of the north.[3] In the
three centuries between Cæsar and Constantine, the
productivity of northern Europe had considerably increased; and the country could hold and feed more men.
Those energetic youths who wanted a career could find
a very profitable one in the Roman army. Central
Europe was less than ever in her history under any necessity of bursting her bounds. If she began to overflow
the Roman frontier, it was not wholly over-population
that urged her. That frontier was becoming artificial,
unreal, and meaningless. It was not so much broken as
forgotten.

[1] Even Prof. J. B. Bury seems to think so in *History of the Later Roman Empire*, I, p. 97.

[2] V. Gordon Childe, *Dawn of European Civilisation*, 1925, Chaps. XI, XII, XV,-
XIX.

[3] Charlesworth, *Trade Routes and Commerce of Roman Empire*, pp. 175-176
and notes on p. 274 and xxiii. Montelius, *Civilisation of Sweden in Heathen
Times*, pp. 97-103.

III

We are usually misled by the way in which the story is told by historians. There never was any general and simultaneous invasion by the northern tribes which destroyed the Roman empire: and probably no recent historian ever said, in so many words, that there was: but the vague general impression to that effect is traditional amongst us. There was a great Gothic war; but evidently something had already happened, for the Roman defence was conducted by a Vandal, Stilico. The English took possession of a Britain from which some years earlier the Roman government had withdrawn. It is true that the Franks conquered Gaul; but the Gaul they conquered was being disputed by Goths, Burgundians and adventurers of various sorts; and the Franks were inclined to look upon themselves as the saviours of civilization. The Lombards first came into Italy as mercenary troops engaged by the imperial government. Far from being conquerors, the Ostrogoths were turned out of Italy, and the Vandals out of Africa. . . . What had really happened was a blurring of boundaries and a growing incertitude as to who was which and which was what. Nobody ever cleared up the mystery. About the time when the Franks were trying to look like Romans, the Romans were trying to look like Franks. The process had begun after the battle of Hadrianople. Theodosius the Great was its chief exponent. Slowly, certainly, the boundaries "ran," and Europe merged into one great area with approximately uniform characteristics.

This process of merging derived its political reality from its economic basis. The tendency to caste in the

Equaliza-
tion of
Europe

Roman empire, the growth of hereditary guilds and hereditary succession in all manner of occupations, brought the empire into harmony with those outlying portions of Europe where the tribal system still survived. In what, indeed, did the tribal system consist, if not precisely in this gentile qualification? The empire was tribalized just when the Germans were picking up the idea of political organization. For a time, therefore, the empire and the outlying north, hitherto beyond its frontier in the economic and the social as well as in the political sense, were equalized. The old frontier vanished; or at least it became a ghostly and unmeaning line, no longer separating two deeply distinguished systems of organization.

Merger

This process had obviously to be gone through at some time or other. If civilization were to expand so that it might include the whole of Europe, there had to come some time when the civilized south and the tribal north coalesced and began their new evolution in company. That coalescence came now! . . . The "tribalizing" of the empire was a phase. The old Roman lands went through the nominal process, cast it off, and returned to their methods of civilization; but now the north followed without question. One by one the tribal characteristics dwindled and vanished as the new dawn arose on the horizon.

IV

It was not Constantine who imposed upon the western empire the principle of hereditary caste. The force which did this was the impersonal force of economic development and political evolution; which may be another name for the automatic composition of the sins, weakness and ignorance of men, but is not another name for their deliberate will. . . . What Constantine did was to rationalize this trend. On the other hand he was personally responsible to a far greater degree than any other man for saving, preserving and strengthening the Christian church, which was not only the incarnate revolt against this system of hereditary caste, but was destined to be the power which, centuries afterwards, fought it and broke it. . . . It was he who enabled the Church to defy the attempt of Galerius either to destroy her or to turn her into a tribe of Levites or Magians. All men acknowledge his responsibility. His friends admire him, and his foes detest him, for this reason and no other. Constantine did not enslave humanity. He made sure that her chains should some day be broken. . . . He nevertheless does not stand or fall purely by his attitude to Christianity. He has other claims upon our attention. But there can be no doubt that for a time Christianity stood or fell by his attitude to it.

Caste in Europe

v

Perhaps the main thing we learn from the results of Constantine's career is that civilization is based upon law. The story of Constantine has been falsified by those who imagine that the monarchy he founded was a Tsarist autocracy, and that the long life of Byzantine civilization was due to the exercise of arbitrary will by individuals. We are coming nowadays to a better conception of the true facts. The monarchy founded by Diocletian and completed by Constantine was no more an autocracy than the principate of Trajan. It was a reign of law, in which law transcended even the lawgiver.[1] We may reckon it a weakness to think of law so strong as this; but it is a weakness on the safe side. The examples that burned the lesson into the minds of Byzantine statesmen were the anarchy described in the first chapter of this book and the downfall described in the last. . . . No autocracy dependent on the arbitrary will of an individual was ever the founder of a strong political state. But law will found a state. No kind of will, or command, or desire can make a state strong; but obedience can do so. If Constantine founded an empire to endure a thousand years, it was because he induced men to believe in the virtue of obeying the moral law of God and the political law of man.

VI

The world, in Constantine's day, was not integrating, but differentiating; hence the steady rise of monarchic systems. For it is an easy generalization from the facts, that monarchy and republicanism are not moral principles, but psychological methods; and when states are forming, polities uniting, and men accommodating their minds and feelings into like-mindedness, their government will be of the type which we call republican or parliamentary; but when states are dissolving, old systems passing into new, fresh human combinations arising, and men growing different from one another, then their government will be monarchic. And even

[1] Bury, *History of the Later Roman Empire*, I, p. 4 and p. 13, quoting the edict of A.D. 429. Lot, *La Fin du mond antique*, p. 1.

when other things are fairly equal, the bias to one type or another will be determined by the preference men have for discipline or individuality. . . . And the reason for this is a very simple characteristic of the human mind. It is easier for many diverse men to discover a man they can all obey than an idea they can all believe. Common belief involves an actual common likeness between the believers. To create a common belief where it was not before, we need to create a likeness where it before was not. Such likeness involves a certain equality of degree and quality. . . . Hence, the age of Constantine tended to monarchy without in the least forgetting the principles it had acquired from earlier ages of Rome. If anything, it polished, pointed and perfected them.

Different as their formal constitution may be from that founded by Constantine, the United States are in theory the chief modern exemplar of this attitude towards law. The tradition founded long ago by John Marshall, which put even the legislator under the survey of the judiciary, has given America at least the beginnings of a system calculated to possess the same stability, the same long life, that distinguished the system of Constantine. The cause in both cases was similar. The diversity of the elements out of which the Roman empire was made called for a quality of rigidity in its legal framework, to compensate for the lack of it elsewhere. Modern America is similarly diverse in its constituent elements, and needs a similar rigidity. . . . Old established nations which are more uniform in ethnic composition need not trouble to the same extent. The likeness of their citizens renders possible a much greater

Value of law

legislative liberty; for where men are similar, their agreement is automatic, and they think alike because they are alike. . . . The reign of law is the protection of individuality. Men may differ, and may develop in freedom the most decorative varieties of human personality, so long as their common obedience maintains their unity. They must be all alike, if likeness is the only unity they can achieve.

VII

The age of Constantine, in which many men have imagined that they saw political degeneration and the advent of autocracy, was as a matter of fact the age which evolved those theories which lie at the root of the English, the French and the American constitutions. Not the Athens of Pericles, but the Rome of Severus and Constantine, proclaimed the gospel that men were born free and equal. Most of the legal doctrines which have defended modern liberty were first brought to point by the Roman jurists of that age. . . . All the political principles of later Europe were founded then.

The age
of Con-
stantine

The divine monarchy therefore did not betoken any sudden access of superstition or servility in the Roman mind. The emperors had always been deified after their deaths. The republican magistrates had always been sacred: and that particular magistrate who was most specifically the representative of the people—the Tribune—was super-sacrosanct and especially inviolable. If we were to gather into one the characteristics of all the republican magistrates, and made one magistrate with all those rights and duties, he would necessarily have been sacred, just as he would necessarily have worn the purple. Quintus Fabius, Gaius Gracchus, Diocletian and King George V. are all alike in being sacred persons. The real breach with tradition is in that neither Mr. Hoover nor M. Doumergue is regarded as sacred.

The change in the nature of monarchy which was carried through by Constantine was registered almost simultaneously throughout Europe. The means of communication between north and south were probably not much worse in the fourth century than they were in the sixteenth. Europe was hardly more restless, or travelling more dangerous, and there was little in one age to prevent the same dissemination of ideas that took place in the other. While Constantine was making the change in the Roman world, the first permanent kingships, founded among the Goths on the Vistula, were extending their influence westward. . . . The difference in force, dignity and effect between the old and the new was remarkable. Irminric, Alaric and Theodoric were men different in power and dignity from the elected tribal war-kings of earlier time. None of them graced a Roman triumph. None of them, like King Teutobod, could vault over six horses. They were men like Constantine himself. The difference in tradition between the Roman and the Goth at first left its mark, but by degrees it faded: as centuries went on, the two types coalesced, and became one.

Constantine's influence

Does any trace remain of the process by which the new form of monarchy spread over Europe? The Roman writers did not record it. But does any trace exist elsewhere?

VIII

Whether we elect to believe or not, old northern tradition had a coherent enough story to tell on this head. Some of the earliest tales form a group with peculiar characteristics. They are the mutually interpenetrating histories of a number of persons one of whom is a famous historical figure—Irminric, King of the Goths; while several others are equally famous in the legends of the Scandinavians, the English and the Germans, but their existence is not attested by separate historical record. If we choose to believe that these other legendary persons also are real (and there is nothing improbable in the idea) then the following story emerges.

Spread of Kingship

Irminric—the famous king who in the days of Constantine was spreading the power of the Goths throughout eastern Europe—had a number of cousins, the children of his uncle Budli, his father's brother. They were, first, Atli, the King of the Huns, Brynhild (the Valkyrie —the Brunhild of the Germans), and Bekkhild. Brynhild was married to Gunnar, the Burgundian king, and Bekkhild to a certain King Hama. We thus locate a great Burgundian and a great Hun dynasty contemporary with the Gothic. . . . But a great deal more than this. We all know the romantic tragedy of Brynhild, embodied by Wagner in his operas. She was traditionally involved with the man Sigfrith, known to the Germans as Siegfried and to the Scandinavians as Sigurd Fafni's-bane. But who was he? . . . The answer is, that according to the old poems, he was the descendant of a line of kings who ruled in eastern Europe. He must have been a very famous man to leave the mark he did upon old tradition. He was of nearly the same generation as Irminric, and came from the same quarter. All these earliest royal dynasties date, therefore, about the time of Constantine, and come from eastern Europe.

But the connections and interactions of these dynasties were, as far as we know, entirely with the far north of Europe. They had very little to do with the tribes of the Rhine. Sigfrith's father, Sigemund Waelsing, was well known to the early English; his name survives to this day in Walsingham and Wolsingham: his tale comes down to us in a fairly full Scandinavian version. Sigfrith's half-brother, Helgi Hunding's-bane, conquered the Saxons, and was murdered by them. The English knew King Hama, Bekkhild's husband. They knew Irminric. All these men were of the same generation: and of the same generation was Wihtlæg the first king of the English. The Danish kings counted their descent from Irminric. All the various stories tell one tale—to wit, that all the dynasties arose about the same time, and were founded by a group of men associated on the one hand with the English, Danes and Norwegians, and on the other hand with the Goths. . . . Whether this story is true or not, it is a perfectly probable one, and it is the only one. The traditions of the northern nations agree in giving this account; and they agree in breathing no word or hint whatever of any other story.

According to this account, therefore, the early northern kingship began almost simultaneously with the great change which turned the Roman principes into divine monarchs. Throughout northern Europe, the tribal war-kings and priest-kings gave way to a new political monarchy. That it was based upon the new Roman

Agreement of the evidence

monarchy founded by Diocletian and Constantine we can see from its model. As soon as we can pick up any details of its construction, we can see it to be a guild **The type** with a hereditary head, a court or consistory of great officers, and a body of military members. That there were differences is only to be expected in view of the contrast in economic structure and political development between the north and the south of Europe. The wonder is that the differences were so small. A point had obviously been reached at which the tribal system of the north and the political system of the south began distinctly to approximate to a common type; and the point of fusion was marked by the rise of this new form of monarchy, and its gradual extension over the whole of Europe.

IX

Whence did Diocletian and Constantine derive the ideas which they used to reform the status of the emperor? Part were no doubt the direct tradition of the military guild that had evolved in unbroken succession from Cæsar. Some were certainly drawn from the Persian monarchy. The testimony of Lactantius is clear on this head. He asserts plainly that Galerius' ideas of monarchy were derived from Persian sources. But even before this, Aurelian had been influenced by Persian ideas. Aurelian, the nominee and successor of Claudius Gothicus, brought back from his eastern campaigns a **Sol Invictus** sun-cult of Sol Invictus which was in all probability of Persian origin. This cult is the likeliest instrument to have held, handed down and spread the political doctrines of the New Monarchy. We have seen that almost to the end of his life Constantine showed signs of his membership of a sun-cult. Its members probably followed him into the Christian Church, and the Order lost its separate existence.

We must be prepared for a good deal of vigorous contrast in the imperial dignity as the Illyrian emperors re-created it. The sacred person, surrounded with its glorious ministers, and approached with meticulous etiquette and particular reverence, was nevertheless still supposed to be the head of a republic. The emperor, ascending the platform to address his troops, was still a magistrate addressing the citizen electors.[1] The army still considered itself the Roman people. It continued to do so until the changes of Theodosius the Great, when the old military guild shrank to the limits of the imperial comitatus.

The later history of this imperial comitatus is not without interest. In western Europe it had to struggle with the similarly organized kingships of the north, and in the contest it sank, with many of its rivals, and dissolved. In the eastern empire it had a somewhat different career. It there enjoyed a period during which the administrative methods of Roman monarchy were developed and perfected; and it then formed a bridge by which this development was carried over to the younger and less experienced royal monarchies of the west. We are accustomed to the truth that when western monarchy was powerful, Byzantine monarchy was weak. We are not so well accustomed to the equal truth that when western monarchy was weak, Byzantine

The imperial comitatus

[1] Ammianus Marcellinus, XIV, 10 (10-16); XXI, 13 (9-15). Lactantius, *De M.P.*, XIX.

monarchy was a powerful system which taught it its methods and principles of organization and administration. Its educative influence penetrated throughout Europe.

But while western monarchy continued on its course, weaving first its web of landed aristocracy with its feudal council outside the royal comitatus, and then its web of commercial oligarchy and industrial democracy, with its representative Parliamentary system outside the feudal council—the Byzantine monarchy never entered upon those stages, but degenerated first into lethargy, and then into incapacity. The fact that eastern Europe and western Asia have for centuries been backward in development is wholly due to this constricted nature of the political tradition they derived from the eastern empire. . . . It was a system strong and stable in its day: and the Turkish Sultanate, which was copied from it, possessed to the last a similar extraordinary vitality. But it was a system without the power of development to its consummation. It could not mature. It left the east permanently in the stage of the military guild, while western Europe was growing vigorously, stage after stage, into fresh forms of political organization and economic life.

The results are plainly before our eyes even to this day. No reader of these pages needs to be told of the immense practical differences which divide modern Persia and Turkey (once the foremost countries in the world) from the prospering and expanding powers of the west. The causes which lie behind this arrest of development are another matter, which does not concern us here.

Strength of the Roman system

X

Practically all the historians who have studied the age
of Diocletian [1] and his successors agree in one point—
the corruption of the administration. But the use of
the word "corruption" is going a great deal too fast,
and prejudges questions which must be discussed, not
taken for granted. What was this quality which we dismiss as corrupt? And, when it comes to that, what is
corruption in the political sense?

We most of us possess certain handy tests, or Awful
Examples, by which we estimate political corruption.
The Englishman looks back to the old unreformed Theory of
franchise; the American to whatever chance to be his political
corruption
favourite instances of graft. But we all of us acknowl-
edge, in one form or another, that political corruption
argues some peculiar condition of affairs. A very old
system, no longer corresponding to the facts of contemporary life, or a very new system, not yet properly
settled down to its work—either of these may be corrupt. No system is ever corrupt in the heyday of its
power. No men are ever wantonly, unnecessarily corrupt, without cause or reason. Or, to be a little subtler
—let us consider the political fact of undue influence
without consideration passed: the clique, the "old gang,"
the "inner circle"—those little rings of happily associated persons who co-operate to exclude the people they
don't like. Very often they are not enriching themselves by the process. Sometimes they are ruining themselves. . . . But what is the meaning of their existence?

[1] See, e.g., Mr. Heitland in *Agricola*, Chapter LI onwards, but particularly
Chapter LII, and the immediately following sections.

All use of the word "corruption" is a way of expressing the fact that men are guilty of a divided loyalty—
that is, that they are loyal in theory and in form to one
sovereign power, but in truth and fact to another. A
man is corrupt if he purports to be unswervingly loyal
to the state, when in reality he is loyal only to some
party within it. Every kind of political corruption can
be classified under this formula. The whole conception
involves this division of interest and loyalty—this secret

**Divided
loyalty**

negligence in one thing for the benefit of another. Not
every man in practical life is capable of the largest-sized
loyalties. Exactly how many Britons really and truly
put the Empire before any sectional interest is a question
which it is needless to press home too severely. It is
probable that the number of Americans with a really
heroic zeal for the Federal Government is smaller than
we should wish. We hear from time to time of governments threatened and at least morally coerced by sectional organization within the state, ranging in degree
from the Church to the Camorra or what not. The
truth is that the claim of the large political unit upon the
warm emotions and earnest zeal of men is sometimes a
little too distant to be effective. It is over-borne by the
smaller, stronger pull of near ties and local connections.
There are times when it seems wicked to sacrifice a
brother to the state. His friends get him off, or put
him in, or whatsoever it may chance to be; and no com-
punctions disturb the dinner with which they celebrate
the event.

In addition to this, circumstances arise in which the
small unit seems to possess not merely the stronger but
morally the higher claim. This was certainly the opin-

ion of the Christians, who regarded devotion to their religious body as a virtue far transcending mere obedience to the law of the state. They were not the only people who cultivated a quarrel with the imperial government. A hundred other bodies existed, diverse in nature and objective; and although the list may have concluded with the enterprising official who felt that nothing could be done till the applicant had made a donation towards the support of his family, it began much higher up, in a more dignified, more philosophical way.

We have, then, to face the fact that this characteristic which we call corruption is something much more considerable in nature than we should be led to suppose by the historians. When it becomes visible on a large scale, and is shared in by important and high-minded persons,[1] it is due to the development of a greater associative strength in the minor societies than in the major society, the sovereign institution, the state itself. That such minor societies frequently do possess such greater strength is a matter of common knowledge. At intervals, which are determined by considerations that need not here be discussed, there are whole periods of many years or several generations in length, during which the minor societies are stronger than the major society. The results must be attributed to the true cause, not to imaginary lapses in the moral nature of man.

This same moral nature of man produces both the power of the large unit and the power of the smaller one. It is not good in one place and bad in another. We may, indeed, at times, realize the necessity of putting

Claims of the small unit

[1] Take Symmachus as a perfect example. Heitland, *Agricola*, pp. 406-407.

the large unit, the supreme patriotism of mankind, first in our thoughts and of resisting and repressing those men who insist upon putting local and sectional interests first. But we can only do so by demonstrating the claim of those large general interests upon the devotion of men: for men will work for those which seem to be made for men: and they will not work for those which seem to argue that man was made for them. In that lies the secret.

XI

More than one modern scholar has attempted a theory to explain the fall of the Roman empire. Some of the most learned have frankly given up the task.[1] But did the Roman empire ever fall in the sense they mean? . . . A government may indeed have collapsed, but there was no interruption of the evolution of political institutions. The eastern empire, centred at Constantinople, preserved itself for a thousand years by refusing all risks and all fundamental change, and sacrificing its future to secure its present. The western empire took another course. By abandoning the peculiar basis on which it had stood, it lost the whole of its material power and visible organization: it "fell." But that "fall" enabled civilization to revive with fresh vigour and infinite potentialities; and while Constantinople was teach-

"Fall" of the empire

---

[1] Prof. Bury, in *The Later Roman Empire*, I, Chap. IX, § 7, suggests that there was no general cause, but only a succession of accidents. M. Rostovtzeff winds up his monumental *Social and Economic History of the Roman Empire* by confessing that no solution seems adequate. "But the ultimate problem remains . . . Is it possible to extend a higher civilisation to the lower classes without debasing its standard and diluting its quality to the vanishing point? Is not every civilisation bound to decay as soon as it begins to penetrate the masses?" . . . Truly remarkable words to come from a citizen of the United States! . . . Another view will be found in Mr. W. E. Heitland's *The Roman Fate* (1922).

ing the youthful nations of the east the outworn principles of the Military Guild as a system of government,
the west was building up a system of national monarchy
that rendered possible aristocracy, and developing aristocracy until it in turn created commercial oligarchy,
which was the origin of industrial democracy. Constantinople perished: but the civilization of the west, its
youth renewed, is still alive. It never fell: it only
entered upon another cycle of activity.

XII

One of the factors, however, which play a great part
in the decline and fall of states, is very little noticed by
historians. It may be called Fatigue: and it is very
deeply entwined with the typical nature of man. . . .
All men tend to become sated with the constant repetition of any action, and even presently to acquire a dislike of it, and at last, if the repetition extends to monot- **Principle
of**
ony, an active hatred of it. . . . A vigorous people **Fatigue**
which has for several generations carried on any activity
—commercial, industrial, or any other—will in the stage
of satiation begin to slacken its energies; in the stage of
dislike it will neglect its work and seek some other kind
of occupation; in the stage of hatred it will destroy its
idols, defy its conventions and its laws, and take the part
of revolution. . . . The reason for this is, that man is
of all animals the least specialized. He positively needs
to do everything there is to do; he must have variety and
change, or he will die, or go mad and kill. He needs
variety in his conduct as he does in his food. There is
no torment like the hideous hell of monotony.

This general law works in all circumstances, with every rank or class, and in every age. It is a universal law. The astutest statesmen have instinctively realized it, and have left loopholes in their policies. No laws were ever founded on a keener insight into human nature than the seventh-day sabbath and the year of jubilee. Give men a rest, and they will go on all the longer. The modern psychologist has rediscovered this law, and has brought his knowledge of it to a more exact form—but it was known from the beginning of things by every wise man who pondered over the ways of his fellows, and noted the rise and fall of their tribes.

Most of us can produce out of our own experience the evidence necessary to demonstrate the social significance of fatigue. We all know saints who provoked in their children a hatred of morality, and of sinners who produced in theirs a zeal for good. . . . We know the rich families whose members loathed their life and yearned for the life of the people; and the man from the back street who fought his way with tooth and nail to the heaven of Sheraton tables and evening dress. Every family of educated men is liable to produce members who turn faint at the very idea of learning. . . . We are all, both individually and in the mass, liable to become super-charged and poisoned with the products of our own activity, and to produce children who react against it.

The super-charged mind

This element of fatigue plays an active part in the formation and decline of political power, in the composition of classes, and the circulation of human beings like blood through all the permanent institutions of social life. We find families rising to power, and falling from it; new men coming forward; holders of power who have no heart or will to struggle against aggression; ambitious new men whose hearts and souls are devoured by the determination to succeed. And because of this law, small states are (as regards their prospects of survival) usually at a great disadvantage. They exhaust their material, have no reserves, and collapse; and by the time the cycle has gone its round, and men are turning once more to the things they rejected, it is too late to build up the little state again. . . . Small states tend, for this reason, to disappear.

Disadvantage of small states

A large state is correspondingly at an advantage. Some part of it may always be refreshed and eager for the labours of government. . . . The history of the process in the Roman empire is traceable. Productive as Italy had been, her men began to weary round about the time of Cæsar. We can mark the time when she fell back upon raw sons of the people like Vespasian; when she turned to the great Spaniard, Trajan, and the humane Gaul, Antoninus. Africa played her part under the Severi. It was the Illyrians who rescued her from the great anarchy: the British, who placed Constantine upon the throne. In days to come, stout country-bred men were to come from Asia Minor to rule the eastern empire. But in Europe, the tired Roman was submerged by a flood of ardent northerners who had never been sated with ease, comfort, sunshine, wealth or happiness, and who were willing to go to any length to gain them. . . . The South European had been highly civilized for a very long time, and civilized for longer still. . . . The ordinary sensual man was weary of being good. He was weary of subordinating himself to the good of the

**Men
weary of
civilization**
community, of being regular in his habits, punctual in his appointments, and prompt in his payments. He wanted—as the Revolting Sons and Daughters, our own uncles and aunts wanted—to break the rules, to neglect his duties, and to do what he liked. . . . And so amid the reprimands of emperors and the rebukes of moralists, the western empire began to dissolve into a welter of uproarious barbarism. . . . Probably most men keenly regretted that their neighbours were imitating their own deficiencies, and wished that someone other than themselves would make an effort to preserve the amenities of civilized society. . . .

The fall of the western empire was due to a complex of causes: but this was the cause which gave all the other causes their chance to operate. The mine was laid with other elements; but fatigue was the element that fired the mine.

XIII

So, at the end of it all, human nature remained, with all its opinions, and views, and passions and romances, and its hopelessly eccentric orbit, and its quite incalculable tendencies—remained, pervasive as air, insinuating as water, universal as time and space—remained insubstantial, indestructible and permanent. It raised a cry of woe and consternation as it saw all the serious things of life, the property, and the figures, and the hard facts, the brick walls and logs of wood, escape like insubstantial gleams of light into the vast inane.

INDEX

345